Paul's Concept of Justification

Paul's Concept of Justification

God's Gift of a Right Relationship

RICHARD K. MOORE

WIPF & STOCK · Eugene, Oregon

PAUL'S CONCEPT OF JUSTIFICATION
God's Gift of a Right Relationship

Copyright © 2015 Richard K. Moore. All rights reserved. Except for brief quotations in critical publications or reviews, no part of this book may be reproduced in any manner without prior written permission from the publisher. Write: Permissions. Wipf and Stock Publishers, 199 W. 8th Ave., Suite 3, Eugene, OR 97401.

Wipf and Stock
An Imprint of Wipf and Stock Publishers
199 W. 8th Ave., Suite 3
Eugene, OR 97401

www.wipfandstock.com

ISBN 13: 978-1-4982-0282-4

Manufactured in the U.S.A.   02/10/2015

First published by Murdoch University in 2002 with the title *Justification: God's Way of Bringing Us into a Right Relationship*. Re-issued with minor amendments 2009. Extensively revised and reset 2014.

Dedicated to
my friend and fellow-pilgrim of long standing

Kent Miller Logie

who c. July 1958 introduced me to
Charles B. Williams' translation of the New Testament,
The New Testament in the Language of the People (1937).

Contents

Preface | ix
Abbreviations | xi

1 Introduction | 1
2 A Profile of Paul's View of Rectification or the Good News according to Paul | 10
3 The Doctrine of Rectification in Historical Perspective | 24
4 Paul's Doctrine of Rectification in English Translations | 53
5 An Anatomy of Paul's Use of the δ-Family | 93
6 Applying These Insights to Paul's Letter to the Romans | 110
7 Conclusions | 161

Appendices

A Glossary | 171
B All Occurrences of the δ-Family in Galatians and Romans (In Order) | 173
C The Relationships among the δ-GR Words in R-Contexts | 176
D All Occurrences of the δικαιοσύνη / θεοῦ Combination in the Pauline Corpus | 180
E Law-Righteousness | 182
F Faith-Righteousness | 183
G Paul's Use of λογίζεσθαι in Galatians and Romans | 185
H The Allusions to Psalm 143:2 in Galatians 2:16 and Romans 3:20 | 189
I Two Perceived Approaches to Establishing a Right Relationship with God in Paul's Letters | 191
J Three Approaches to Englishing Paul's δ-Family Illustrated from Romans 3:21–26 | 197

Contents

Select Bibliography | 199

Indices
Scripture Index | 207
Greek Index | 211
Latin Index | 213
Persons Index | 215
Subject Index | 217

Preface

My doctoral dissertation of 1978 examined Paul's understanding of "justification" and how that doctrine was expressed in English translations.

After considerable additional research, I reworked and expanded the dissertation, publishing it as *Rectification ('Justification') in Paul, in Historical Perspective, and in the English Bible* (3 volumes; New York: Edwin Mellen, 2002-2003). The first volume focused on Paul's concept of God's rectifying activity; the second on how the doctrine of "justification" developed historically; the third on how Paul's doctrine has been expressed in English translations. The three volumes occupy 1372 pages.

Recognizing that the three volumes constituted a technical work intended for a theologically trained readership, in 2002 I also wrote a small volume of 150 pages, publishing it through Murdoch University for the benefit of busy theological students and non-specialists. The present monograph is a revised and expanded update of that earlier work. It states my case succinctly, but without providing all the detailed evidence and argumentation found in the three-volume work.

I have long desired that the case made in this volume and in the larger work be placed before a much wider readership. That desire arises from the firm conviction that it presents more clearly and more accurately than many contemporary presentations the "Good News" Paul expounded so passionately.

Further, while a number of translators and translation societies (including the British and Foreign Bible Society and the American Bible Society) have opted to utilize the "relational" view of "justification" for their English translations, I am not aware that the case for doing so has ever been presented in any comprehensive way. That was what I set out to do in the three-volume work published in 2002-3, and now summarized in the present monograph.

Preface

Over three decades of tertiary theological teaching it has been my privilege to benefit enormously from the insights of numerous scholars, colleagues, students, and lay friends. For any defects that remain in this monograph, however, the responsibility is mine alone.

Richard K. Moore

Research Associate
Vose Seminary
Western Australia
2014

Abbreviations

AB	Anchor Bible
ABS	American Bible Society
BETL	Bibliotheca Ephemeridum Theologicarum Lovaniensium
c.	circa = around about
CE	Common Era
CEB	Common English Bible (2011)
CEV	Contemporary English Version (1995)
diss.	dissertation
DMH	Darlow, Moule, and Herbert; *s.v.* Herbert, A. S.
EETS	Early English Text Society
esp.	especially
ESV	English Standard Version (2001)
ET	English Translation
EvQ	*Evangelical Quarterly*
GNB	Good News Bible (1976 ^{2}1992)
HCSB	Holman Christian Standard Bible (2004)
ICC	International Critical Commentary
JPS	The new JPS [Jewish Publication Society] translation (Second Edition, 1999).
KJV	King James Version (Authorized Version)
LN	Louw and Nida
LS	Liddell and Scott
Lxx	Septuagint
MT	Masoretic Text (the form in which the text of the Hebrew Bible has come down to us)

Abbreviations

NAB	New American Bible (1970, ʳ1987)
NABRE	New American Bible Revised Edition (2011)
NASB	New American Standard Bible (1971, ʳ1999)
NCV	New Century Version (1991)
n.d.	no date
NET	NET Bible (New English Translation, 2001)
NICNT	The New International Commentary on the New Testament
NIV	New International Version
NIV2011	New International Version (2011)
NJB	New Jerusalem Bible (1985)
NRSV	New Revised Standard Version (1990)
NT	New Testament
OT	Old Testament
PS	Parker Society
REB	Revised English Bible (1989)
ʳ	revised
r.	reigned
r.i.	re-issued
s.v.	*sub verbo/sub voce* = see under the word
USC	*Under the Southern Cross: The New Testament in Australian English* (2014)
WUNT	Wissenschaftliche Untersuchungen zum Neuen Testament

1

Introduction

BY ITS VERY DEFINITION, religion is concerned with how human beings relate to the divine, the divine usually being understood as a divine being (or beings). In the Christian religion the means by which such a relationship is formed between God and humankind has often been expressed by the doctrine commonly referred to as "justification by faith."

In the historical development of Christianity the doctrine of "justification" came into prominence early in the sixteenth century with the advent of the religious phenomenon in Western Europe known as the Reformation. For the first time a major rift developed in the Western church that was to prove permanent. The doctrinal issue dividing the Roman Catholic Church from the emerging Protestant churches was "justification." Even today, notwithstanding increasing rapprochement between the Roman Catholic and Lutheran communions, significant differences remain over this issue.

The term "justification" is derived from the family of words that characterize the expression of the doctrine in the New Testament. Throughout this study we will refer to this family as the δ-family (delta-family). The three most prominent members of this word-family are the noun δικαιοσύνη (*dikaiosune*), the verb δικαιοῦν (*dikaioun*), and the adjective δίκαιος (*dikaios*).

In treatments of the doctrine of "justification," the term "justification" is sometimes applied in a very broad sense, so that any material that touches on the concepts fundamental to the doctrine are included, even if the language characterizing "justification" in the New Testament (i.e., the δ-family) is not present.¹ In this book the term is applied more precisely, referring only to those passages where the δ-family is present.

1.1 "JUSTIFICATION" IN PAUL

Defined in the way just described, the doctrine of "justification" is almost exclusively a doctrine of the Apostle Paul. He expounds "justification" in three of his letters. In order of importance they are Romans, Galatians, and Philippians. However, in the present work these letters will be treated in what is generally regarded as their order of composition, namely, Galatians, Romans, and Philippians. In addition, there are significant echoes of "justification" language in the two Corinthian letters (1 Cor 6:11; 2 Cor 3:9; 5:21). We have now accounted for five of the seven letters whose Pauline authorship is widely regarded as authentic: only 1 Thessalonians and Philemon lack any use of "justification" language. In the case of Philemon this is hardly surprising due to its brevity and the personal nature of the issues Paul is addressing; Philemon contains theological principles rather than theological exposition. Among the six letters whose Pauline authorship is widely disputed, the Letter to Titus has a significant passage utilizing the δ-family.²

Early in the days when the Christian faith was being shaped, the author of 2 Peter wrote:

> **15** . . . regard the Lord's patience as salvation, just as our dear brother Paul also wrote to you in accordance with the wisdom granted to him, **16** as he also speaks about these matters in all his letters. There are some things in them that are hard to understand, things that the uneducated and unstable will twist, just as they do the rest of the Scriptures also—to their own destruction!³

Among the things Paul wrote that are "hard to understand" the doctrine of "justification" has proved, over the last two millennia, one of the most intractable. From the earliest post-apostolic writings and through the next two millennia, we find that the apostle's doctrine of "justification" is frequently ignored or seriously misrepresented.

---

1. E.g., Carson, *Right with God*.
2. Titus 3:3–8a.
3. 2 Pet 3:15–16.

Introduction

1.2 DEVELOPMENT OF THE DOCTRINE OF "JUSTIFICATION" IN THE WESTERN CHURCH

In the early centuries of the development of Christianity, the Roman Empire was divided (on the basis of language) into East and West, the East being predominantly Greek-speaking, the West Latin-speaking. In church life the differences went beyond language to embrace different ways of understanding and practising the Christian faith. East and West developed different models of salvation and different understandings and estimates of the doctrine of "justification."

In the West, which is the focus of this monograph, the doctrine of "justification" did not feature prominently at all until late in the fourth century, when the North African church father, Augustine of Hippo Regius (354–430), began to give grace (Latin *gratia*) a prominent place in his theology. In the opening decades of the following century he employed a grace-based theology against the claims of the monk Pelagius and his followers.

The views of Augustine were enormously influential during the Middle Ages and among the Reformers, and even today exercise a powerful influence, although their source is not always recognized.

Fundamental to the view of "justification" held by Augustine and his heirs in the Middle Ages was the understanding that the verb *iustificare* (standing for Paul's δικαιοῦν in the Greek) meant "to make righteous." "Justification" was seen as the *process* by which a person becomes—ideally—increasingly righteous during their lifetime. The "righteousness" involved is a moral righteousness. This view is often referred to as the realist view of "justification": a person becomes righteous in reality. In Augustine and in the Middle Ages, a person became righteous only because God, through his grace, took the initiative and supplied the means making it possible. The necessity of grace marked off the orthodox view of "justification" from those views which accorded grace a lesser role. Formally it was described as "anti-Pelagian." This term is derived from Pelagius, a contemporary of Augustine. Augustine vehemently opposed Pelagius, claiming he had a defective view of human nature, especially in assuming that a person is capable of taking the first steps towards salvation without the aid of God's grace.

In spite of its anti-Pelagian stance, the actual practices of the Western church at times belied the formal reliance on divine grace. The practice of selling indulgences provides just one example. Associated with the elaborate system of penance prevailing at that time, it provided the spark which ignited the sixteenth-century Reformation that was soon to affect the whole of the Western church and ultimately to make its impact felt universally.

Behind the opposition to the sale of indulgences was a profoundly spiritual movement which was impatient with artifice and called for a return to the original sources of Christianity, the Scriptures of the Old and New Testaments. With the catchcry of *sola scriptura* there was a repudiation of the ecclesiastical traditions which had grown up alongside the Bible and a demand that the Scriptures be the touchstone for all matters of faith and conduct.

One of the streams contributing to the new way of thinking was the Renaissance, with its veneration for the ancient world. The revival of the Greek language was a direct consequence of the Renaissance, and made the original language in which the New Testament writings were composed more readily available again to the Latin-speaking West.

It was inevitable that these developments would impact on the theology of the Reformers. Very quickly an alternative view of "justification" surfaced, and over the next decade or so it was elaborated to the point where certain features would become permanent in the emerging Protestant articulation of "justification."

The foundation stone for the Protestant doctrine was a different understanding of the verb δικαιοῦν (Latin: *iustificare*) in the key Greek word-family. Instead of "make righteous," the Reformers held its meaning to be "declare righteous." In time the Reformers made a separation between the divine act of "justification" and the process of sanctification. In "justification" a person was declared righteous, in sanctification a person became righteous in reality (i.e., in a moral sense).

The theological rationale for "justification" developed on the Protestant side can be summed up as follows:

> What did Paul mean by justification? The term is a legal or forensic one. It refers to the acquittal of an accused person in a court of law. In Paul's mind, a sinner is charged with breaking the law of God (Romans 3:10, 19, 23). The penalty is death (6:24). The justice of God demands that the penalty be paid. However, God is also merciful and wishes to save the life of the accused. How then can both the justice and mercy of God be satisfied? The divine dilemma is solved through the atoning death of the Lord Jesus Christ, who bears the penalty on behalf of the accused (3:25; 4:25; 5:6-11). Justice having been done through a substitutionary atonement, God

Introduction

is free to offer pardon to the accused (3:24-28), who is discharged a free man (5:1-2; 8:1). This is what Paul meant by justification.[4]

The Reformers thus came to understand "justification" in terms of the law court (forensic justification). They frequently spoke of *the imputation of Christ's righteousness* to believers as the basis for their righteousness.

Luther and the tradition he established considered the doctrine of "justification" to be at the heart of Christianity. For him it even had a canonical function, so that its presence or absence in a writing of the New Testament determined the canonical status of that writing. Since the Reformation the Lutheran communion has been the most consistent among the world body of Christian denominations in promoting the centrality of the doctrine of "justification" for the Christian faith.

Each of the two models of "justification" just reviewed is problematic.

The realist view suffers from the reality that Christians do not attain full moral righteousness in this life. Had Paul been convinced they do, he would have had no need, after outlining his doctrine of "justification" in Romans 3–5, to go on to urge his addressees to become righteous in reality, that is, in a moral sense (Romans 6–8).

The forensic view typical of the majority of Protestants has other flaws. It is built up on concepts which have no place in Paul's discussions of "justification." For example, the notion of the imputation of Christ's righteousness to the believer is entirely foreign to the apostle. Terms such as "penalty" and "substitution" are also completely absent from his discussion. If the apostle didn't find it necessary to use them, we ought to be suspicious about explanations of "justification," such as that above, which depend so heavily on them.

Another obvious problem with the Protestant explanation of "justification" is seen in Rom 4:5, where, according to this understanding, God declares the ungodly to be in the right, or righteous. Such an approach justly deserves the criticism of being a "legal fiction."

A third explanation of Paul's doctrine gained considerable support during the twentieth century. It has often been combined with other views. However, it is able to stand in its own right.[5] According to this explanation, the verb δικαιοῦν means "to bring into a right relationship." This right relationship is a divine gift, arising from God's grace and embraced by faith when a person listens to the good news of what God has done through Christ. Since

---

4. Clifford, "Gospel and Justification," 253–54.
5. Moore, *Rectification*, vol 1.

1937 this view has been applied to some English translations of the New Testament, though never embraced for the "standard" English versions.

The twentieth century was also notable for the unprecedented level of ecumenical dialogue which developed. Since the issue over which the Western church split was the doctrine of "justification," many of the dialogues and conversations, particularly between the Roman Catholic Church and various bodies representing the Lutheran churches, concerned that doctrine.

During the last quarter of the twentieth century, and extending into the twenty-first, new perspectives on the Apostle Paul claimed a great deal of attention among the New Testament community. It is probably no exaggeration to say that they have dominated scholarly discussion during this period.

1.3 "JUSTIFICATION" IN ENGLISH VERSIONS OF THE NEW TESTAMENT

Inevitably, any English version of the Scriptures reflects the historical matrix, including the theological trends, in which it arose.

From the time English translations became available in the Middle English of the fourteenth century, a further factor influencing the way "justification" was understood in them came into play. The key word-family in the Greek (the δ-family, which is characterized by the δικαι-stem) was represented in English translation by *two* English word-families: "righteousness" and cognates (the R-family) and "justify" and cognates (the J-family). These two English word-families have no obvious semantic connection. This two word-family pattern still dominates the "standard" English versions of today (e.g., the NJB, REB, NRSV, NIV2011 and NABRE).

1.4 WHERE TO FROM HERE?

The three areas touching on the doctrine of "justification" that we have just outlined, namely, (1) the New Testament in its original language of Greek, (2) the historical development of the doctrine, and (3) English versions of the New Testament, form a three-way conversation.

For most of us it is likely that our first acquaintance with the doctrine of "justification" came through (3) reading an English version of the New Testament or through preaching, group study, conversation, or secondary reading, all of which rely on those English versions. We are unlikely to have met it first in (1) the New Testament in its original language of Greek, or

Introduction

to have had an awareness of (2) the historical development of the doctrine. Since most contemporary English versions use specialized vocabulary to convey Paul's doctrine, employing words (such as "justify") or phrases (such as "the righteousness of God") that do not have their usual meanings, it should not surprise us that most people find the doctrine unintelligible in the English Bible. Further, the vocabulary of "justification" utilized in the other areas mentioned above, such as preaching and secondary literature, is largely drawn from the vocabulary used in the standard English versions.

There is therefore a certain circularity in the way we meet the doctrine of "justification" in English. Over time various factors have conspired to encrust Paul's doctrine with successive layers of meaning far removed from the apostle's original intention. How is this vicious circle to be broken? How are the layers to be peeled back?

To understand the apostle on his own terms we need to make every effort to enter his world—its vocabulary, its culture, its worldview. While we may not be able to achieve this to a level of one hundred per cent, we should be skeptical of those who, motivated by an unhealthy skepticism, claim such an exercise is futile. That is, it is possible to attend to no. (1) above.

A second approach is to trace the ways in which the understanding of Paul's doctrine has developed over the two millennia separating his time from ours. As we do so, we need not merely to document what happened, but to *evaluate* it. For out of the enormous variety of ways of understanding Paul which emerge from such a survey, it is plain that not all of them can accurately represent the apostle's meaning. In this exercise we are attending to no. (2) above. It is tantamount to peeling back the encrusted layers that have accumulated over the centuries, layers which obscure the original Pauline treasure, and in some cases powerfully influence our basic assumptions and the way we think about "justification" today.

A third approach is to study how Paul's doctrine, as established in no. (1), has been represented in English versions of the New Testament: no. (3) above. By doing so, we become aware of the tenacious persistence of the approach adopted initially, of using two English word-families for Paul's single Greek word-family, but also of approaches which have broken out of this mold.

In this way we are able to engage in a three-way conversation, in which each partner can contribute to clarifying what Paul intended to convey by his doctrine of "justification."

Now an explanation of how the material is presented in the following chapters.

We begin with the conclusions reached about Paul and his doctrine (chapter 2). This is, in one sense, back to front. However, the present work is concerned with expounding the apostle's doctrine. Those who wish to work through the evidence inductively and systematically, reaching conclusions only at the end of that process, are referred to my three-volume technical treatment of the topic: *Rectification ('Justification') in Paul, in Historical Perspective, and in the English Bible: God's Gift of Right Relationship*.

We then survey the major developments in the doctrine of "justification" with special reference to the Western church (chapter 3). Since in this chapter we move forwards in time, it is, of course, the reverse of "unpeeling," but is intended to have the same benefit.

Chapter 4 focuses on a particular aspect of the historical development of "justification": how the doctrine has been expressed in English versions of the New Testament from their beginnings in the fourteenth century to early in the third millennium.

There follows an anatomy of how Paul develops his doctrine of "justification," including the influences which helped inform it (chapter 5).

In chapter 6 these insights are then applied to the major Pauline letter concerned with "justification," namely, his letter to the Christians of Rome.

Chapter 7, the concluding chapter, reiterates the main issues and points to their significance for our ongoing understanding of this Pauline doctrine.

From this point on, the doctrine usually known in English as the doctrine of "justification" is normally referred to as "rectification." It involves the change of just three letters from *jus* to *rec*, both words being derived from Latin roots! There is a small but significant trend to adopt and/or advocate this change among others working professionally in the field of New Testament.[6] In this book it constitutes an attempt to encourage a more accurate and more meaningful way of referring to the doctrine concerned, which is about how God rectifies our human dilemma.

On the grounds of sound translation principles, however, I personally do not advocate the use of "rectify" and cognates for English translations of the Scriptures; while this works quite well for the verb and as a translation of the rare noun δικαίωσις ("rectification"), the "rectify" word-group in English has no suitable equivalent for δικαιοσύνη, the most commonly occurring noun—indeed, the most commonly occurring word—of the

---

6. Moore, *Rectification*, 1:1 n. 4.

Introduction

δ-family in the New Testament. It is better, in my view, to focus on "right" and to adapt it to context—as has been done by a number of English translators, and in the translation I provide in this monograph (*Under the Southern Cross: The New Testament in Australian English*).

2

A Profile of Paul's View of Rectification

or,

The Good News according to Paul

2.1 GOD'S RIGHTEOUS CHARACTER: GOD IS ALWAYS IN THE RIGHT

FUNDAMENTAL TO PAUL'S UNDERSTANDING of God and of ultimate reality, is a notion he had acquired during his upbringing as a Jew, namely, that God by his very nature is righteous. By this understanding God always acts in a way that is right, and in fact he is incapable of acting in any other way. Indeed, God's attitudes and actions define what is right. If it were possible to put God on trial in a court of strict justice, the inevitable verdict would be that God is in the right. Such a hypothetical scenario had already been anticipated by the Psalmist (Ps 50:6 Lxx), whom Paul quotes at Rom 3:4b: "that you [God] may be shown to be in the right by what you say, and may emerge victorious when you are tried in court."

In Romans Paul was especially concerned that his readers understand one particular action of God as a right action on his part. In a play on words from the Greek word-family which expresses "right" (δικαιοσύνη and cognates) Paul explained that, in putting forward and accepting Christ's sacrifice for sins, God was both "in the right" and the one who "brings into a right relationship" the person who puts their faith in Jesus (Rom 3:25–26).

2.2 THE UNIVERSAL SINFULNESS OF HUMANITY

Human beings ultimately owe their existence to God, their Creator. Because they bear the image of their Creator they are capable of a personal relationship with him. However, they have alienated themselves from God by their behavior, by the way they have thought, spoken, and acted. To describe such wrong conduct Paul uses the term ἁμαρτία ("sin"). He speaks of the "exceeding sinfulness of sin" (Rom 7:13).

How does God regard and respond to sinful human behavior? Paul sums up the divine attitude by the word ὀργή ("anger, hostility"). In Romans he states that God's ὀργή is directed against sin (specifically, ἀσέβεια and ἀδικία, "ungodliness" and "wrongdoing," Rom 1:18). It was to deal with the world's sin that God put Christ on public display during his death as a sacrificial, expiatory sacrifice (Rom 3:25).

Paul held that sin is a universal human condition. Although his statement in Rom 3:23 is incidental to the main point he is making, the rendering "all have sinned and fall short of God's glory," fairly represents his view. It is also evident earlier in that chapter as he quotes a catena of Old Testament quotations beginning: "There is not even one who is righteous, no, not one . . . " (Rom 3:10, citing Ps 14:1–3 // Ps 53:2–4).

Paul makes the same point in Romans 5. Although Adam is representative of sinful humanity, the reason all experience death is "because all have sinned" (Rom 5:12).

The apostle's basic position is well summed up later in the letter: "For God consigned everyone to disobedience, so that he might have mercy on all" (Rom 11:32). He had used similar language earlier, when addressing the churches of Galatia: "But scripture has declared the whole world to be prisoners in subjection to sin, so that faith in Jesus Christ should be the ground on which the promised blessing is given to those who believe" (Gal 3:22 REB).

2.3 THE ROLE OF THE LAW

Contrary to the view widely held among his fellow Jews, that the intended function of the Law was to give life to those who observed it (Gal 3:21), Paul regarded the primary function of the Law as negative: far from having any power to save, the Law merely provided the knowledge that a person is sinful (Gal 3:22; Rom 3:20). Indeed, the Law addresses itself to those under its jurisdiction, "so that every mouth may be muzzled and the whole world may be held accountable to God" (Rom 3:19).

Not that the Law is to be set aside (Rom 3:31). In order to demonstrate that the Law endorses the view of faith he is putting forward in Romans, Paul appeals to the Law (Torah), specifically, the experience Abraham had, as recorded in the Torah at Gen 15:6 (cited Rom 4:3). In a similar way he had earlier, when addressing those in the Galatian congregations who wished to be "under Law" (Gal 4:21-31), appealed to a complex argument based on the book of Genesis. For, as he went on to point out, those wishing to be brought into a right relationship with God through observing one part of the Law, namely circumcision, were "under obligation to keep the Law in its entirety" (Gal 5:3).

Earlier in Galatians Paul had put his view of the relationship between Law and faith as follows:

> . . . if a Law had been given which was able to impart life, then right relationship would certainly have been based on Law, but the Scripture subsumed everything under sin, so that the promise, based on faith in Jesus Christ, might be given to those who have faith.[1]

2.4 GOD'S SAVING PURPOSES

In the Scriptures God's deliverance of human beings from the consequences and the power of their sin is often expressed as "saving" or "rescuing" them. The giving of the Law was just one step in his provision for humanity's salvation. In the Old Testament (especially in Isaiah) the concept of "salvation" was often linked with that of God's "righteousness," i.e., of God's acting in a right way. Paul picks up this link between "salvation" and "righteousness" at several points in Romans (e.g., Rom 1:16–17; 10:9–10). However, in Galatians and Romans his strong preference is for expressing God's saving purposes not by using the language of "salvation," but through words of the "right" family (the δ-family).

---

1. Gal 3:21–22.

2.5 GRACE, THE DIVINE MOTIVATION UNDERLYING GOD'S RECTIFYING ACTIVITY

What is it that motivates God to make provision for saving human beings, for bringing them into a right relationship with himself? For Paul the key term is "grace" (χάρις), occurring 25x in Romans. It may be defined as the gracious and generous attitude God shows towards human beings in their need—a need brought about by their sinful condition and activities. Typical of Paul's use of the term is Rom 3:23–24: "since all have sinned and fall short of God's glory, they are brought into a right relationship freely, by his grace, through the liberation purchased by Christ Jesus," or Rom 11:5-6: ". . . at the present time a remnant has come into being, chosen by grace. However, if it is by grace, it no longer depends on human behaviour, otherwise grace would no longer be grace."

While χάρις is the most common term for describing this divine motivation, it also serves as the overarching term for a cluster of words broadly in the same semantic domain. They embrace the concepts of love (ἀγάπη), forbearance (ἀνοχή), forgiveness (ἀφιέναι), gift (δωρεά, δωρεάν, δώρημα, χάρισμα), mercy (ἐλεεῖν), longsuffering (μακροθυμία), compassion (οἰκτιρμός, οἰκτίρειν), generous wealth (πλουτεῖν, πλοῦτος), patience (ὑπομονή), and goodness (χρηστός, χρηστότης).[2]

2.6 CHRIST, GOD'S AGENT IN RECTIFICATION

God's desire to bring human beings into a right relationship with himself was not sufficient of itself to bring this about. Human sin, forming a barrier between God and humanity, needed to be dealt with. To achieve the reconciliation God desired, it was necessary for sin and its effects to be removed. Here, in the Pauline conception, we see God's grace and generosity at work. For to achieve a restoration of relationships, God was willing to send his Son into the world to do what was necessary to remove human sin.

So we find Paul writing in Gal 4:4–5:

> But when the time had fully arrived, God sent his Son, born to a woman, born under the Law, so that he might redeem those who are under the Law, so that we might be adopted as his children.

---

2. Moore, *Rectification*, 1:79.

Paul's Concept of Justification

In his later letter the apostle explained the role of Christ in his central statement on God's rectifying activity in this way (Rom 3:21–25):

> Now, however, quite apart from the Law, the way to a right relationship with God, attested to by the Law and the Prophetic Writings, has come to light, a right relationship with God through faith in Jesus Christ for all who have faith. For there isn't any difference: since all have sinned and fall short of God's glory, they are brought into a right relationship freely, by his grace, through the liberation purchased by Christ Jesus. God put him on public display as a reconciling sacrifice though faith in his blood to demonstrate the rightness of his action in disregarding sins committed previously . . .

Note that in both passages above, it is *God himself* (not Christ) who takes the initiative.

In using sacrificial imagery when speaking of Christ's death in Galatians and Romans, Paul was following the general practice of the New Testament writers. He never speaks of Christ's death as being necessary to fulfil a legal requirement. Even the "curse" language of Galatians is religious rather than legal in nature, both in its application to the person who steps outside the Law and to the death of Christ (Gal 3:10, 13).

Nor does Paul speak directly of Christ's death in connection with the removal of divine ὀργή in Galatians and Romans, the two letters where he develops his doctrine of rectification in detail. Rather, the fact that God's ὀργή has been dealt with is something he assumes there.[3]

A second reason for Christ's salvific mission was to make it possible for the rectified person to receive the Holy Spirit (often referred to as the Spirit of Christ, e.g., Rom 8:9). For it is the presence of the Holy Spirit in the Christian (rather than the Law) which makes it possible for the Christian to become δίκαιος (righteous) in reality, δίκαιος in a moral sense, personally δίκαιος. Or, to use another Pauline expression which moves in the same direction, the Christian is to submit to God and to do "what is right" (δικαιοσύνη) with a view to holiness or sanctification (Rom 6:19): "I am using everyday illustrations because of your human limitations. For just as you presented the various parts of your bodies as slaves to impurity and lawlessness, with lawlessness as the consequence, so now present the

---

3. God's ὀργή is not, in fact, referred to at all in Galatians, and in Romans in the one passage where it is used in an R-context (Rom 5:9), its use is incidental or subsidiary rather than central, being used of a *future* situation (cf. ἡ ἡμέρα ὀργῆς, Rom 2:5) or possibly in a *gnomic* sense.

various parts of your bodies as slaves to what is right, with holiness as the consequence."

[See also 2.12–14 below.]

2.7 FAITH, THE ESSENTIAL PREREQUISITE FOR RECTIFICATION TO OCCUR

For God's δικαίωσις (rectifying act), or God's salvation, to be actualized in any individual instance, the condition of πίστις ("faith") or πιστεύειν (the act of "believing," or of "coming to faith") must first be present, exercised by the person who would be rectified. Since rectification can only occur on an individual basis, and is meaningful only on that basis, Paul expresses what is involved in the second person *singular*: "For if you ['thou'] acknowledge the Lord Jesus with your ['thy'] lips and believe in your ['thy'] heart that God raised him from among the dead, you ['thou'] will be saved" (Rom 10:9; cf. the KJV).

All people, presumably, have faith. Faith differs from individual to individual, however, depending (in part) on the object of faith in each case. Rectifying faith has value precisely because, and only because, it is faith *in Christ*.[4]

Paul quarries much of his key material on faith from the Jewish Scriptures, notably in his treatment of Abraham in Romans 4. There he argues that faith is essential if a person is to be brought into a right relationship with God. As the model for one who has been brought into a right relationship with God, Abraham set an example of faith for both Jew and non-Jew, and indeed he is the "father" of all those who have faith in both these groups (Rom 4:10–12). At a later point in Romans the apostle is even prepared to state that "everything which is not motivated by faith is sin" (Rom 14:23).

When Paul speaks of rectifying faith as being faith in Christ he has in mind the two great events (or the two great aspects of the one central event) in Christ's incarnate life—his cross and his resurrection. Indeed, while he speaks more clearly of "Christ crucified" in the Corinthian correspondence and in Galatians, in Rom 10:9 (in the context of discussing rectification)

---

4. Almost certainly Paul intended his several uses of the phrase πίστις Χριστοῦ in Galatians (2:16 [2x], 20; 3:22) and Romans (3:22, 26) to be understood as *objective* genitives ("faith in Christ") rather than genitives of *possession* ("Christ's faithfulness"). But even if this were not the case, parallel expressions make it clear that he had in mind faith in Christ (Gal 2:16; 3:26; Rom 3:25; 10:14); see the discussion in Moore, *Rectification*, vol. 1, §7.5.

faith is especially directed towards Christ's resurrection: "if you . . . believe in your heart that God raised him from among the dead, you will be saved."

2.8 THE PROCLAMATION OF THE GOOD NEWS IS THE CONTEXT IN WHICH FAITH COMES INTO BEING

How does a person obtain the faith that is associated with God's rectifying activity? Certainly Paul nowhere suggests in Galatians or Romans that the faith that leads to a right relationship comes to a person as God's gift.

Paul's own understanding of this issue emerges from his statement in Rom 10:17 where faith arises in the context of the proclamation of the good news: "faith is the consequence of listening (ἀκοή), and listening occurs through the message about Christ." In his parlance, the "message about Christ" is simply another way of expressing the "good news" to which he refers so frequently. The background to the statement of 10:17 is the logical sequence he provides in Rom 10:14–15.

In Pauline thought, faith is closely associated with obedience. In both the opening of his letter, and towards its close, he uses the phrase "the obedience of faith" (Rom 1:5; 16:26). Here it is probable that faith is intended to be exepegetic, that is, it is the faith that consists of obedience, or the faith that constitutes obedience, or the obedience that is motivated by faith.

As far as God is concerned, such faith is regarded as δικαιοσύνη. Paul utilizes the statement about Abraham in Gen 15:6 as a model for Christian faith and rectification: "Abraham put his faith in God, and for him that was regarded as the basis for a right relationship" (cited Gal 3:6; Rom 4:3. Romans 4 serves as an extended commentary on this quotation, and an application of it).

2.9 GOD (NOT CHRIST) IS THE RECTIFIER

Once the factor of faith or personal trust in Christ is present, God's action of bringing the ungodly person into a right relationship (δικαιοῦν τὸν ἀσεβῆ, Rom 4:5) becomes possible; the prior condition required of the recipient has been met.

It is to be observed that it is *God* who rectifies. Although Christ's action in coming to earth so that he might be "handed over because of the offences we have committed" and "raised so that we might be brought into a right relationship" (Rom 4:25) is vital in making reconciliation between

God and humankind possible, nevertheless in Paul's writings the rectifying act is consistently attributed to God, not to Christ. So in Galatians we find Paul writing, "The Scripture, anticipating that God would bring people who aren't Jews into a right relationship as a consequence of faith, proclaimed the good news to Abraham in advance: 'Through you all the non-Jewish nations will be blessed'" (Gal 3:8). Similarly, in Romans we read: "Who will lay charges against those whom *God* has chosen? Will it be *God*, who brings people into a right relationship?' (Rom 8:33).

What is the meaning of the verb δικαιοῦν?

The view developed in the Western (Roman Catholic) tradition is that Paul's reference is to God's making the ungodly (morally) righteous. Since this patently does not occur at the very beginning of the Christian life, Roman Catholics viewed (and continue to view) "justification" as a (lifelong) process.

Early in the development of their distinctive thought, Protestants abandoned this interpretation in favor of regarding God's act of δικαιοῦν as the act by which God initiates the Christian life. They subsequently divided God's work into two: (1) an initial declaratory act, "justification," in which the ungodly person is declared or pronounced to be righteous, followed by (2) the continuing process of sanctification, by which the Christian continues to become righteous in a moral sense.

A third view builds on the Protestant insight that God's work is carried through in two stages. However, it understands the nature of God's initiating act differently, taking δικαιοῦν to refer to God's setting right[5] of the ungodly in the sense of bringing the ungodly into a right relationship [with himself]. It originated in the nineteenth century, but gained considerable ground, especially in the twentieth century. It is this view which best explains the Pauline data. In support of it we may note the following considerations:

1. 2 Cor 5:18–21 and Rom 5:9–11 make it clear that the concepts of "rectification" and "reconciliation" come very close to each other.

2. In Romans 14 and 15 Paul uses προσλαμβάνειν to speak of the Christian's *acceptance* by both God (Rom 14:3) and Christ (Rom 15:7).

3. Rom 2:13 makes it clear that experiencing (passively) the action of δικαιοῦν is equivalent to being δίκαιος παρὰ τῷ θεῷ, right before God:

---

5. "Set right" is the first of three meanings given by Liddell and Scott [LS 429]; LN §34.46 give: "to put right with, to cause to be in a right relationship with."

οὐ γὰρ οἱ ἀκροαταὶ νόμου δίκαιοι παρὰ τῷ θεῷ, ἀλλ' οἱ ποιηταὶ νόμου δικαιωθήσονται [For it isn't those who hear the Law who are right before God, but those who do the Law who will be righted (brought into a right relationship).]

4. It is clear that while Paul varies his expression when using the words of the δ-GR family, the referent he has in mind is the same for each: thus, for example, while in Rom 4:5 he can speak of God setting right (δικαιοῦν) the ungodly, this is no different in essence from God's granting the gift of δικαιοσύνη (Rom 5:17), or manifesting his δικαιοσύνη in such a way that the person who responds may be described as ὁ δίκαιος (Rom 1:17).

2.10 THE SCOPE OF GOD'S OFFER OF RECTIFICATION IS UNIVERSAL

The salvation proclaimed in the New Testament has meaning only in the context of the Old Testament Scriptures and the salvation-history unfolded in them. While that salvation-history involved God's choice of a people of his own, beginning with Abraham, right from the very beginning the Old Testament Scriptures make it clear that the terms of reference for God's blessing are much wider than Abraham and his descendants, even though his blessing will come through them (e.g., Gen 12:3). It is this wider vision that the New Testament writers appeal to in their contention that what God has achieved through Christ is available to all who will avail themselves of it, irrespective of race, class, or gender (e.g., Gal 3:28). As Paul styles himself "apostle to non-Jews" (Rom 11:13; cf. Gal 1:15; 2:7–9; Rom 15:14–15) this universal availability of rectification is particularly prominent in the Pauline writings (e.g., Rom 15:8–12). Paul states the point being made very succinctly in Rom 15:8–9: "let me point out that Christ has become a servant to those who are circumcised for the sake of God's truth, so that the promises given to the ancestors might be kept, that is, that non-Jewish people might glorify God because of his mercy . . ."

2.11 THE CONSEQUENCES OF GOD'S RECTIFYING ACT IN THE INDIVIDUAL

What are the consequences for a person when God has brought them into a right relationship with himself? The following list is not exhaustive, but endeavors to identify the main outcomes for the Christian:

1. Peace with God (Rom 5:1). Through Christ the hostility that alienated us from God is removed, and reconciliation is effected (Rom 5:9–11; 2 Cor 5:17–21). To use the old English expression (favored by some of the early English translators) we are "at one" with God.

2. Very close to reconciliation is the notion of acceptance by God or Christ (προσλαμβάνεσθαι), drawn from the sphere of social relations. Though referred to only incidentally (Rom 14:3; 15:7) it, too, is clearly a consequence of rectification.

3. Forgiveness of sins. Paul never uses this expression in Galatians, and only once in Romans (Rom 4:6–8). Nevertheless his statement there is strong and clear.

4. It is also clear that rectification has dealt effectively with anything that stood against the Christian in a religious sense (the "curse" of Gal 3:10, 13, Christ having redeemed us from the curse of the Law), or in a legal sense (we will be saved from anger, Rom 5:9; there is no punishment [κατάκριμα] to those in Christ Jesus, Rom 8:1). Thus, while rectification is not set in a legal framework (it comes about χωρὶς νόμου [apart from the Law], Rom 3:21) it nevertheless has "legal" consequences (Rom 8:1). What is explicit in Galatians (Gal 3:10–14) is stated only incidentally in Romans (Rom 8:1).

5. The gift of the Holy Spirit. The fact that a Christian receives the gift of the Holy Spirit is not spelt out in Paul; instead, it is assumed. In writing to the Galatians, for example, he appeals to their conversion experience by asking (Gal 3:2–3, 5):

   > There is just one thing I want to find out from you: Did you receive the Spirit as a consequence of doing what the Law requires, or as a consequence of the faith associated with listening? Having begun with the Spirit, are you so stupid as to now be concluding on the merely human plane? . . . does he who supplies the Spirit to you . . . do so as a consequence of your doing what the Law requires, or as a consequence of the faith associated with listening?

In Romans he makes the same point negatively, stating, "You, however, aren't under the control of human nature, but are under the control of the Spirit—if God's Spirit resides in you. Now if any person doesn't have Christ's Spirit, that person doesn't belong to Christ" (Rom 8:9).

6. Eternal life. Depicting the change from being in a situation of alienation from God to one of being brought into a right relationship with God as a change of masters, the apostle writes: "... the wages sin pays is death, but the gift God freely gives is eternal life through Christ Jesus, our Lord" (Rom 6:23).

7. Assurance of salvation. Provided their sense of assurance is based firmly on the love of God and of Christ for them, a Christian need not doubt their acceptance with God and with Christ (Rom 14:3; 15:7), for there is nothing that is capable of standing between the Christian and that love (Rom 8:31–39). As Paul had stated earlier: "The Spirit himself testifies together with our spirits that we are God's children" (Rom 8:16).

2.12 GOD BRINGS A PERSON INTO A RIGHT RELATIONSHIP WITH HIMSELF IN ORDER THAT THAT PERSON MIGHT LIVE A RIGHT LIFE

While it is the ungodly for whom Christ died (Rom 5:6) and the ungodly whom God brings into a right relationship with himself (Rom 4:5), the underlying purpose of God's rectifying act is that the rectified person might escape the dominance and mastery of sin and serve a new master: righteousness, or "what is right" (Romans 6). Both Galatians and Romans contain extensive passages in which Paul exhorts his addressees to work out the implications of being a "new creation" of God in the moral sphere. God's people are not only to be in a right relationship with God, but in their lives they are to do what is right—in a personal, moral, sense. The very reason for Christ's coming was so that what the Law quite rightly and properly requires of us might be fulfilled in those who live, not according to human desires, but in accordance with the Spirit (Rom 8:3–4).

2.13 THE LAW CANNOT HELP THE RECTIFIED PERSON TO LIVE RIGHTEOUSLY

Viewed in terms of their subjective experience, the person who has been brought into a right relationship with God is not able to progress from being ungodly to being righteous simply by endeavoring to keep the Law. As the endeavor to fulfill the Law was ineffective as a means of coming into a right relationship with God (Romans 2–3), so for the person who has been brought into a right relationship by God, endeavoring to fulfill what the Law quite rightly and justly requires also proves ineffective for moral transformation (Romans 7).

2.14 ONLY BY COOPERATING WITH THE HOLY SPIRIT CAN THE RECTIFIED PERSON LIVE RIGHTEOUSLY

Instead, the divinely appointed means of bringing about moral transformation is through the Holy Spirit, who resides in a Christian. In both Galatians (5:13–18, 22–25) and Romans (8:1–13), Paul makes a strong appeal to his addressees to be led by the Spirit, to conform to the Spirit within them, as the means of moral transformation, of becoming righteous in a moral sense. By "walking by the Spirit," i.e., by conducting our lives in sensitivity to his presence, guidance, and leading, and by adopting a mindset focused on the Holy Spirit—rather than following a merely human mind-set—the Christian will not fulfill the desires of human nature, but will live in accordance with the Spirit (Rom 8:1–8, 12–14).

2.15 BAPTISM SYMBOLIZES THE CHRISTIAN'S REORIENTATION

All the evidence of the New Testament suggests that the standard way of declaring one's allegiance to Christ was through Christian baptism, understood (in the context of that time) as an immersion rite undergone in the name of Christ or of the Father, Son, and Holy Spirit. In the case of the Galatian congregations to whom he writes, Paul no doubt had been personally involved in administering baptism, or at least witnessed it, as it was through him that they first heard the good news. So he takes for granted the baptism of those to whom he writes (Gal 3:27). Similarly, although he had not yet visited Rome, his letter there was addressed to "all ... in Rome who are dearly loved by God" (Rom 1:7), that is, all the Christians of Rome. He therefore assumes that they have all been baptized, and appeals to this universal Christian experience, which signals one's entry into the Christian life, in order to apply moral teaching to his addressees (Rom 6:1–11).

As Paul presents it, Christian baptism is essentially a means of identifying with Christ. The change in orientation effected by God's rectification of the ungodly, and the consequent transformation of the rectified person's life, is graphically depicted by the three stages involved in the immersion rite:

1. being plunged into the water is a means of being identified with Christ in his death;
2. the momentary submersion figures burial;
3. being raised (passively, through the strength of another person!) is a means of identifying with Christ in his resurrection.

The person who is baptized (immersed) is plunged into the water just as Christ was plunged into death. The act of immersion symbolizes a "death to sin"; but the baptized person is also raised up out of the water of baptism, just as Christ was raised from the dead, symbolizing being raised to a new life. Consequently, Paul writes (Rom 6:4):

> ... through baptismal immersion we were entombed with him in the realm of death, so that just as Christ was raised up from among the dead through the Father's glory, so we too would be able to live in the newness life brings.

He goes on to apply it as follows (Rom 6:11):

> On this basis, you are to consider yourself to be dead as far as sin is concerned, but alive through Christ Jesus as far as God is concerned.

2.16 THE DIVINE INITIATIVE IN RECTIFICATION BEGINS WITH ELECTION

Throughout the presentation of his doctrine of rectification Paul emphasizes the divine initiative. The very motivation underlying it is God's love and God's grace; it is he who sent his Son into the world as an atoning sacrifice (Gal 4:4; Rom 3:25) that there might be "good news." (It is the good news about his Son: Gal 1:7; Rom 1:9; 15:19.) It is God who sends those who proclaim the good news (Rom 10:15); it is God who brings people—the ungodly—into a right relationship with himself (Rom 4:5) on the basis of the faith with which they respond to the good news (Rom 1:16–17; 10:14–17). Through that same faith, they receive the gift of the Holy Spirit in the divine act of rectification (Gal 3:5).

But behind this whole plan and process, in God's foreknowledge and planning lies the exercise of his own divine prerogative—to elect (that is, choose or select) people to salvation, thereby ensuring that *some*, at least, will be saved. Paul spells out this divine prerogative most fully in Romans 9.

It provides further evidence that rectification is to be understood as something God initiates and does—the fundamental insight of the sixteenth-century Reformers. God's rectifying act became possible through the sacrificial death of Christ, whom God sent into the world for the very purpose of dying on behalf of the ungodly (Rom 4:5; 5:6).

What role then does the individual have in God's plan? Clearly there must be some involvement by the human recipient of God's grace, otherwise God's actions would be wholly deterministic, overriding any sense in which the human benefactor has a choice.

For Paul the answer lies in faith, not as a new species of "work" (in the sense of the "works of the Law") but as the obedient response ("the obedience of faith," Rom 1:5; 16:26) to the good news proclaimed by messengers God has sent, a good news made possible in the first instance because God sent his Son into the world. For "the good news" is no more and no less than "the good news about Christ"—the message and significance of his death and resurrection.

When faith (i.e., faith in Christ) has arisen in an individual, in the context of the proclamation of the good news [about Christ], God is able to undertake the action of δικαιοῦν (setting right, rectifying) that individual. With that divine action comes all the benefits noted, some with immediate effect (e.g., forgiveness), some of long-term significance (e.g., the presence of the Holy Spirit, enabling that person to become increasingly righteous in reality, in a moral sense).

The discussion above makes it clear that God's rectification of the ungodly is overwhelmingly brought about on the basis of divine initiative. When a person responds to God in faith, that faith-response, that act of obedience, is simply the response which the Creator and Redeemer can rightly and justly require of his own creatures.

3

The Doctrine of Rectification in Historical Perspective

3.1 THE PATRISTIC PERIOD

IN ALL PROBABILITY IT was not long after copies of Paul's letters had been gathered together and made available as a collection that the author of 2 Peter, while speaking appreciatively of them, also observed that some things in them are hard to understand.[1]

Certainly the evidence of the sub-apostolic period, i.e., of those who followed immediately after the apostles, indicates that Paul's major concerns, as expressed in his letter to the Galatian churches and his letter to the Christians at Rome, were not only of no interest to Paul's spiritual successors, but were seriously misunderstood by them. Indeed, it is not overstating the case to say that in the sub-apostolic era Paul's concepts were completely turned on their head.

On the other hand, the New Testament evidence suggests that Paul regarded rectification as the primary expression of salvation in the good news he proclaimed: see, for example, the pivotal soteriological statements at Gal 2:15–21, Rom 1:16–17, and Rom 3:21–31, each of which is crammed with rectification language. Yet Paul's doctrine of rectification is conspicuously absent among the apostolic fathers and the apologists who make up the earliest strata of the patristic period.[2] In its place was a soteriology that presented Christ as the new Lawgiver, whose laws were to be obeyed! Scholars

---

1. 2 Pet 3:16.

2. The anonymous second century *Letter to Diognetus* appears to be the sole exception (on this see Gundry, "Nonimputation," 17 n. 1).

The Doctrine of Rectification in Historical Perspective

are virtually unanimous in recognizing the ignoring or distorting of Paul's doctrine of rectification in the early patristic period.[3]

In the East, there is evidence from early on that the language and concept of rectification developed particularly by Paul was subordinated to other expressions of salvation, notably the notion of humankind's deification.

In the West, theological developments proceeded along different lines. In describing the relationship between God and humanity, sin occupied a much more significant place than it did in the East. The major developments that were ultimately to impinge on the doctrine of rectification were largely confined to one area of the Latin-speaking West, namely, Roman North Africa.

Early in the third century Tertullian (c. 150–c. 220), the first of three influential figures in North Africa, introduced into the vocabulary of theological discussion three terms that were destined to feature prominently in the doctrine of "justification." They were: (1) freewill; (2) merit; (3) satisfaction. None were biblical terms (or concepts for that matter), but each soon came to have a technical meaning and a role in theological enterprise and debate, particularly with respect to the doctrine of "justification."

Following Tertullian in consular North Africa was Cyprian, of the next generation (†258). His contribution was much more modest; nevertheless, he contributed to later discussion by applying the term "satisfaction" to humanity, just as Hilary of Poitiers (c. 315–367) in Gaul was to be the first to apply it to the death of Christ.

However, of all the church fathers it was the third of the Africans who made by far the greatest impact on the doctrine of rectification. The view of Augustine of Hippo Regius (354–430) underwent development, such that we can speak of his earlier view to c. 396, his mature view from 396/397. It was the latter which Augustine was to direct against Pelagius and his followers from c. 411. The outstanding feature of Augustine's view was a recovery of Paul's doctrine of grace. Augustine came closer than any of his predecessors to understanding the apostle's view of rectification. Yet his understanding is not to be presented as being identical with Paul's, or even approaching it. Its great strength was that it rehabilitated the grace of God as the supreme factor motivating the divine action of rectification. At the same time Augustine's writings became a quarry for the medieval period

---

3. Torrance, *Doctrine of Grace*; Stuhlmacher, *Gerechtigkeit Gottes*, 11–18; Stendahl, *Apostle Paul*, 83, 83 n. 7; McGrath, *Justification*, 19–20; Snyder, "Major Motifs", 44; *pace* Oden, *Justification Reader*.

that was soon to dawn. Without question, they came to exercise a much greater influence over subsequent generations in the West than was the case with the work of any other church father.

However, as well as drawing closer to Paul, Augustine left a legacy of concepts and methods that, in hindsight, can only be judged as negative. Already he was starting to divide grace into different categories; his view of infancy and childhood was completely at odds with the teaching and example of Jesus; the doctrine of original sin he developed rested on a mistranslation of the Latin Bible he used; it was he who was most responsible for extending the practice of infant baptism to the many areas of the Western church where it was not yet standard; he portrayed saving faith as a divine gift rather than an act of trust or commitment in obedience to the Creator and Redeemer.

3.2 THE MIDDLE AGES

The thousand years or so making up the medieval era constitute a lengthy and complex period.

In the Western church (which is our focus from this point on) the influence of Augustine was dominant. While this was so for the medieval period, aspects of Augustine's view continued to make an impact on the Reformation tradition which, to date, have proved permanent.

Unsettled conditions prevailed for several centuries following the Barbarian invasions at the beginning of the medieval period. They affected all of Europe and the former Roman Empire. At that time the spread of Christianity was largely the result of monasticism, chiefly in its Benedictine and Celtic forms. In the monasteries *lectio divina* kept alive the reading of the Christian Scriptures, primarily for the purpose of edification. As conditions became more settled in central and southern Europe, the pattern of Christian life began to diversify. New monastic orders came into being. Then, as part of the reforms introduced by Hildebrand (†1085), came rapid growth in the numbers and influence of cathedral schools. It was in them that the methodology referred to as scholasticism developed. Its great respect for the past led to the glossing of the entire Bible by early in the twelfth century. By the middle of that century Paris had become the most significant center for biblical and theological studies. It was at about this time that one of the very first universities came into being, in Paris. By the end of the twelfth century Aristotle was being mediated to the West through the Iberian Peninsula, which had connections with the Islamic east, where Aristotle's works had been kept alive. Early in the thirteenth century the two mendicant orders of Franciscans and Dominicans were founded. These events set the stage for the dominance of the Dominican Thomas of Aquino, who was a leading figure in applying the new Aristotelian insights to theological studies. The separation of theology as a discipline in its own right, distinct from biblical exposition, was now complete.

With the rise of theology came a renewed interest in Paul's doctrine of rectification, and an increasing refinement in the understanding of that doctrine. Armed with the accumulated exegetical experience of preceding generations of expositors, medieval scholars concerned themselves with issues such as the relationship between nature and grace (both of which have their source in God), whether the initiative in rectification is human or divine, what the process of "justification" involved, and the role played by the sacraments. They worked within an essentially Augustinian, anti-Pelagian framework, affirming that "justification" is by *faith*, not works. They considered that grace was manifest in a variety of forms to effect a diversity of functions in the salvation process; the process itself was at first regarded as threefold, ultimately as fourfold. Scholastic methodology proceeded by making ever more subtle distinctions in the categories under which "justification" had come to be discussed. Consequently, the concept of *grace*, which for Paul had been a divine attitude towards humankind, was conceived of basically as a medicine-like substance that could be dispensed (primarily through the sacraments, especially baptism, the Mass, and penance). It was treated atomistically, and given a wide variety of descriptors intended to differentiate between the varied functions and different circumstances in which it was believed to operate. Similarly, *merit*, an extra-biblical term and concept, was subjected to categorization designed to cover the variety of situations medieval ingenuity devised.

Granted that medieval exegetes and theologians operated within a framework of shared presuppositions, their work manifested considerable diversity. They were agreed that *iustificare* (the equivalent of Paul's δικαιοῦν) referred to the divine activity by which the *viator*[4] was made righteous in a moral sense. All envisaged this as a process that lasted throughout life. All were agreed that there were no grounds on which to establish the certainty that a person enjoyed a state of divine acceptance. The crucial Pauline phrase *iustitia Dei* (standing for δικαιοσύνη θεοῦ) was understood as

4. Pilgrim or wayfarer.

a personal attribute of God that operated in a punitive sense much as ὀργή θεοῦ functions in Rom 1:18.

Their points of difference related to how humankind, who share God's gift of nature, yet at the same time inherit it though Adam in the form of a fallen human nature, could become participants in God's gift of grace, which they envisaged as operating in the sphere of supernature. Hence they differed on such issues as (1) the conditions under which a person may transfer from the realm of nature to the realm of grace; (2) the respective roles of God and human beings in the process of justification; (3) whether it is God or humankind who initiates the "justification" process or whether it may be either.

While a significant number of features pervade the entire medieval period, there are nevertheless numerous developments which made unique contributions either to a particular age or to the ongoing understanding of Paul's doctrine of rectification.

What, then, were the features that characterized the period as a whole? Here it is possible to highlight only the main features and trends.

1. The Bible was read, studied, and known almost exclusively in a Latin translation: the Vulgate of Jerome. The original biblical languages played little part in biblical studies, and consequently had little influence. Given that one of Augustine of Hippo's most central and influential doctrines, his doctrine of original sin, rested on a mistranslation in the Latin versions (at Rom 5:12), that doctrine remained unchallenged throughout this period. This was just one means by which Paul's doctrine of rectification was effectively sidelined throughout the Middle Ages. For under Augustine and the medievals, the profile of divine salvation assumed a very different shape from its profile in Paul's theology.

2. While Augustine, the Doctor of Grace, had rehabilitated grace to a large degree (compared with his patristic predecessors) he had also sown the seeds of the de-personalization and reification of grace and its mediation through the sacraments, another feature pervading the entire medieval period. Instead of grace being a gracious attitude on God's part (as it was in Paul) it became a commodity to be dispensed by the church on earth. The sacraments of baptism and the eucharist, but especially of penance, were the means by which grace was mediated to the faithful. While the atomization of grace reached a peak

during the period of high scholasticism, already the seeds of that atomization were present in Augustine.

3. Faith, the prerequisite for rectification in Paul's view, was no longer conceived of as an attitude of trust (in God or Christ)—as it had been for the apostle—but was defined in terms of *a body of beliefs*.

4. Throughout the Middle Ages a formal anti-Pelagian[5] stance was maintained—another feature inherited from Augustine and his age. Notwithstanding, in various ways the essence of this stance was circumvented. It was precisely this sort of circumvention which brought about Luther's stand against indulgences.

5. In the medieval view, "justification" was conceived of as both an (initiating) event and a process. By his action of *iustificare* God makes the sinner right—in a moral sense. It is a process which lasts throughout one's earthly life.

6. Instead of the central place which rectification occupied in Paul's understanding of salvation, during the Middle Ages it was subordinated to other doctrines. Indeed, the medieval period effectively continued the situation that had prevailed for most of the patristic period.

7. In Paul's theology, God's gift of the Holy Spirit comes about as a consequence of God's rectifying act, and in the ongoing Christian life it is through the Holy Spirit that the Christian is to be remade into a person who is morally right. In medieval thinking, however, the Holy Spirit was not presented as a person or in personal categories, and his role in the saving process was greatly diminished.

In spite of these stable factors, however, the medieval period is not to be regarded as a static period. It witnessed numerous developments, and it was some of the later of these developments that eventually made possible, and indeed led to, a major break with a thousand years of a relatively uniform theological and ecclesiastical tradition. One British historian has helpfully subdivided the medieval era into three periods: (1) The Primitive Age, c. 700–c. 1050; (2) The Age of Growth, c. 1050–c. 1300; (3) The Age of Unrest, c. 1300–c. 1550.[6] These provide convenient headings under which

---

5. To Pelagius was attributed the view that human beings are able to fulfill God's commands by exercising God's gift of free will, unaided by divine grace (Gerald Bonner in Hart, *Dictionary*, 422.) Augustine strongly opposed this view.

6. Southern, *Western Society*, 24–52.

to discuss the major factors contributing to the way an understanding of the nature and function of Paul's doctrine of rectification developed during the Middle Ages.

(1) The Primitive Age (c. 700–1050)

Following hard on the collapse of the Roman Empire, the early centuries of the medieval period witnessed a socially and politically unsettled time. Nevertheless, even in these conditions Christianity continued to expand its influence geographically, chiefly through the spread of monasticism, especially in its Benedictine and Celtic forms. In the monasteries the Scriptures continued to be read on a regular basis through the practice of *lectio divina* and the use of lectionaries for divine service.

A significant ninth-century development was the adoption in Europe of the Celtic form of regular private penance, replacing the earlier public and much more occasional practice.

Towards the end of the period, under the influence of the Cluniac reforms of 910, many monasteries underwent reform. There was also a blossoming of new monastic movements, extending from the last quarter of the tenth century and into the first quarter of the twelfth.

(2) The Age of Growth (c. 1050–c. 1300)

The most striking phenomenon of the eleventh and twelfth centuries was the spread of cathedral schools. Their purpose was to train the secular clergy for their parish duties. Rising late in the tenth century, by the following century they had overtaken the monasteries as the most significant centers for the study of the Bible; by the twelfth century they were well established on a wide front. While they retained the practice of *lectio divina* characteristic of the monasteries, they went beyond this largely devotional function of the Bible to utilize it for doctrinal and moral instruction.

Within the cathedral schools, and early in their development, came scholasticism. Inspired by Fulbert of Chartres (c. 960–1028) and his pupil Lanfranc (c. 1010–89), who became Archbishop of Canterbury in 1070, it was systematized by his successor, Anselm of Canterbury (c. 1038–1109).

Scholasticism was greatly enhanced by the glossing of the entire Bible. Glossing took the form of adding marginal and interlinear notes (extracted from the writings of the church fathers) to the (handwritten) copies of the biblical text (in Latin). The *Glossa Ordinaria* was a standardized system developed under the leadership of Anselm of Laon (†1117). By the mid-twelfth century it had become the basis for teaching the Bible, as exemplified by such teachers as Peter Lombard (c. 1100–60) and Peter Comestor (†1179) of the great schools in Paris. (This latter Peter was also dubbed "Manducator"; both "Comestor" and "Manducator" mean "Eater," a reference to the perception that he had thoroughly "consumed" the Scriptures!)

Others, too, were very involved with the study and teaching of the Bible at this period. The Victorines, Hugh (c. 1096–1141), Richard (†1173), and Andrew (†1175) pursued the quest for a more literal interpretation of the Bible (that is, over against the traditional medieval approach of the fourfold sense in which the literal sense was subordinate to the three "spiritual" senses: the allegorical, the moral, and the anagogical.

For at least the first half of the medieval period, the Bible was everywhere regarded as a kind of encyclopedia of all knowledge. In some quarters at least, this perception began to change under Gregory VII (Hildebrand), Pope from 1073 until his death in 1085; he separated the study of Scripture from the study of natural science. Another significant shift in thinking occurred around 1200, with the separation of theology from biblical studies as a discipline in its own right.

Traditionally the philosophical base for Christian thought in the west had been Plato, mediated through Neo-Platonism. However, during the late twelfth and thirteenth centuries the full corpus of Aristotle's works entered Europe through Islamic influences in Spain. Early in the thirteenth century two orders of mendicant friars came into being which were to achieve considerable significance: the Franciscans (founded 1209) and the Dominicans (founded 1216). Before long the Dominicans under Albertus Magnus (c. 1200–80) and his even more famous pupil, Thomas Aquinas (1225–74) were applying Aristotelian concepts to theology.

The Processus Iustificationis

During the second half of the twelfth century a long neglected area began to be addressed: in a phenomenon referred to as the *processus iustificationis*, the attempt was made to define the doctrine of "justification" and to show its relationship to other major theological concepts and to ecclesiastical practice.

The development of the *processus iustificationis* coincided with the separation of theology from biblical studies and with the time when several Parisian schools were being formed into the University of Paris.

By this time Lombard's work of systematic theology, the *Sentences*, was in the process of being adopted ever more widely until it eventually, between the mid-thirteenth and the end of the fifteenth centuries, formed the basis for Western theological education.

The first scholar to use the term *processus iustificationis* and comment on it was Peter Comestor (†1179), Chancellor of the University of Paris from 1164. Comestor proposed a scheme involving three elements or stages in the process of "justification." The first was the infusion of grace, the last the forgiveness of sins. The middle term was concerned with free will. In its classical fourfold form a fourth element was created by subdividing this middle term.

The fourfold version first became explicit in the work of Peter of Poitiers (†1205), who had sat under both Peter Lombard and Peter Comestor in Paris and who had taught there himself between 1167 and 1205. In the course of his lecturing, Peter of Poitiers produced an abridged version of Peter Lombard's *Sentences* (a "Lombard without tears"!) which became very influential. It contained the *processus iustificationis* with the following elements or stages:

1. The infusion of grace;
2. a movement arising out of grace and the exercise of free will;
3. contrition;
4. remission of sin.

From around 1200 the fourfold *processus* came to be adopted by a number of scholars, some of great influence. It became a standard feature of the commentaries on the *Sentences* which mushroomed at this time. It received its most detailed treatment at the hands of the summit Albert the Great (c. 1200–80), while Bonaventure (1221–74) and his contemporary, Thomas Aquinas (c. 1225–74), each made influential contributions to how it was understood.

From the elements or stages in the *processus*, it is abundantly clear that a very close link was made between the doctrine of "justification" and the sacraments, particularly penance. This raises the further question of how the medieval understanding and practice of "penance" relates to the notion of "repentance" as we find it in the New Testament. One thing is certain: Paul nowhere makes such a linkage directly.

(3) The Age of Unrest (c. 1300–c. 1550)

From c. 1310 the friars engaged in a further great effort aimed at promoting biblical studies. It came to an end with the Black Death of 1348–49, which took such an enormous toll on Europe's population, reducing it by about one third.

By this time, however, there were signs of a different kind of change. The Franciscan, Johannes Duns Scotus (c. 1264–1308), opposed a number of Aristotelian principles and established alternative theological positions. His order adhered to some of these for many centuries. Another English Franciscan, William of Ockham (c. 1285–c. 1347) developed an approach which came to be known as the *via moderna* ("the modern way"). Ockham was ejected from his order in 1331.

3.3 THE REFORMATION AND ITS LEGACY

It is beyond dispute that the doctrinal issue at the heart of the sixteenth century Reformation was "justification."

In its early phases the Reformation had developed in two distinct geographical areas: Germany and German-speaking Switzerland. For the early Swiss reformers, the doctrine of rectification held no special significance; however, for the much more influential Reformers in the east of the German-speaking territories, it was not only dominant, but accorded first place.

By the second half of the 1530s Martin Luther (1483–1546) was hailing this doctrine as "master and chief, ruler and judge above every kind of doctrine."[7] In the ecclesiastical tradition which took his name, "justification" has continued to hold a central place, even though some individuals from Lutheran contexts, such as Albert Schweitzer (1875–1965) and Krister Stendahl (1921–2008), later accorded it a much less significant role in their understandings of the Christian faith.

Within the Lutheran tradition, Luther and his younger colleague Philip Melanchthon (1497–1560) were very different personalities. While Luther was the inspiring genius behind the German Reformation,

---

7. Luther's preface to 45 theses drawn up June 1, 1537.

Melanchthon was its systematizer. His *Loci communes*, first produced in 1521, went through four major editions, during which time Melanchthon's view of "justification" underwent significant changes.

Melanchthon arrived at Wittenberg, where Luther was professor of biblical exegesis, in 1518. Although he was Luther's junior by fourteen years, he evidently assisted Luther with Greek and encouraged him to embrace the humanism which was so influential in his own life, epitomized by Erasmus. On the other hand, Melanchthon had been an admirer of Luther before taking up the post of Professor of Greek at Wittenberg, and continued to be influenced by him down the years.

Their views of "justification," while sharing much in common, also had significant differences. From 1531 at the latest, and probably much earlier, Melanchthon developed a forensic view of "justification," that is, the view that envisages God's role in "justification" as that of a judge. Later he incorporated into this understanding the notion that in God's act of "justification" Christ's righteousness is imputed to the believer (as the means enabling God to pronounce the believer righteous):

> ... in this mortal life, that by which we are pleasing to God is the righteousness of *Christ*, which is imputed to us. . . . Thus we are clothed with a strange [alien] righteousness. Although our nature itself is still not uniform with God, nevertheless, as the Mediator Christ in his complete obedience is uniform with God and covers our sins with his righteousness, so we are justified, have forgiveness of sins, and are pleasing to God, for *Christ's* sake, whose righteousness is accepted on our behalf. . . . Thus righteousness means this imputed righteousness.[8]

The initial impetus in a forensic direction may have come from the first printed Greek New Testament, published by Erasmus in 1516. Erasmus's Greek New Testament was actually a diglot, in which the Greek and his own translation into Latin were on facing pages. At numerous points Erasmus's Latin translation differed from that of the Latin Vulgate, the standard version of the Bible in use in the Western church throughout the Middle Ages, at the time of the Reformation, and, in the Roman Catholic Church, until well into the twentieth century.

When translating one of the two key Pauline quotations on rectification from the Old Testament (Gen 15:6, cited Gal 3:6 and Rom 4:3),

---

8. Melanchthon, *Melanchthon*, 161–62.

Erasmus utilized *imputatem* instead of the Vulgate's *reputatem*, thereby echoing language used by the lawyers of that day.[9]

Already in Article 4 of the *Apology* for the Augsburg Confession (1531) Melanchthon had written, "In this passage 'justify' is used in a judicial way to mean 'to absolve a guilty man and pronounce him righteous,' and to do so on account of someone else's righteousness, namely, Christ's, which is communicated to us through faith."[10] In his 1532 commentary on Romans he introduced the illustration of Scipio's acquittal by the people of Rome (even though they knew him to be guilty). The Scipio illustration was also placed in the 1533 edition of Melanchthon's *Loci communes*.[11]

In time it was largely Melanchthon's views that came to be mediated by the Lutheran formularies; these, after all, had Luther's tacit endorsement. Of particular significance among the later post-Luther formularies was the *Book of Concord* (1580), which set the standard for Lutheran orthodoxy. It embodied nine documents, three ecumenical in nature, six of Lutheran origin. Of the latter, three were drawn up by Luther, two by Melanchthon, while six Lutheran divines were responsible for the last, the *Form of Concord* (1577).

The third of the three most influential sixteenth-century Reformers was French-speaking John Calvin (1509–64). Twenty-six years younger than Luther, twelve years younger than Melanchthon, Calvin came to a Reformation position some time during the first half of the 1530s, considerably later than they had. By that time a number of positions had been adopted by the German Reformers. While Calvin was certainly an independent thinker, and was to provide Reformed theology with its own characteristic stamp, in the matter of "justification" the evidence suggests that he simply took over the essentials established particularly by Melanchthon. (Melanchthon's *Loci communes* was available in Latin, the language of scholarly writing of that day, and so was readily accessible to Calvin.)

Melanchthon had provided Protestant theology with an apologetic that was able to deny the Roman Catholic position that God's action of justifying involved *making* a person righteous, by affirming that justification was a *forensic* act on God's part in which God (acting as judge) *declared* a person to be righteous. This, it came to be argued, was possible on the basis of the imputation of Christ's righteousness. (Neither the Protestant Reformers nor their Catholic opponents seem to have noticed that Paul nowhere

---

9. Fitzmyer, *Romans*, 374.
10. Melanchthon, "Apology," §305.
11. He evidently alludes to Scipio Africanus Major (236–184/3 BCE).

even mentions Christ's righteousness in association with his doctrine of rectification, and certainly doesn't use the verb "impute" [λογίζεσθαι] in this connection. See appendix G.)

There was one point on which Calvin's view of "justification" differed significantly from Luther's, and from Lutheran theology as a whole: unlike Luther and the Lutherans he did not regard the doctrine of "justification" as "master and chief, ruler and judge above every kind of doctrine." Calvin's position has, almost without exception, been followed by his spiritual heirs in the Reformed and Presbyterian traditions.

Generally speaking the Reformers retained much of the language of "justification" that had arisen in the patristic period and continued to be developed in the medieval period. Whereas the NT was silent on the notion of "merit," medieval theologians referred to "the merits of Christ and the saints"; the Reformers dispensed with the merits of the saints, but continued to speak of the merits of Christ. Many of them also continued to describe Christ's death in terms of "satisfaction," another extra-biblical concept.

In the later sixteenth century, and especially in the seventeenth, the Protestant world witnessed the growth of what has been dubbed "Protestant scholasticism." As in the high scholasticism of the Middle Ages, it became fashionable among Protestants to refine their understanding of the faith by systematizing it in great detail and providing definitions for each component and its relationship with other aspects of belief.

In one sense this trend was already present in the systematic works produced by the mainstream Reformers, Melanchthon (the *Loci Communes*) and Calvin (*The Institutes of the Christian Religion*). Each of these works had begun quite small, but had passed through a number of editions (always in the direction of expansion and augmentation). As the heirs of the Reformation multiplied, the number of volumes in these systematic treatments of Protestant belief also multiplied, as did often the aridity of their contents. In this process the doctrine of "justification," rather than being studied afresh by examining its Pauline roots more closely, became entrenched in its Protestant understanding, even where aspects of that understanding owed nothing to the apostle.

The Reformation in England and Scotland

The early English reformers such as Tyndale, Frith, and Barnes, were strongly influenced by Luther and his followers. Lutheran influence was also evident in the life and activities of Thomas Cranmer, under whom the first Anglican confessions and liturgy were shaped. In addition, Cranmer was open to the developing south-west German and Swiss expressions of the Reformation, as Tyndale and his circle had been at an earlier stage.

However, following the reign of "Bloody Mary" (Mary I, reigned 1553–58), it was the Calvinistic-Reformed influence that came to dominate. The 800 or so exiles who returned to England after Mary's death had been influenced primarily by Calvin's Geneva, whether they came directly from that city or from adjacent regions. Their strength was such that in exile they had produced their own New Testament (the *Geneva New Testament*, 1557), and not so long after their return the full Bible appeared (the *Geneva Bible*, 1560). In England and Scotland the Calvinistic form of Protestant Christianity dominated, and the specifically English form of Calvinism, Puritanism, came into being, later to be transplanted across the Atlantic to Britain's American colonies.

3.4 THE COUNCIL OF TRENT AND ITS LEGACY

In the meantime, there was provided for Roman Catholics a conciliar statement of their faith, which took into account the challenges it had faced from the Protestant movement.

The Council of Trent met over a period of almost two decades (1545–63). Its decree on "justification" was promulgated early in the council's deliberations (Sixth Session, Jan. 13, 1547). Entitled *Decree concerning Justification*, it was comprised of sixteen brief chapters, to which thirty-three canons were attached.

It sets out:

> . . . to expound to all the faithful of Christ the true and salutary doctrine of justification, which . . . Jesus Christ . . . taught, which the Apostles transmitted and which the Catholic Church . . . has always retained; strictly forbidding that anyone henceforth presume to believe, preach or teach otherwise than is defined and declared in the present decree.[12]

A selection of the contents of the decree, summarized by chapters, follows:

---

12. Olin, *Reformation Debate*, 14–15.

- Chapter 4: "Justification" is defined as "a translation from that state in which man is born a child of the first Adam, to the state of grace and of the adoption of the sons of God through the second Adam, Jesus Christ."[13] For this, the "laver of regeneration" [baptism] is essential.
- Chapter 5: Adults are called by God, that call constituting "the predisposing grace of God" by which they are "to convert themselves to their own justification by freely assenting and co-operating with that grace."[14]
- Chapter 6: [Adults] are disposed to divine justice when they receive faith by hearing, repent, and are baptized.
- Chapter 7: Once again a "definition" is provided for "justification." It is not only "the remission of sins," but also "the sanctification and renewal of the inward man through the voluntary reception of the gifts whereby an unjust man becomes just."[15]
- Chapter 9: This chapter is directed against Protestant assertions that it is possible to have an assurance of one's salvation.
- Chapter 10: Here the decree argues for an increase in "justification" received: "they [the justified] through the observance of the commands of God and of the Church, faith cooperating with good works, increase in that justice ['justification'] received through the grace of Christ and are further justified . . . ."[16]

It hardly needs pointing out that the several chapters referred to above, which base their exposition on the situation for adults, must have been extremely rare in Western Europe in the second half of the sixteenth century. Most people would have been christened as infants. In such cases, it is hard to see the relevance of much in these chapters.

Further, it is very doubtful indeed whether the way Scripture is appealed to in the decree on "justification" would today be defended as exegetically responsible by the majority of biblical scholars, not only those of Protestant persuasion, but also those who are Catholics. The reasons for this assertion are:

---

13. In Schroeder, *Canons and Decrees*, 31.
14. Ibid., 31–32.
15. Ibid., 33.
16. Ibid., 36.

The Doctrine of Rectification in Historical Perspective

1. The broad scope of the study, which, instead of focusing on the biblical statements about "justification," draws widely on numerous Scriptures not using "justification" vocabulary or not directly related to that doctrine in the Scriptures.
2. The use of extra-biblical terminology, such as penance, merit, venial sins.

Because Roman Catholics regard the decrees of the Council of Trent as continuing to have the status of authoritative statements, and since Trent addresses the doctrine of "justification" specifically and at greater length than any equivalent Catholic documents, the Tridentine decree on "justification" remains significant for Roman Catholic understanding of the doctrine.

This was openly acknowledged by the Roman Catholic theologian Hans Küng when, in the 1950s, he set out to compare Catholic teaching with the doctrine of "justification" set forth in the massive *Church Dogmatics* of the Protestant theologian Karl Barth.

In his response to Küng, Karl Barth was also acutely aware of this situation. He expressed amazement that Küng had discovered that there were no substantive differences between the view he had put forth and Catholic teaching.

> ... taking the statements of that Sixth Session as we now have them before us—statements correctly or incorrectly formulated for reasons then considered compelling—don't you agree that I should be permitted to plead mitigating circumstances for the considerable difficulty I had trying to discover in that text what you have found to be true Catholic teaching? Imagine! So unexpected a view of freedom, of grace, of juridico-real justification and its realization and foundation in Christ's death, of the formulae *simul iustus et peccator* ["a justified person and a sinner at the same time"] and *sola fide* ["faith alone"], and so on! How do you explain the fact that all this could remain hidden so long, and from so many, both outside and inside the Church?[17]

In an extended critique of the Tridentine decree, Barth concluded, "It is difficult to see in the Tridentine doctrine of justification anything better than what Paul meant [in Gal 1:6-7] by another gospel.[18]

---

17. Barth in Küng, *Justification*, xxxix–xli.
18. Barth, *Church Dogmatics*, IV, 1:626.

3.5 DIVERSITY IN THE NINETEENTH CENTURY

The nineteenth century was marked by a greater diversity of approaches, particularly among Protestants, than had been witnessed since the Reformation.

Certainly many Protestants simply continued to defend what had become Protestant orthodoxy. At the popular level this can be illustrated from the very influential preaching of the London Baptist pastor, Charles Haddon Spurgeon (1834-92) who at the height of his influence drew Sunday congregations approaching six thousand. A moderate Calvinist and admirer of the Puritans, Spurgeon had his Sunday sermons published simultaneously in his native Britain and in the United States. Ultimately they were translated into many languages. They run to sixty-two substantial volumes. Yet in spite of Spurgeon's commitment to the doctrine of "justification by faith," the number of occasions when he spoke directly on this doctrine amounts to only eleven sermons for the thirty-seven years covered by *The Metropolitan Tabernacle Pulpit* (1855-92). Further, while the doctrine of "justification" Spurgeon expounded owed a lot to the Calvinistic and Puritan traditions, much of that tradition (for example, the imputation of the righteousness of Christ to the believer as a forensic act on God's part) lacks any basis whatever in the writings of the Apostle Paul.[19]

Much earlier in the century an Anglican priest, John Henry Newman (1801-90), had published his *Lectures on Justification* (1838, ²1840). During the years 1843 to 1845 Newman made his transition to the Roman Catholic Church.

In the earlier editions of his *Lectures* Newman set out to expound his understanding of the authentic Anglican view of "justification" as the *via media* between the Protestant and Roman Catholic stances respectively. He affirmed both the forensic understanding of the Protestant view and the Roman Catholic insistence that by "justification" the Christian becomes morally righteous, righteous in reality. Thus for him it was not possible to distinguish between "justification" and "sanctification," as it is in the Protestant understanding. He emphasized the creative power of the divine (forensic) declaration of "justification." He considered that the sacraments of baptism and especially the eucharist played a vital role in "justification." In his view "justification" could be repeated again and again, and there were degrees of "justification."

---

19. Moore, *Rectification*, 2:234-40.

The Doctrine of Rectification in Historical Perspective

As a Roman Catholic, Newman published a third edition of his *Lectures on Justification* (³1874). Significantly, this third edition contained no substantive changes from the earlier ones!

While the two nineteenth-century persons treated so far endorsed the forensic view of "justification," there were two influential leaders working within a Protestant framework who denied it.

Following his conversion to Christianity, Charles Grandison Finney (1792–1875), a lawyer by training, initially became an evangelist, later a theological educator. In his *Lectures on Systematic Theology* published in 1846–47, Finney argued against the notion that "justification" is forensic, likening it rather to the granting of a pardon, which is never the function of a law court, but rather of the executive or law-making department of government. He argued that the ground of our "justification" is the love and mercy of the Godhead, while Christ's atoning death is a condition for it (along with repentance, faith in Christ, sanctification, and perseverance). While Christ's obedience to the Law could benefit none but himself, his suffering (which he did not owe to the Law) could benefit others, giving his death a substitutionary character.

Working in an entirely different context, the German scholar Albrecht Benjamin Ritschl (1822–89) also concluded that "justification" is not the act of a judge. Rather, for him, in "justification" God acts as a ruler, as King and Lord of his kingdom. He further pointed out (1) that "justification" can not be, at one and the same time, an act of divine justice and of divine grace; (2) that the Law makes no provision for the transfer of punishment from the guilty to another party.

Finally, there is evidence in the nineteenth century of the beginnings of the understanding that God's act of "justification" is primarily concerned not with moral transformation or the declaration of a judge, but the establishing of a right relationship as a divine gift. This concept was to be developed much more fully in the twentieth century. At this stage it was often regarded as just one dimension of "justification," and was usually linked with more traditional understandings.

Such a viewpoint can be seen in the exegetical writings of the German New Testament scholar Heinrich August William Meyer (1800–73). At the turn of the century it was also evident in the German lexicographer, Hermann Cremer (1834–1903). The British exegetes, William Sanday

(1843–1920) and Arthur Cayley Headlam (1862–1947) also made a brief reference to it in their Romans commentary in the ICC series.[20]

Several North American scholars also embraced the concept in writings published towards the end of the century: David Worthington Simon (1830–1909) in his *Reconciliation by Incarnation: The Reconciliation of God and Man by the Incarnation of the Divine Word* (1898) and in his article on "Justification" in *Hastings' Dictionary of the Bible* (1899); and George Barker Stevens (1854–1906) in his article on "Righteousness in NT," also in *Hastings' Dictionary of the Bible*.

3.6 TWENTIETH-CENTURY TRANSLATION INSIGHTS, INTER-DENOMINATIONAL DIALOGUE, THE "NEW PERSPECTIVE" ON PAUL, AND THE ONGOING DEBATE

Our focus in this section is on various attempts during the twentieth century either to refine how "justification" was understood or to provide new insights into its meaning, particularly in relation to the writings of Paul the apostle.

3.6.1 Twentieth-Century Translation Insights

Although the notion that "justification" was primarily about God granting a repentant sinner the gift of a right relationship had been put forward occasionally in the nineteenth century, no attempt had been made to express that concept in English translations of the New Testament. In the twentieth century a number of translations did precisely this.

The earliest was the work of Frederick Brooke Westcott (1857–1918), son of B. F. Westcott, the Cambridge New Testament scholar. In 1913 Westcott produced an attractive little work in which he provided translations of those parts of Galatians and Romans which use "justification" vocabulary. He argued that "justification" refers to "being set right with God."[21] His preferred way of rendering the verb (δικαιοῦν) was "to set right." Westcott published his book with some diffidence, and it is likely to have had only a limited circulation.

---

20. Sanday and Headlam, *Critical*, 30.
21. Westcott, *St. Paul*, 11.

More popular in appeal was a translation of the New Testament by the Southern Baptist scholar, Charles Bray Williams (1869–1952): *The New Testament in the Language of the People* (1937). Instead of the traditional English rendering "to justify," Williams' preferred way of rendering the verb δικαιοῦν in the passive was "to come into right standing with God."

Quite independently, but from the same ecclesial tradition, Robert Galveston Bratcher (1920–2010) translated the New Testament of the *Good News Bible* for the American Bible Society (1966). Typically, he rendered the verb δικαιοῦν as "to put [someone] right with God." In its first decade, the *Good News New Testament* sold over fifty million copies, setting a new paperback record. In 1976 it was incorporated in the Good News Bible.

Whereas most earlier English versions from the very beginning had traditionally rendered Paul's *single* word-family (δικαιοσύνη and cognates) by *two* English word-families ("righteousness" and cognates and "justify" and cognates), all of the translators just discussed showed a strong preference for using only one English word-family, that family being "right" and cognates. Greek-English lexicons produced by Bible societies supported this approach. While Barclay M. Newman's useful *A Concise Greek-English Dictionary of the New Testament* (1971) runs to only 203 pages, the larger work by Johannes P. Louw and Eugene A. Nida *Greek-English Lexicon of the New Testament Based on Semantic Domains* (1988) occupies two substantial volumes of more than 1,200 pages.

3.6.2 Inter-Denominational Dialogue

Interest in the doctrine of "justification" was re-awakened in 1957 with the publication of Hans Küng's *Rechtfertigung. Die Lehre Karl Barths und eine katholische Besinnung* (ET: *Justification: The Doctrine of Karl Barth and a Catholic Reflection*, 1964). This exchange between a Roman Catholic scholar and a scholar in the Reformed tradition provided the stimulus both for debate within the Roman Catholic Church and for ecumenical discussion.

During the second half of the twentieth century the interest in "justification" intensified, resulting in numerous inter-denominational dialogues or conversations in which "justification" played a significant role. These exchanges between the various denominations were on a scale not previously known.

In this chapter we will focus on the outcomes of two major conversations between the Roman Catholic Church and Lutheran bodies, limiting the scope to their considerations of "justification" as the issue which had caused the initial divide.

The Roman Catholic–Lutheran Dialogue, whose findings on "justification" were published in 1983, had commenced in July 1965, almost six months before the Second Vatican Council (1962–65) concluded. Catholics were represented by the USA Roman Catholic Bishops' Committee, while the Lutherans were drawn from the USA National Committee of the Lutheran World Federation. "Justification" was the seventh area they considered together. Its deliberations extended over five years and culminated in the publication *Justification by Faith (Common Statement)* in 1983. It consisted of some 24,000 words of text, presented in 165 numbered paragraphs.

The authors of the *Common Statement* insisted it resulted from a common search, and was not merely a compromise between initially opposed views.[22] Both partners were able to affirm the following position wholeheartedly:

> our entire hope of justification and salvation rests on Jesus Christ and on the gospel whereby the good news of God's merciful action in Christ is made known; we do not place our ultimate trust in anything other than God's promise and saving work in Christ.[23]

Those responsible for the *Common Statement* openly acknowledged that it did not have official status in either of the two participating denominations.[24]

It was, nevertheless, a significant milestone in Catholic/Lutheran relations. While recognizing that there were still a number of areas on which the two bodies were not of a common mind, they also raised the question whether, in view of the agreement reached on the significant doctrine of "justification," such differences as did remain need be "church-dividing."[25]

Whereas the 1983 Dialogue was limited to the United States, in 1995 representatives of the world bodies of the two dialogue partners commenced conversations with a view to exploring whether a consensus could be reached on a more widely representative basis. By then other national dialogues had occurred, notably those in Germany in 1986 and 1994. In

---

22. Anderson et al., *Justification*, 9.
23. *Common Statement*, §4, in Anderson et al., *Justification*, 16.
24. Anderson et al., *Justification*, 9.
25. *Common Statement*, §4, in Anderson et al., *Justification*, 16.

the present case, Lutherans were represented by the Lutheran World Federation, Catholics by the Pontifical Council for Promoting Christian Unity. They did not start afresh, but built on the work and outcomes of earlier dialogues. By 1997 their work had been completed. The report, titled *Joint Declaration on the Doctrine of Justification* (1997) was ratified by the relevant bodies in June of the following year. In October, 1999, a series of joint celebratory ceremonies were held in the city of Augsburg, which lends its name to one of the most important of the Lutheran Confessions.

The *Joint Decla*ration states its intention as:

> . . . to show that on the basis of their dialogue the subscribing Lutheran churches and the Roman Catholic Church are now able to articulate a common understanding of our justification by God's grace through faith in Christ. It does not cover all that either church teaches about justification; it does encompass a consensus on basic truths of the doctrine of justification and shows that the remaining differences are no longer the occasion for doctrinal condemnations.[26]

Several phrases in this statement invite comment. The reference to " . . . the *subscribing* Lutheran churches" (emphasis mine) alerts us to the fact that not all Lutheran bodies are members of the Lutheran World Federation. One notable group outside the world body, for example, is the Lutheran Church–Missouri Synod.

The concluding reference to "doctrinal condemnations" draws attention to one of the major concerns of this dialogue, namely, that during the sixteenth century each of the participating denominations had condemned the position of the other on "justification" in historical documents. The *Joint Declaration*, while taking these condemnations seriously, argued they should no longer be a cause of division:

> Like the dialogues themselves, this *Joint Declaration* rests on the conviction that in overcoming the earlier controversial questions and doctrinal condemnations, the churches neither take the condemnations lightly not do they disavow their own past. On the contrary, their *Declaration* is shaped by the conviction that in their respective histories our churches have come to new insights. Developments have taken place which not only make possible, but

---

26. §5 of the Preamble.

also require the churches to examine the divisive questions and condemnations and see them in a new light.[27]

Not one of the joint statements on "justification" produced by the various dialogue partners has lacked critics—and often well-informed critics—from within the participating denominations. The *Common Statement* and the *Joint Declaration* discussed above are no exceptions. Yet whatever force the critics' arguments carry, the spirit in which the dialogues have been conducted deserves to be recognized as a great advance over the earlier standoffs and written condemnations.

Given that "justification" constituted the doctrinal heart of the sixteenth-century controversy between the Roman Catholic Church and the Lutheran Reformers, there is a sense in which these twentieth-century dialogues and conversations culminated in the celebration of the *Joint Declaration on the Doctrine of Justification*. It was held by these two denominations on Reformation Sunday (October 31) 1999 and took the form of joint services in the historic city of Augsburg. The first was held in the (Catholic) Cathedral, the second in the (Lutheran) Church of St. Anna, where the *Declaration* was signed.

3.6.3 The "New Perspective" on Paul

Other factors were at work in New Testament scholarship in the last quarter of the twentieth century which augmented the renewed ecumenical interest in "justification."

The most important of these was the publication in 1977 of E. P. Sanders' monograph *Paul and Palestinian Judaism: A Comparison of Patterns of Religion*. The responses generated by the issues it raised caused those issues to eclipse all other aspects of New Testament scholarship for the remainder of the century and even beyond. The phrase coined to describe this phenomenon was "the new perspective" on Paul. In essence it argued that the common understanding of first-century Judaism as aspiring to earn a works-based righteousness was mistaken. Rather, it was by God's grace that a Jew enters the covenant; the means of remaining in the covenant is observing the works of the law. Sanders dubbed this "covenantal nomism."

In his 1977 monograph, Sanders identified six aims, the two main ones being:

---

27. §7 of the Preamble.

1. to argue a case concerning Palestinian Judaism (that is, Judaism as reflected in material of Palestinian provenance) as a whole.
2. to carry out a comparison of Paul and Palestinian Judaism.

He took strong objection to the prevailing view of Palestinian Judaism in New Testament scholarship, and hoped to overturn it.

According to the prevailing view Palestinian Judaism was a religion based on fulfilling the works of the Law. Against this, the "covenantal nomism" for which Sanders argued, has the following features:[28]

1. God has chosen Israel and
2. given the law. The law implies both
3. God's promise to maintain the election and
4. the requirement to obey.
5. God rewards obedience and punishes transgression.
6. The law provides for means of atonement, and atonement results in
7. maintenance or re-establishment of the covenantal relationship.
8. All those who are maintained in the covenant by obedience, atonement and God's mercy belong to the group which will be saved.

An important interpretation of the first and last points is that election and ultimately salvation are considered to be by God's mercy rather than human achievement.

As the sources for Palestinian Judaism at the time of Paul, Sanders relies on (1) apocryphal and pseudepigraphic literature; (2) the Dead Sea Scrolls; (3) Tannaitic literature (in particular, the Mishnah, and the Palestinian and Babylonian Talmuds). The limitations of this material for recovering Palestinian Judaism as it operated in Paul's day should be self-evident. The Mishnah was not committed to writing until late in the second century CE; the two Talmudim were composed around 400 and 500 CE respectively. If we had to rely on the writings of say, Irenaeus, for our knowledge of Christianity, the picture we acquired would be vastly different from the picture that emerges from the New Testament writings. Yet Irenaeus is separated from Paul's day and Rabbinic Judaism by about the same interval as the Mishnah is.

---

28. Sanders, *Paul and Palestinian*, 422.

The Dead Sea Scrolls, while serving a community which was contemporary with Paul, were produced not by mainstream rabbis, but by a sect of Judaism.

While Sanders devoted about 400 pages to Palestinian Judaism, his treatment of Paul occupies less than 100 pages. Instead of undertaking a detailed examination of the apostle's writings, he limits himself to a mere handful of Pauline texts and relies on a selection of twentieth-century scholars and their views of Paul. Given that the crucial Pauline doctrine for his area of interest is "justification," his treatment of that topic can only be assessed as woefully inadequate.

Sanders' work was the catalyst for a stream of articles and monographs taking up aspects of the issues he had raised. Especially prominent was the relationship between Paul and the Jewish Law. Sanders himself devoted a book to this topic: *Paul, the Law, and the Jewish People* (1983).

Eight years after the appearance of *Paul and Rabbinic Judaism*, the New Testament scholar Robert Gundry provided an informed, penetrating, and devastating critique of Sanders' thesis, targeting especially Sanders' later work *Paul, the Law, and the Jewish People*. He drew attention to shifts in Sanders' position between the two works, a situation Sanders himself acknowledged.[29] Responding to Sanders' covenantal language of "getting in" and "staying in," Gundry took issue with Sanders' assertion that there is "an in principle agreement between Paul and Palestinian Judaism: a person gets in by God's grace and stays in by works of law."[30] He pointed out that in Galatians the circumcision issue related to "staying in," not "getting in":

> . . . Paul attacks the Judaizers' teaching as a corruption of grace and faith (again see Gal 3:3,10; 5:4,7). For Paul, then, getting in and staying in are covered by the seamless robe of faith as opposed to works, with the result that works come in as evidential rather than instrumental. Sanders' bisection of getting in and staying in cuts a line through Paul's religion where the pattern shows a whole piece of cloth.[31]

He concluded that for Paul faith was the key not only to "getting in" but also to "staying in." Gundry is only one of a growing number of scholars critical of Sanders' thesis and the "New Perspective."

---

29. Sanders, *Paul, the Law*, ix.
30. Gundry, "Grace, Works," 8.
31. Ibid., 12.

Finally, on the matter of sources, it is to be noted that in their quest to recover the Palestinian Judaism of Paul's day, Sanders and others have failed to take seriously Paul's criticisms of Judaism which, after all, he knew from the perspective of an "insider." To put it another way: for those interested in the Palestinian Judaism of Paul's day, the authentic Pauline corpus is one of the very few contemporary written sources available.

A second factor contributing to the intensification of interest in "justification" was the publication of Richard Hays' *The Faith of Jesus Christ: An Investigation of the Narrative Substructure of Galatians 3:1-4:11* (1983). The work sparked a debate over the meaning of πίστις Χριστοῦ (or equivalent). Although the phrase is used only seven times in contexts where Paul is expounding his doctrine of "justification" (Rom 3:22, 26; Gal 2:16 [2x]; 2:20; 3:22; Phil 3:9) the genitive may be understood as either a possessive (subjective) genitive: "the faith (or faithfulness) *of* Christ," or as an objective genitive: "faith *in* Jesus Christ." Hays argued for the former. After the earlier exchange over the same issue between T. F. Torrance and C. F. D. Moule in 1957, in which Moule evidently presented the more convincing case in favor of an objective genitive, it seems the more favored view today is to take these genitives in the way Hays advocated, as possessive genitives. Although, as Beilby correctly points out,[32] the πίστις Χριστοῦ debate is not properly part of "the new perspective" on Paul, nevertheless many devotees of "the new perspective" have adopted it. It has also been incorporated in some English versions published in the twenty-first century.

3.6.4 The Ongoing Debate over "Justification"

During the twentieth century, the ecumenical debates and the two factors just discussed, intensified interest in "justification." This impetus has carried over into the twenty-first century, so that in the view of one writer, by its second decade the "justification" debate had reached "fever pitch."[33]

This ongoing debate is multifaceted.

While it has involved scholars from the entire spectrum of New Testament scholarship, debate has been particularly vigorous among those identifying as evangelicals. It attests to the very diverse understandings of "justification" within that faction alone.

---

32. Beilby and Eddy, *Justification*, 80.
33. Ibid., 9, 13.

There follows a catalogue of issues which have been taken up in the debate. It makes no pretence to being an exhaustive list, but hopefully it does include the major issues.

- Fundamental to what developed as Protestant orthodoxy was the notion that in "justification" the righteousness of Christ is imputed to the believer. Such a notion is no part of Paul's expositions of the doctrine. He does not even mention the righteousness of Christ, let alone state that it is imputed to the believer. It is sad to see Protestants defending such a notion, which entirely lacks New Testament evidence, Protestants who would be the first to condemn Mariolatry or purgatory as doctrines lacking adequate biblical evidence. It is hard to avoid the conclusion that advocates of this view are putting one facet in the historical development of the doctrine above the data contained in the biblical texts.

- With the publication of Alister McGrath's *Iustitia Dei: A History of the Christian Doctrine of Justification* in 1986, a history of the doctrine became available that could fairly claim to be comprehensive and taking into account recent scholarship. (It was subsequently updated in 1998 and 2005.) It filled a much-needed gap, and has undoubtedly led to a greater interest in how the doctrine has developed. As well as renewed study of the Reformation, it has generated a lively debate on the role of "justification" during the patristic period.

- The role played by "justification" in God's saving purposes was evaluated differently by the major Reformers, notably Luther and Calvin, and their followers. It continues to be discussed in the current debate. While some warn against the notion of placing any one aspect of salvation at the center (such as Luther did for "justification"), others have argued that fundamental to Paul's exposition was a narrative story or metanarrative rooted in the salvation-history of Israel and the New Israel.

- The relationship between "justification" and participation or incorporation in Christ.

- A widespread assumption in many discussions is that "justification" and divine covenant are closely linked. Tom Wright is an example of someone who has gone much further than that, and made it explicit in his argumentation and his translation of the New Testament (2011).

- The relationship between "righteousness" as it is expressed in the Old Testament with the explicit doctrine of "justification" in the New, is another area of debate. One example of this is discussion as to the identity of the "righteous one" in Hab 2:4 (quoted in both Galatians and Romans).

Inevitably, older controversies are re-visited in the current debate. Among these we may note:

- Whether Christ's sacrificial death is presented primarily as a propitiation or an expiation.
- The critique of the notion of "faith alone" in James 2.
- The role played by works in "final justification"/judgment.

One of the most high profile debates in the first decade of the twenty-first century took place between Tom Wright, Anglican Bishop of Durham, England, at that time, and John Piper, Pastor of Bethlehem Baptist Church, in Minneapolis, USA. The debate was initiated by Piper with *The Future of Justification: A Response to N. T. Wright* (2007), while Wright responded with *Justification: God's Plan and Paul's Vision* (2009). Piper's concern was that N. T. Wright's "portrayal of the gospel—and of the doctrine of justification in particular—is so disfigured that it becomes difficult to recognize as biblically faithful."[34]

Wright opened his response with an analogy from the history of science: the replacement of the geocentric view of the solar system by the heliocentric view. He went on to plead for a replacement of a self-centered view of the gospel by a theocentric one,[35] arguing that Piper's loyalty to the old paradigm established by the Reformers was preventing him from seeing those insights gained through the "new perspective" on Paul which are helpful for understanding "justification" in today's world.

The Piper-Wright debate provides a good example of the widespread differences in understanding "justification" which can arise in an intra-evangelical context.

In this chapter we have traced in broad brush strokes the way that the New Testament doctrine of rectification has been interpreted from the beginning to the present day. Attention has been drawn to key people and key

---

34. Piper, *Future*, 15.
35. Wright, *Justification*, 3–9.

concepts influential for how future generations understood the Apostle Paul, as the chief exponent of the doctrine. At times the aircraft of interpretation has been put back on track, but all too often it has been hijacked, preventing it from reaching the destination of an accurate understanding of what the apostle was really concerned to convey. Inevitably, the way in which rectification is understood, or misunderstood, in any given generation will be reflected in the translations that generation produces. It is to translations in the English language that we turn in the following chapter.

4

Paul's Doctrine of Rectification in English Translations

So far we have covered two major areas, considering (1) the main features of Paul's doctrine of rectification; (2) how the doctrine of "justification" developed over a period of almost two thousand years. We now turn to consider (3) how Paul's doctrine of rectification was conveyed in English translations of the primary documents, particularly Paul's letters to the Galatians and to the Romans.

As well as documenting how Paul's use of the δ-family was handled in English versions, the following account provides a broad sketch of the main features of English biblical translation as the context in which the translation of the δ-family was handled.

4.1 THE EARLIEST PHASE OF ENGLISH BIBLICAL TRANSLATION: THE MANUSCRIPT TRADITION

While isolated examples of English biblical translation can be traced as far back as the seventh century, it is not until the Middle English period of the fourteenth century that we find examples of Pauline texts containing renderings of words of the δ-family. It was also in the fourteenth century that the first complete Bible in English appeared.

As mechanical printing was not invented until the following century, we are dealing here solely with the manuscript tradition.

The major enterprise of the fourteenth century was the Lollard Bible. Evidently inspired by the Oxford scholar, John Wycliffe (c. 1330–84), it appeared in two editions, the earlier late in his lifetime, the later after his death. We will refer to these versions as the Early Lollard Version (ELV, c. 1382) and the Later Lollard Version (LLV, c. 1395).

In addition, two independent fourteenth-century translations of parts of the Bible contain renderings of the δ-family in the Pauline letters. We will refer to them as the *Southern Epistles*[1] and MS Parker 32, a manuscript located in the library of Corpus Christi College, Cambridge.[2]

This spate of Middle English vernacular translation came to an abrupt end when the Constitutions of Oxford were promulgated in 1407–8. They effectively proscribed translation of the Scriptures into English for the next 120 years, when the first of William Tyndale's translations became available (1526).

When we examine how words of Paul's special rectification vocabulary were brought over into English in these fourteenth-century versions, the most striking feature is that *all four used two English word-families for Paul's single δ-family*. Generally the noun *iustitia* (for δικαιοσύνη) was Englished as "rightwesness" [modernized as "righteousness"] belonging to the R-family; the verb *iustificare* (for δικαιοῦν) as "to justify," belonging to the J-family; while the adjective *iustus* (for δίκαιος) was divided between the R- and J-families ("righteous," "just").

These fourteenth-century versions were all based on the Vulgate translation (in Latin). Like the original Greek, however, the Latin had only one word-family. This suggests that already by the fourteenth century this two-family approach had established itself in English, most likely through sermons, possibly through theological debate, religious instruction, and hymnody. (It must be borne in mind that serious scholarly writing at this period was in Latin.)

Where different meanings are involved, the translation even of words of the same word-family by different word-families may be appropriate. However, in the present case we are talking about a family of words which, in their Pauline usage in rectification contexts, have only *functional* differences (as noun, verb, or adjective), not differences in *meaning*.

---

1. Paues, *A fourteenth-century*.
2. Powell, *The Pauline Epistles*.

4.2 THE ENGLISH REFORMATION AND THE EARLY PHASE OF THE PRINTED BIBLE

The beginnings of the English Reformation were during the reign of Henry VIII (r. 1509–1547). Among the early Reformers was a gifted linguist and priest by the name of William Tyndale (c. 1494–1536). Tyndale translated the New Testament not from the Latin Vulgate, but from the Greek New Testament, which, in 1516, had become widely available through being printed by the Renaissance scholar Desiderius Erasmus (1466/9–1536). Tyndale's translation was printed abroad, in Germany. After an attempt at Cologne in the previous year had to be aborted when the authorities intervened, it was published at Worms in 1526.

When Tyndale came to the realization that not only was there no room in the Bishop of London's palace to translate the New Testament (as he had requested), "but also that there was no place to do it in all England,"[3] he went into voluntary exile on the Continent, where he resided from about 1524[4] until his martyrdom in 1536.

Although Tyndale made no use of earlier English versions, like them he used the two English word-families approach for Paul's δ-family, suggesting that this approach had already become firmly entrenched in the English language.

In the following years, Tyndale revised his NT and continued his current project of translating the OT from Hebrew. The latter enterprise was cut short by the betrayal, arrest, and eventually the martyrdom of Tyndale, when it was about half complete.

Others picked up the baton. Miles Coverdale, a colleague of Tyndale's, produced his own translation of the whole Bible, the first complete English Bible to be printed (1535). The NT was largely his own work, and has much to commend it. Although Coverdale also used a two-family approach, he showed a very marked preference for "right" and cognates over "just" and cognates, especially when translating the verb. As a consequence, at some points his handling of the δ-family is superior to Tyndale's. In the OT Coverdale made use of Tyndale's work where it was available; where Tyndale was lacking, Coverdale, who had good facility in Latin, but not in Hebrew, evidently translated from the Vulgate.

---

3. Tyndale's preface to the Pentateuch in Daniell, *Tyndale's Old Testament*, 5.
4. Daniell, *William Tyndale*, 108.

Meanwhile, the political and religious map of Western Europe was changing rapidly. By the close of the year in which Coverdale's Bible appeared, the secession of the English church from Rome was complete. Tyndale was martyred the following year (1536). Yet by 1537 two complete English Bibles were circulating with the royal assent. One of these was Coverdale's, the other went under the name of Thomas Matthew (a pseudonym for John Rogers, who had also been one of Tyndale's collaborators). The Matthew Bible (1537) contained Tyndale's translations wherever they were available, i.e., the NT and about half the OT (considerably more than had been the case in the Coverdale Bible).

Although he was thoroughly committed to the Reformation position, Coverdale had managed to gain the confidence of the king and of the ecclesiastical authorities. In those uncertain times, he was charged with the task of revising the English Bible for official use. Ironically, the starting point was not to be his own work, but the Thomas Matthew Bible.

Consequently, in the Great Bible which resulted from Coverdale's revising activity (1539), it was Tyndale's two-family pattern which was preserved, rather than his own.

In 1557 another significant English version was produced by English exiles on the Continent, who had been strongly influenced by John Calvin: The Geneva New Testament (revised for the complete Bible of 1560). Its two-family pattern resembled Tyndale's. It quickly enjoyed great popularity.

In the influential conservative leadership of the Elizabethan church, however, the Geneva Bible was met with distaste, and in 1568 the Bishops' Bible appeared as an official revision of the Great Bible. The Bishops' Bible was the direct antecedent to the King James (Authorized) Version of 1611, although the revisers who produced it took an eclectic approach, not hesitating to draw on renderings in the Geneva Bible or even the Catholic Rheims New Testament of 1582.

4.3 THE BIBLE OF ENGLISH-SPEAKING CATHOLICS

In the meantime, another significant translation endeavor, which was entirely independent of these developments, came to fruition. As Tyndale had been obliged to produce the first printed English New Testament in exile on the Continent, so in Elizabethan England English-speaking Roman Catholics living in exile in France produced their own English version. That they carried out the work with great reluctance will be obvious to anyone who takes the time to read the preface of the Rheims New Testament. Their reluctance grew out of the deeply held conviction that it was dangerous to place a vernacular Bible in the hands of untrained laity. They were prepared to do so only if their translation was supplied with extensive explanatory and dogmatic notes.

Their reluctance is also borne out by the fact it was fifty-six years after Tyndale's New Testament before Roman Catholics published their first English translation of the New Testament.

With their resources and influence greatly diminished by the Protestantization of England, initially they were able to print only the NT at Rheims, hence the Rheims NT (1582); the OT appeared at Douay, only a little ahead of the KJV, in 1609-1610.

Unlike the Protestant versions, the Rheims NT (RhT) and the Douay OT were based not on the original languages of Greek and Hebrew/Aramaic respectively, but on a Latin translation: Jerome's Vulgate. The version they produced lacked that feel for English idiom that was Tyndale's special contribution, tending to excessive Latinisms and to obscurity at many points. This is well illustrated by their handling of Paul's doctrine of rectification. Paradoxically, while they achieved for the first time in English biblical translation the representation of the single word-family in the original Greek (the δ-family) by a single family of English words, by choosing the J-family (with "justice" as the key term) they succeeded in making the doctrine of rectification even more obscure than it was in the Protestant versions with their two word-family approach. For the Latin-based English equivalents for which the RhT translators opted ("justice," "justify," "just" for *iustitia, iustificare, iustus*) did not communicate as effectively as their Anglo-Saxon equivalents ("righteousness," "make righteous," "righteous").

The Rheims-Douai Bible was extensively revised by Bishop Challonor in 1749–50; it remained the Bible of English-speaking Catholics until the second half of the twentieth century.

4.4 THE BIBLE OF ENGLISH-SPEAKING PROTESTANTS

At the turn of the seventeenth century the two versions used most widely in England were the Bishops' Bible and the Geneva Bible. Sales of the Geneva Bible outnumbered the Bishop's Bible more than fourfold, despite the fact that the latter was the officially sanctioned version.

The impetus for the King James Version came from a conference convened at Hampton Court by James VI of Scotland, soon to be officially recognized as James I of England. At that conference Dr. John Reynolds, President of Corpus Christi College, Cambridge, suggested that a new translation be made which would have the approval of the whole church. Although Reynolds's suggestion received at best only lukewarm support from the church's hierarchy, it appealed to the King, and over the next few months steps were taken to appoint six "companies" to oversee the work: three for the Old Testament, one for the Apocrypha, two for the New Testament.

The basis for the new version was to be the Bishops' Bible, which was to be "as little altered as the truth of the original will permit."[5] In the outworking of this and the other guidelines laid down, the pattern of words representing Paul's δ-family differed from the Bishops' Bible in only three places, and from Tyndale's version in six places.[6] By contrast, the King James Version differs from Coverdale's own version of 1535 (with its preference for the "right" family) in seventeen places.[7]

Within eight years of the publication of the King James Version, the original objective, of producing a version approved by the whole church, had been achieved. By 1619 the Geneva Bible had gone through only twelve printings, whereas the KJV had gone through forty-one. Thereafter, the frequency of reprints declined even more dramatically for the Genevan version.[8] The King James Version had become the Bible *par excellence* of the English-speaking world, a status it was to retain for well over three and a half centuries. During the 1980s, however, the popular appeal of contemporary versions, particularly the *Good News Bible* (1976) and the *New International Version* (1978)—both strongly promoted with modern marketing methods—greatly reduced its market share.

The consequence of these sixteenth- and seventeenth-century developments in English biblical translation among Protestants was twofold: (1) the two word-family approach to translating Paul's δ-family became firmly entrenched in English versions; it remains the predominant pattern in all the "standard" versions at the present day; (2) the doctrine Paul expounded with the δ-family at its heart continued to be known as "justification," i.e., by a theological technical term. As such, its meaning differs from the

   5. Wescott, *General View*, 114.
   6. Moore, *Rectification*, 3:412, 424, 428.
   7. Ibid., 3:414, 428.
   8. Ibid., 3:108 n. 20.

meaning of "justification" in everyday English usage and must be specially acquired. Thus the prevailing Protestant understanding of "justification" is that it is an act in which God, as Judge, declares a person to be righteous.

However, English-speaking law courts simply do not function in this way, even though it is commonly assumed by those using this kind of language that they do: judges do not "justify" those accused persons brought before them who are found "not guilty," nor do they "declare them to be righteous" or "declare them to be in the right" or "declare them to be innocent." Where they do pronounce a "favorable" verdict, it takes the form of pronouncing a person "Not guilty" of the charges brought against them, simply because the evidence is inadequate or does not support the charge(s). (A verdict of "not guilty" is quite different from a declaration of innocence.)

4.5 THE FIRST SERIOUS CHALLENGES TO THE KING JAMES VERSION

4.5.1 Official Versions

By the mid-nineteenth century several factors conspired to motivate scholars and church leaders in the United Kingdom to work on a revision of the King James Version. Later, scholars in the USA formed a parallel committee. Initially they simply responded to the English committee's work; later they published their own version. The translations these committees produced were, respectively, the *Revised Version* (RV: NT, 1881; Bible, 1885) and the *American Standard Version* (ASV: 1901).

Since 1611 the number, and particularly the quality, of the manuscript witnesses to the Greek text of the New Testament had grown enormously. Two fourth-century manuscripts in Greek held particular significance for New Testament textual critics, namely, Codex Sinaiticus and Codex Vaticanus. During the nineteenth century their contents became more widely available through being published and through the publication of critical editions of the Greek New Testament produced by Tischendorf and others. Further, the techniques of textual criticism had undergone significant refinement during this period.

A second factor was that the English language continued to evolve. By the nineteenth century a number of words were obsolete. Notable among them was the KJV's use of the second person singular pronoun (thou, thee, thy, thyself, thine). These pronouns also affected the verb form with which they were associated. They had gradually been dropping out of common usage in mainstream English from as early as 1650.

The Revisers were concerned mainly with the first area, adjusting the English text to correspond with the Greek text, which had been established on critical lines as the form of text most likely to be original. Since the KJV had been based on a late form of the Greek text, one which contained the accumulated errors of centuries of copying, particularly in the form of additions to the text, the New Testament they produced was shorter than the KJV by around a page and a half.[9] As to the second area, the currency of the English in which the translation was expressed, the revisers did replace many obsolete words and phrases, but overall they were content to retain what even then was old-fashioned language.

While the RV and the ASV each enjoyed a measure of support, particularly from scholarly communities, the KJV continued unrivalled as the English Bible in popular usage. Half a century was to elapse before another "official" version was produced in the USA: the Revised Standard Version (RSV) of 1952 (NT, 1946). In the UK revision was abandoned altogether in favor of a fresh start. Eighty years after the RV New Testament came out, the New Testament of the New English Bible was published (1961; Bible, 1970).

4.5.2 Private Translations

Among some in the British scholarly community, the appearance of the RV was greeted with a sense of despair. The chief point of contention was the Revisers' retention of seventeenth- (or even sixteenth-) century language. Towards the end of the nineteenth century and early in the twentieth, four British translations of the New Testament came out which were largely in reaction to the efforts of the British revisers: Ferrar Fenton (1895); *The Twentieth Century New Testament* (1901), Richard Weymouth (1903) and James Moffatt (1913). The last three were particularly concerned to express the New Testament in contemporary English.

As to their renderings of the δ-family, Fenton's translation showed a strong preference for the "right" family. Of the 77 occurrences of the δ-family in the original Greek, only two were rendered by words of the "just" family, while another eight used expressions falling outside

---

9. A convenient list of omissions may be seen in Strong, *Exhaustive Concordance*, under "Comparative concordance–Notanda."

the "right" and "just" families, such as "to declare to be free from guilt" (Gal 3:8) and "rectification" (Rom 5:16).

The Twentieth Century New Testament showed an even stronger preference for the "right" family; it too used words of the "just" family only twice, but made use of only four expressions falling outside the traditional two families.

Weymouth had been one of the advisers for *The Twentieth Century New Testament*, but his own version (published posthumously) relied a great deal more on expressions falling outside the traditional "right" and "just" families, making use of them 24 times, particularly when rendering the verb δικαιοῦν. While he used words of the "right" family 50 times, he drew on words of the "just" family only four times.

Moffatt actually produced two English translations of the New Testament. The first, *The Historical New Testament*, appeared in 1901 and was more traditional in language, but the second (1913) was a rendering in contemporary English with the goal of making the same impact on modern readers as the original was presumed to have had on its readers. It ultimately became part of the Moffatt Bible (OT 1924, final revision 1935). Of Scottish birth, from 1927 until his death in 1944 Moffatt lived and worked in the USA, where his translation was especially popular. With regard to his rendering of the δ-family, Moffatt adopted a more traditional two-family approach than had been the case with the translations of Fenton, the *Twentieth Century New Testament*, and Weymouth. In addition, however, he made considerable use of expressions falling outside the traditional two families (11 times).

The United States also saw the publication of private translations; that of Edgar Goodspeed (1923) was particularly popular. For the 13 occurrences of words of the δ-family in Galatians, Goodspeed used only words of the "right" family. In this respect he showed a strong preference for "uprightness" and cognates over the traditional "righteousness." In Romans, while "upright" and cognates predominate, he utilizes words of the "just" family four times, and expressions falling outside the traditional two word-families eight times. One significant innovation in his translation, which a number of later translators were to adopt, was the use of "way" in his expression "God's way of uprightness" (Rom 1:17; 3:21–22).

4.6 A NEW DEPARTURE: WESTCOTT, WILLIAMS, AND THE BIBLE SOCIETIES

In the first half of the twentieth century two private translators developed an approach to the translation of Paul's δ-family (evidently independently) that was to be taken up by both British and American Bible societies during the second half of that century.

This new approach had the following characteristics:

1. A strong preference for the "right" family;

2. The presentation of "justification" as God's establishing of a right relationship with the ungodly, rather than making the ungodly righteous (the Catholic view) or declaring the ungodly righteous (the Protestant view).

3. To accomplish this, it was often necessary to use a number of English words for a single Greek word.

4.6.1 F. B. Westcott

In 1913 Frederick Brooke Westcott (1857–1918), son of the eminent New Testament scholar Brooke Foss Westcott (1825–1901), published *St. Paul and Justification, Being an Exposition of the Teaching of the Epistles to Rome and Galatia*. Out of his classical background and examination of the Septuagint, he argued that the basic meaning of the verb δικαιοῦν is neither "make righteous" nor "account as right-doing" but to "set right."[10]

With his exposition Westcott provided his own English translation of considerable portions of Galatians and Romans, covering all those passages where Paul used the δ-family while expounding his doctrine of rectification. Westcott's frequent rendering of the verb δικαιοῦν as "set right" brought a certain freshness to his translation when it is compared with the English versions prevailing at the time.

Westcott's translation remained incomplete, and was available only in the book just referred to.

---

10. Westcott, *St. Paul*, 7.

4.6.2 Charles B. Williams

Charles B. Williams (1869–1952) worked on his translation of the New Testament for some twenty years, while undertaking the busy schedule of a professor of New Testament in Southern Baptist seminaries. It was published in 1937 as *The New Testament in the Language of the People*.

In 1923 the translation of a fellow Baptist, Edgar J. Goodspeed, had appeared. Williams made considerable use of it for his own translation. In rendering Paul's δ-family he picked up the "way of" that Goodspeed had introduced into the stream of English translation to render Paul's "righteousness of God" (δικαιοσύνη θεοῦ) at Rom 1:17 and elsewhere: "God's way of uprightness." However, Williams's own approach went far beyond Goodspeed; he rendered Rom 1:17: "For in the good news God's Way of man's right standing with Him is uncovered, the Way of faith that leads to greater faith, just as the Scripture says, 'The upright man must live by faith.'" He made extensive use of "right standing," emphasizing that Paul was concerned with a person's status before God (as Westcott had argued earlier).

Williams did make use of the "just" family, but in only four of the 77 occurrences of the δ-family in Galatians and Romans. In five cases he used renderings falling outside the traditional two English word-families. For the remaining 68 instances he utilized words of the "right" family.

Williams's translation was groundbreaking because it is the first English version to bring out the concept that rectification is about God bringing people into a right relationship with himself. Since 1937 a considerable number of translations have taken up this approach. Many of them are private translations, but the use of this approach by Bible societies in both the USA and Britain, not only in the translations they sponsored, but also in the lexicons they produced, is significant.

4.6.3 Bible Societies

The relational approach outlined above was taken up by Dr Robert Bratcher when he produced the *Good News New Testament* for the American Bible Society (1966).

In Britain the British and Foreign Bible Society also adopted this approach when it produced a translation for its many translators around the world: the *Translator's Translation New Testament* (1973). It was more consistent in its application of the relational approach than the *Good News New Testament*, but had a very much more restricted market.

In addition to these translations, the Bible societies produced lexicons which reinforced this approach in the definitions they gave for Paul's use of words of the δ-family. Barclay M. Newman's *A Concise Greek-English Dictionary of the New Testament* (203 pages) was issued both separately and bound with the standard Bible Society's *The Greek New Testament* (1973). The two-volume *Greek-English Lexicon* by Johannes P. Louw and Eugene A. Nida (1988) ran to 1218 pages. Both were issued by the United Bible Societies on behalf of the various national Bible societies.

The effect of the approach currently being discussed may be gauged by consulting appendix J. There, in parallel columns, the following three English versions of Rom 3:21–26 are shown:

1. The NJB (1985): This Roman Catholic version uses the J-family exclusively in this passage, reflecting the situation of the *Rheims New Testament* of 1582, the *Douay Bible* of 1609–10, and its revision by Dr. Richard Challonor (1749–50).

2. The NIV (2011) enables us to assess the impact of using the two word-family approach (in what is undoubtedly the most widely used version at the present time): the etymological (and semantic!) links between the words of the δ-family are lost by the use of two English word-families, which not only lack a stem in common but, more seriously, are not directly related in meaning.

3. *Under the Southern Cross: The New Testament in Australian English*, by the author (2014), expresses the δ-family in relational terms, using only the R-family.

4.7 THE MULTIPLICATION OF ENGLISH VERSIONS (1945–1999)

Following the second World War (1939–1945) there was an explosion in the number of English versions produced. Several of these were "official" revisions or translations enjoying wide support among the various Protestant denominations or by the Roman Catholic Church. All of these underwent revision towards the end of the period under review. Others were more sectional in character, such as the version produced for Jehovah's Witnesses or some produced by fundamentalist organizations. Others again were private translations, some of which proved extremely popular.

Here it is possible to draw attention only to the more influential versions and to note the more significant trends, particularly as they impacted on the rendering of the δ-family. More detailed information will be found in Moore, *Rectification*, volume 3.

4.7.1 "Official" Protestant Translations

In designating the following versions "official" translations we flag that the bodies that produced them commanded wide support from the major (Protestant) Christian denominations. In time, as genuine ecumenical progress was made, they tended to bridge the fundamental Catholic/Protestant/Orthodox divide.

In the year following the end of the Second World War, the New Testament of the *Revised Standard Version* was published (RSV: NT, 1946; Bible, 1952). It was based on the *American Standard Version* (ASV) of 1901, the American Revisers' equivalent of the British *Revised Version* (RV). As a revision in the KJV line, the RSV used the traditional two-family approach. It underwent revision in 1990, resulting in the *New Revised Standard Version* (NRSV). Changes to the way the words of Paul's δ-family were rendered were minimal in both revisions, so that even in the NRSV the profile for these words is very similar to that of the KJV.

In Britain the notion of revision was abandoned in favor of making an entirely new translation. The result was the *New English Bible* (NEB: NT, 1961; Bible, 1970). In spite of the fresh start, the translators felt obliged to use the traditional two English word-families for Paul's single δ-family in a way very similar to the KJV. One small innovation at two vital points, "God's way of righting wrong" (Rom 1:17; 3:22), was abandoned when the NEB was revised and published as the *Revised English Bible* (REB, 1989). In my view, this was a retrograde step. Other modifications made to the way the REB brought Paul's δ-family across into English were not of any substance.

4.7.2 Official Catholic Translations

The *Jerusalem Bible* (JB, 1966) was undertaken by a team of British Catholics who modeled it on a French translation produced by Dominican scholars in Jerusalem. It has special significance as the first Catholic translation into English to be based not on the Latin Vulgate, but on the original biblical languages of Hebrew-Aramaic in the Old Testament and Greek in the New. Setting aside the Catholic tradition of Englishing the words of Paul's δ-family by "justice" and cognates, the JB translators distributed the English equivalents among the "right" and "just" families as well as drawing significantly on means outside the traditional two families (twelve times). The *Jerusalem Bible* was revised in 1985, resulting in the *New Jerusalem Bible* (NJB). (This also followed a French initiative.) There was a significant shift in the NJB from the "right" family and "other means" to the "just" family, especially in Romans, where the commonest way of rendering δικαιοσύνη was "saving justice."

The *New American Bible* (NAB: 1970) was a product of American Catholics. In contrast to the JB translators, they retained the long-standing Catholic preference for representing Paul's δ-family by the "just" family, although other means were used in six cases. When the NAB was revised in 1986, the original title was retained, even though extensive changes had been made. With respect to Paul's δ-family, the profile of the NABr (as we shall refer to it = *New American Bible* revised) now resembled a Protestant version: the ratio of the "right" family (R) to the "just" family (J) to other means (O) was 38:33:6 (cf. KJV 46:30:2; RSV 40:30:5).

In 2011 the NAB was revised again, although it seems that the revision did not affect the New Testament, for which the revised text of 1986 (published 1987) was used.

4.7.3 Bible Society Translations

The *Good News Bible* (GNB: NT 1966, Bible 1976; revised 1992) began as an initiative by the American Bible Society to cater for the needs of people for whom English was a second language. The large Hispanic population residing in the USA was especially in mind. The New Testament was undertaken by Dr Robert Bratcher (1920–2010), who had been a missionary in Brazil. By the end of its first decade the NT had set an all-time paperback record, selling over 50 million copies. It was initially marketed under the dual description of *Good News for Modern Man* and *Today's English Version* (TEV). While Bratcher used means outside the traditional two English word-families in seven instances, all other renderings of Paul's δ-family drew on the "right" family, with "God putting people right with himself" as the central concept. The revision of the GNB in 1992 did not alter the pattern established for Paul's δ-family.

The *Translator's Translation* (TT: NT 1973) was produced by the British and Foreign Bible Society for the benefit of translators, especially those for whom English was a second language. Prior to 1973, for some books of the NT this "clear, accurate and straightforward translation of the Greek"[11] had been printed as a diglot opposite the Greek of the New Testament. Publication of the English only version in 1973 widened its potential appeal, though—in spite of its merits—it enjoyed only limited circulation when compared with the GNB. As to Paul's use of the δ-family, its translators adopted a similar approach to the GNB, with a strong preference for the "right" family (predominantly God "puts men right with himself" or "makes men right with himself"), although in the case of the TT the "just" family was used eight times, and extensive use was also made of "other means" (27 times).

However, it was another version, which came out in the same year and was also produced by a Bible Society, that eventually was to become the most widely used English version, supplanting the King James Version. It was the *New International Version* (NIV: NT, 1973; Bible, 1978; revised 1984), sponsored by the New York Bible Society International (founded 1809; subsequently renamed the International Bible Society, then Biblica, its current name). It has now sold 150 million copies. Like the "official" versions discussed above, the NIV utilized a predominantly two-family pattern for Paul's δ-words. In 1996 an inclusive-language edition was published in Britain, but this did not affect the pattern of rendering for the δ-family. It was revised to appear as the TNIV (NT, 2002; Bible, 2005) and again in 2011 (NIV 2011).

In 1991 the American Bible Society brought out the New Testament of a new translation, the *Contemporary English Version* (CEV: NT, 1991; Bible, 1995). It was initially marketed as *The Bible for Today's Family*. Research for this version was based on extensive observation of TV programs beamed to the five to thirteen year old age group—"The generation of cartoon character Bart Simpson." A radically different approach was taken to translating words of the δ-family. The traditional "right" and "just" families did not appear at all in Galatians, while in Romans only the "right" family was used, and that very sparingly (three times: 3:5, 25–26). The key phrase adopted for representing the δ-GR words was "accept/acceptable" in the

---

11. Chamberlin, *Catalogue*, 586.

sense that in rectification God accepts people, or they become acceptable to him. Abandonment of the notion of "right" for the δ-family, however, can only be regarded as unfortunate and problematic. In the first place, "right" is the nearest English equivalent; in the second, the highly significant link between "right" relationship and "right" behavior is entirely lost. Yet it is just this link that Paul was able to encompass in the word of the δ-family he used most frequently—the noun δικαιοσύνη.

The following year the same society published a revision of the *Good News Bible* (GNB; 1992). Its treatment of the δ-family was unchanged, retaining the relational approach noted for the GNB (NT, 1966; Bible, 1976). It is perhaps the sole representative of the "relational" approach to Paul's δ-family which is still available in English.

1995 saw the appearance of *God's Word* (GW). It origins lay in a translation by the Lutheran scholar, Dr. William F. Beck († 1966). In time plans for the completion and revision of Beck's work passed into the hands of the Luther Bible Society, subsequently renamed God's Word to the Nations Bible Society. The principle adopted for the new translation was described as "closest natural equivalence," the stated goal "to communicate clearly to contemporary Americans without compromising the Bible's message." In the case of Paul's δ-family this involved almost total abandonment of the traditional two English word-families. This is essentially the approach adopted for the CEV, and in fact, like the CEV, words from the traditional two English word-families were used only three times. Each of these occurrences was in Romans where the "just" family was used twice (Rom 3:4, 26b), the "right" family once (Rom 7:12). Like the CEV, the GW replaced the traditional two-family approach with a single word-family, but in this instance the core concept is "approval/approve." To illustrate, Rom 4:5 GW depicts God as "the one who approves ungodly people." If this really is what Paul meant, and if this is how he would say it if he were writing in English today, one wonders why the cross and resurrection were even necessary! "Approving" is very different from "rectifying" or "bringing an ungodly person into a right relationship." Of course, in context the translators intend their readers to understand that God's approval comes only with the faith of ungodly people, but enough has been said to demonstrate that their approach to the rendering of Paul's δ-family, involving the abandonment of "right," is fundamentally flawed.

4.7.4 Sectional Translations

The Amplified Bible (NT, 1958; Bible, 1965) was not intended as a standard version, but took the opportunity of "amplifying" words to indicate their range of meaning in a way that a word-for-word translation is not capable of doing. The "amplifications" were placed in round or square brackets or were signaled by conjunctions or prepositions in italics. While the primary text was very traditional, the amplifications made very little use of the "just" family (only five times), "right" words were often expressed in relational terms, and considerable use was made of vocabulary falling outside the two families (3/23 in Galatians; 22/59 in Romans).

The *New World Translation* (1961) was an official translation of Jehovah's Witnesses. With respect to the δ-family it is remarkable in using the R-family in all but two places (one using the J-family, the other means outside the traditional two families). Typically, it renders the main noun δικαιοσύνη as "righteousness," the verb δικαιοῦν as "declare righteous."

The *New American Standard Bible* (NASB: NT, 1963; Bible, 1971; revised 1999) was sponsored by the Lockman Foundation (also responsible for *The Amplified Bible*). Its renderings of the δ-family are almost identical with those of the ASV on which it was modeled. It therefore stands firmly in the two-family tradition.

With respect to its rendering of Paul's δ-family, the *New King James Version* (NKJV: NT, 1979; Bible, 1982) marketed in Great Britain as the *Revised Authorized Version* (RAV) is very similar to the NASB. It was, after all, regarded as an "edition of the Authorized Version of the Bible." The sixty renderings of the two main words, δικαιοσύνη and δικαιοῦν, are identical in NASB and NKJV, with inconsequential changes in some of the occurrences of δίκαιος and the three less-frequent δ-R words.

On the other hand, the *New Century Version* (NCV: NT, 1984; Bible, 1991) adopted a relational approach, abandoning the "just" family entirely in favor of the "right" family (with "making [someone] right with God" the dominant concept). Means outside the traditional two families were also utilized ten times.

4.7.5 Private Translations

On the Catholic side, Monsignor Ronald Knox translated the New Testament from the Vulgate "in the light of the Hebrew and Greek originals."

Initially it was produced as a "trial edition" for private circulation (1944) and received the imprimatur of the Roman Catholic Hierarchy of England and Wales later that year, seeing publication in 1945. The Old Testament followed in two volumes in 1949. After some modifications, the imprimatur was extended to the whole Bible (1954), which appeared in 1955. Knox was critical of the way Paul's δ-family and its Old Testament antecedents had been Englished. He was particularly critical of the use of "righteousness" by the KJV revisers. His own solution was to give preference to the "just" family, in which "justification" and "justify" and cognates dominate. He did make limited use of the "right" family (six times), but next to the "just" family were various other means (24x) in which "accept" and cognates are prominent. Although his renderings are much less wooden than the Rheims-Douai version which served as the standard Bible for the English-speaking Catholics of his day, his use of "justification" and cognates and the variety of his renderings left his translation open to the more serious charge of obscurity than the critique he brought against the use of "righteousness" in Protestant versions.

Soon after the conclusion of the Second World War, J. B. Phillips published *Letters to Young Churches* (1947), his own translation of the Pauline letters. These were followed by a translation of the entire New Testament (1958) which Phillips revised for the 1972 edition. For the δ-family Phillips utilized the two-family approach in the main, though he made greater use of means outside the traditional two families, and even within the "right" family extended some of the language to phrases such as "plan for imparting righteousness to men" (Rom 1:17a) and "Act of Perfect Righteousness" (Rom 5:18a). The 1972 revision extended this tendency very slightly.

The Living Bible was the work of Kenneth Taylor (b. 1917). Responding to a perceived need in his daily family devotions, Taylor began paraphrasing the ASV in 1954-55. He continued to work on the letters of the NT over the next seven years, but, unable to get a publisher, he took out a loan and had 2,000 copies printed. Shortly afterwards he left his employment at Moody Press and founded his own publishing company. In the years that followed, he continued to paraphrase portions of both the Old and New Testaments until the whole Bible had been treated in this way. The NT was published as *The Living New Testament* (1967), while *The Living Bible* came out in 1971. Taylor's work enjoyed phenomenal success and his paraphrasing technique was extended to over one hundred other languages through Living Bibles International, which he had set up.

It needs to be emphasized that *The Living Bible* was in fact no translation at all (Taylor did not have competence in the original biblical languages), but merely a paraphrase of an earlier English version, and a very antiquated one at that. Of the traditional two families used to English Paul's δ-family, Taylor preferred the "right" family (21x) over the "just" family (3x), but the majority of his renderings drew on means outside the traditional two families (62x). The enormous variety of expressions employed makes it impossible for an English reader to make the kind of word (and concept) connections which Paul no doubt consciously intended. Most serious of all, however, is Taylor's imposition of his personal theology on the reader, while purporting to convey what the apostle intended.

In 1996 the *New Living Translation* (NLT) made its appearance. Ostensibly it is a revision of the *Living Bible*. However, two quite distinct approaches were used for these two versions: whereas the LB was the work of one man, Kenneth Taylor, and no translation at all, but an updated English rendering of the ASV of 1901, the NLT was undertaken by a team of more than ninety "evangelical scholars" taking as its primary base for its New Testament *The Greek New Testament* (^{4}1993) and the Nestle-Aland *Novum Testamentum Graece* (^{27}1993).

While the translators showed a strong preference for the R-family (64 percent), drawing on the J-family at only three points, means other than these two word-families account for 25 percent of their renderings. In their use of the R-family they made use of a wide range of expressions. Frequently they represent a Greek noun by an English verb. While the NLT frequently offers improvements over the LB renderings, its failure to render consistently words of the δ-family which clearly have the same referent, is a distinct weakness.

After a number of years in pastoral ministry, William Barclay (1907–78) spent the last three decades of his working life as an academic at Glasgow University. He is best known for his success in popularizing the fruits of NT scholarship and the gospel message through his writing and radio broadcasting. Trained in the classics as well as theology, he was involved in several biblical translation projects apart from his own, namely, the *New English Bible* Apocrypha and the *Translator's New Testament* of the British and Foreign Bible Society. His *The New Testament: A New Translation* appeared in two parts: the Gospels and Acts (1968) and the Letters and Revelation (1969). Like many private translations, Barclay's NT is considerably "wordier" than the "standard" translations. This is illustrated by his approach to the δ-family, where typically he uses an English phrase for a single underlying Greek word. Understanding the δ-family in relational terms, Barclay majored on the "right" family (55x) in which "right relationship" was the key concept; other means were used seventeen times, while the "just" family was employed only nine times. This approach resulted in a very clear presentation of Paul's message in the crucial δ-family passages, which in English versions are often laden with theological technical jargon as well as other disadvantages spawned by the two-family pattern.

Jewish-born Heinz Cassirer (1903-1979) escaped from Nazi Germany to pursue a career in philosophy in British universities, converting to Christianity around the age of fifty. In his seventieth year he commenced a translation of the New Testament, drawing on his earlier training in the classics. Cassirer died unexpectedly in 1979. By that time he had entrusted the publication of his NT translation to his secretarial assistant, Ronald Weitzman. With the aid of Cassirer's widow, Weitzman was finally able to publish the translation in 1989. Cassirer took a very traditional approach to rendering the words of the δ-family Paul had used in Galatians and Romans, though he showed a strong preference for the "right" family (64x) using the "just" family only eight times and other means six times. The main noun δικαιοσύνη is almost always Englished as "righteousness," while the verb δικαιοῦν is mostly "to accept [someone] as righteous." This approach offered considerable advantages over the traditional two English word-family pattern, but still did not communicate as effectively as translations using the relational approach.

In 1993 the New Testament of Eugene Peterson's *The Message* came on to the market (Bible, 2002). Promoted in its subtitle as "The New Testament in Contemporary English," it proved immensely popular, and no doubt—on the basis of the claim made in its subtitle—many users have treated it as the New Testament. However, the message which emerges is Peterson's message, not Paul's; the messenger has taken the original and changed it, so that what is finally delivered bears only a shadowy resemblance to the original. At point after point it is simply not possible to establish a relationship between Paul's Greek and *The Message*. Peterson's handling of a complex Pauline statement like Rom 3:21–26 makes this abundantly clear.

4.8 ENGLISH BIBLICAL TRANSLATION SINCE 2000

The third volume of *Rectification ('Justification') in Paul, in Historical Perspective, and in the English Bible* (published in 2002), described forty-five English translations of the New Testament or Bible from the fourteenth century to the *International Standard Version* of 1999. After each description was an analysis of how that version handled Paul's use of the δ-family in Galatians and Romans.

Since the end of that period, English biblical translation has continued unabated. In fact, it has been necessary to limit our survey to the major translation projects and any that are of special interest for the way they treat Paul's δ-family.

Those that have been considered and analyzed are shown in the following table. The right column summarizes the approach used for Paul's δ-family in Galatians and Romans in each version.

Year	Version	Approach
2000	*Holman Christian Standard Bible* (HCSB) NT	T
2001	*English Standard Version* (ESV)	T
	NET Bible (NET)	T
2002	*Today's New International Version* (TNIV) NT	T
2005	*New International Reader's Version* (NIrV)	R
2011	*New American Bible, revised edition* (NABRE)	T
	New International Version (NIV 2011)	T
	Tom Wright *The New Testament for everyone*	T
	Common English Bible (CEB)	R
	The [Expanded] Bible	R
2012	*The Voice*	T

T = Traditional 2-family approach. R = R-family predominates.

Of these eleven versions, eight have been selected for more detailed treatment.

As the table indicates, 2011 was an especially fruitful year for English versions of the Bible or New Testament.

In the case of the *New American Bible* (NABRE), the revisions it contained were limited to the Old Testament; for the New Testament the 1986 text was retained. As this has already been treated in its place, it will not be discussed below.

Three scholars contributed to *The [Expanded] Bible* (2011): Tremper Longman III, Mark L. Strauss, and Daniel Taylor. The main text of their translation, shown in bold, is a modified version of the *New Century Version*. Extensive use is made of square brackets within the main text to provide alternative translations, various forms of commentary, and references. For Paul's use of the δ-family in Galatians and Romans, the R-family predominates, the key phrase being "make right with God." No use was made of the J-family at all. In the nine occurrences where the R-family is not used, means falling outside the traditional two word-families are employed. The widespread use of brackets in this version means that while it is suited to private study, it is quite unsuitable for public worship or as a standard version. For this reason it has not been included below.

The Voice (2012) results from collaboration among biblical scholars, pastors, writers, musicians, poets, and other artists. Its producers aspired to be both "faithful and accurate" in relation to the original languages, while expressing the Scriptures in "beautiful and readable" English. In rendering words of the δ-family in Galatians and Romans, they made use of a very wide range of English equivalents indeed, so wide that it can only leave us incredulous that the words of this family, which provide the key to the apostle's exposition of the good news, could mean so many different things. This wide range of renderings draws on both the R-family and the J-family as well as means outside these traditional two families. The style adopted for their enterprise means it does not really constitute translation, but paraphrase, and for this reason it is not considered below.

Brief descriptions of the eight selected versions and of the way they translate Paul's δ-family in Galatians and Romans follow, before general observations are made on the situation as it obtains at the time of publication.

4.8.1 Holman Christian Standard Bible (2000)

The origins of the *Holman Christian Standard Bible* (HCSB) date back to 1984, when Arthur L. Farstad (1935–98) commenced a new independent Bible translation project. In 1998 he entered an agreement with LifeWay Christian Resources, the publishing arm of the Southern Baptist

Convention, by which LifeWay would fund and publish the completed translation. Farstad died shortly after this. As the source text for the Greek New Testament, Farstad had had in mind the text underlying the King James Version, as represented in *The Greek New Testament According to the Majority Text*, which he had edited with Zane C. Hodges (1982; ²1985). Following Farstad's death, the editorial team replaced this text with the modern scholarly texts, Nestle-Aland *Novum Testamentum Graece* (²⁷1993) and the United Bible Society's *The Greek New Testament* (⁴1993) whose texts are identical; they differ only in punctuation and formatting.

In the meantime, Holman Bible Publishers, the Bible publishing arm of LifeWay, had assembled a team of more than a hundred scholars, editors, stylists, and proofreaders that was both interdenominational and international. All were committed to biblical inerrancy. With every translation decision they pursued two ideals: each word must reflect clear, contemporary English and each word must be faithful to the original languages of the Bible. Initial drafts were circulated to consultants and reviewers, who contributed suggestions from their areas of expertise. The final manuscript was then edited and polished by an executive team.

The HCSB retained a number of traditional features such as personal names and place names as well as theological vocabulary. On the other hand, a number of valuable formatting features were introduced to bring the translation more into line with modern usage. They included setting Old Testament quotations in the New Testament in boldface type, the use of "dynamic prose," using Arabic numerals for numbers 10 and above. Use is made of superscripted bullets for certain foreign, geographical, cultural, or ancient words when they first occur in a chapter, and in a few cases more than once per chapter. For each of these bullet terms a brief explanation is provided in an appendix.

In stating in their "Introduction" that they had retained traditional theological vocabulary, the HCSB translators made explicit mention of a number of terms, "justification" among them.[12] Unsurprisingly, their renderings of the δ-family in Galatians and Romans utilize the traditional two word-family approach. All thirty-eight occurrences of the noun δικαιοσύνη are rendered "righteousness." On the other hand, in Romans the verb δικαιοῦν is divided between "justify" (9x) and "declare righteous" (5x), while the adjective δίκαιος is divided between "righteous" (5x), "just person" (1x) and "just"

---

12. In reality the word "justification" is only used twice in their translation, in each case for δικαίωσις, which only occurs twice in the NT.

(1x). In these last two cases, it is arguable that in the vast majority of cases the Greek verb and the Greek adjective respectively, have the same referent. Overall, the HCSB makes use of the R-family 51x, the J-family 22x, other means, 3x. In assessing this approach, we need to remind ourselves that all of these renderings derive from just the one Greek word-family!

4.8.2 English Standard Version (2001)

The publishing team behind the *English Standard Version* (ESV) included more than a hundred people whose work was carried out under the auspices of the Good News Publishers Board of Directors. Fifty "biblical experts" served as Translation Review Scholars while the comments of more than fifty members of the Advisory Council were also taken into consideration by the fourteen-member Translation Oversight Committee. All involved shared "a common commitment to the truth of God's Word and to historic Christian orthodoxy." The team was international in scope and included leaders from many denominations.

The ESV stands in "the classic mainstream of English Bible translations over the past half-millennium." It is essentially a revision of the Revised Standard Version of 1952, as revised in 1971, replacing archaic language with current English and making "significant corrections . . . in the translation of key texts" in the light of the standard scholarly texts in the original languages (*Biblia Hebraica Stuttgartensia* for the Old Testament, Nestle-Aland *Novum Testamentum Graece* (^{27}1993) and the (identical) text of the UBS's *The Greek New Testament* (^{4}1993) for the New. In particularly difficult passages, they exercised the right to draw on other sources for both Testaments.)

The team sought to make the ESV ideally suited to "in-depth study of the Bible," but also "equally suited for public reading and preaching, for private reading and reflection, for both academic and devotional study, and for Scripture memorization."

They endeavor to make a case for their retention of non-inclusive language, claiming it is consistent with their "essentially literal" translation philosophy. In pursing this approach, the team seems to have been entirely impervious to widely accepted changes in the English language for at least the quarter-century before they published. More seriously, in relation to the source language of the New Testament, at places like 2 Tim 2:2 and 3:17 they do not seem to realize that the core meaning of ἄνθρωπος is not "man" but "person" (in the plural "people"). As was the case with the KJV, they have made their version more male-dominated than the Greek of the New Testament authors!

In pursuing their goals, the team retained traditional theological terminology, and in the list of examples make explicit mention of "justification." Not surprisingly, they made use of the traditional two word-family approach, using the R-family 44x, the J-family 28x, and other means, 4x. The noun δικαιοσύνη is rendered "righteousness" on all but three occasions ("justification," Gal 2:21; "justify," Rom 10:10; "it," Rom 9:30b). The verb δικαιοῦν is translated "justify," except at Rom 3:26c ("justifier") and Rom 6:7 ("set free").

4.8.3 NET Bible (2001)

The *NET Bible* (*New English Translation*) project had its beginnings in November 1995 during the annual meetings of the Society of Biblical Literature, held that year in Philadelphia. While those initially involved had in mind to revise and update existing English versions, as discussions progressed the concept of a completely new translation was proposed and felt to be both possible and desirable. The planning group was interdenominational and evangelical. Early on the intention was to create a faithful Bible translation that could be placed on the internet.

Early on it was decided that the translation committee should be kept small, consisting of about twenty scholars who shared a number of basic assumptions, methods of interpretation, and translation philosophy. They were to avoid doctrinal peculiarities and sectarian bias. The small committee strategy paid off, with the first release of the New Testament (Version 1.0) being posted on the internet in just thirty-two months. From the beginning the concept of using the internet was to encourage feedback.

In time the NET Bible became available both on the internet (as a free download) and in hard copy, still with a view to its being open to improvement.

A feature that immediately characterizes the NET Bible is the very large number of notes associated with it. These currently number over 60,000.

In rendering words of the δ-family in Galatians and Romans, the translators took a very traditional approach. In Galatians their use of the J-family and the R-family is fairly even, In Romans, however, the R-family is favored (52x) over the J-family (10x). The noun δικαιοσύνη is consistently rendered "righteousness" (except at Rom 9.30b: "it"). In Galatians, the verb δικαιοῦν is translated "justify" (6x), "declare righteous" only once, whereas in Romans "declare righteous" and "justify" ("justifier" at Rom 3.26c) are each used 7x. It would be interesting to know what criterion was used as the basis to decide which of these two renderings should be used for each place where the verb occurs.

4.8.4 Today's New International Version (NT, 2002; Bible, 2005)

In 2002 the New Testament of *Today's New International Version* (TNIV), a major revision of the *New International Version* (NIV), was published.

The New Testament of the NIV had first appeared in 1973, the whole Bible in 1978. At that time its chief competitor among the new versions was the *Good News Bible* (GNB) of 1976. Over the next decade or so the NIV was to establish itself as the preferred version of English readers. It was at about this time that the long reign of the KJV as the English Bible *par excellence* came to an end.

One of the principles laid down by the original NIV Committee was the provision for regular updates. To this end they established the Committee on Bible Translation (CBT), a self-perpetuating group of biblical scholars. Its mandate was to:

1. keep abreast of advances in biblical scholarship;
2. keep abreast of changes in English;
3. issue periodical updates to the NIV.

The first update was in 1984, when the text of the NIV underwent some revision.

One feature the NIV shared with the KJV was male-dominated language; at a number of points this feature was more prominent in these (and most other) English versions than it was in the Greek in which the New Testament writings were composed, even though the Greco-Roman world was heavily male-dominant. (By contrast, inclusive language had been adopted for the GNB.)

The use of inclusive language in biblical translation was (and still is) a sensitive issue. In 1992 the Committee on Bible Translation resolved to make an inclusive language edition available. It first appeared in 1995 and 1996, but only in Britain, where the NIV was published by Hodder and Stoughton.

In the United States this development brought a violent reaction, with large and influential theological institutions in the South threatening to boycott the NIV if an inclusive language edition were published in the USA.

Notwithstanding this threat, the Committee on Bible Translation proceeded with the TNIV project, publishing the New Testament in 2002, the full Bible in 2005. It is a thoroughgoing inclusive language translation, and thus the Committee addressed what was one of the most serious weaknesses of the earlier editions of the NIV.

With respect to its rendering of words of the δ-family in Galatians and Romans, the TNIV is identical with the NIV, apart from three insignificant changes: at Rom 5:7 "righteous man" of the NIV becomes "righteous person" in the TNIV (in line with the policy of using inclusive language); at Rom 5:18a NIV's "righteous act" becomes "act of righteousness" of the TNIV; at Rom 6:7 "[to] free" of NIV becomes "set free" in the TNIV. Of much greater significance was the alteration of "righteousness from God" (Rom 1:17; 3:21–22) in the NIV to "righteousness of God" in these places in the TNIV. While "righteousness from God" is supported by Rom 5:17 ["gift of righteousness"], utilizing "righteousness of God" immediately suggests to the English reader that Paul's phrase is a possessive genitive, and refers to God's personal attribute of righteousness (cf. Rom 3:25–26).

4.8.5 New International Reader's Version (1998, revised 2005)

Around 1990 Ronald F. Youngblood of the International Bible Society and Zondervan Publishing House was asked to consider heading up the production of a children's Bible aimed at a third-grade reading level. Reluctant at first, he eventually concluded that such a Bible was necessary, and became executive editor of the project. The new version was to be known as the *New International Reader's Version* (NIrV).

Paralleling the organization used for the NIV, a four-tiered system was developed: (1) a relatively large number of "rough-draft simplifiers"; (2) an Initial Simplification Committee; (3) three Committee on Bible Translation Simplification Committees; (4) a Final Review Committee. While the NIV's Committee on Bible Translation didn't produce the NIrV, the work was carried out by several members of the CBT.

The NIrV was to be based on the NIV, and wherever possible, to use its wording. It was recognized, however, that overall the sentences of the NIV had to be shortened and its vocabulary simplified. When a verse is quoted from elsewhere in the Bible, the reference to it is put after the verse. Each chapter was divided into shorter sections. Almost every chapter was given a title, sometimes a title was given to a section. Where a person or a place has more than one name in the Bible, the team fixed on the most familiar name and used it throughout (e.g., Sea of Galilee). The relatively small number of technical terms (e.g., "apostle," "circumcision," "Passover") that it was deemed necessary to retain were explained in a brief dictionary appended to the biblical text.

Accuracy was regarded as of supreme importance. In the New Testament constant reference was made to the oldest and best manuscripts. Verses added to these later in the copying tradition are signaled in the text, and listed and translated in the preface. The longer passages at Mark 16:9–20 and John 7:53–8:11 remain in their place in the text, but are marked in such a way as to indicate their later status.

Following the publication of the TNIV (NT, 2002; Bible, 2005) the NIrV was revised (in 2005) so that its gender language matched that of the TNIV and the forthcoming NIV (2011).

With regard to their rendering of words of the δ-family in Galatians and Romans, the NIrV translators followed the NIV and TNIV in adding "justification" vocabulary at Rom 1:17 and 4:24, while deleting one of the three Greek occurrences of δικαιοσύνη at Rom 10:3. However, the approach they took to bringing the δ-family into English brings us into a whole new world. In contrast to the NIV and TNIV, no use is made of the J-family at all! The R-family is represented 65x, "other means" 13x. The most prominent phrase is "make right with God" with the variations "be right with God," "become right with God," "consider right with God," and "get right with God." For δικαιοσύνη as a moral attribute (Romans 6) "right living" predominates (3x), but "what is right" and "live a godly life" are used once each. It will be obvious that a very wide range of meanings are attributed to this Greek family, taking us past the point of credulity. Nevertheless, the approach taken in the NIrV has considerable merit, and arguably communicates far more effectively than the wooden and traditional two-word family approach used in the NIV and TNIV, for which an English reader needs to understand that the renderings are theological technical terms, not everyday English. The difference between these two approaches, coming from the same translation stable, can be seen in the sample passage, Rom 3:21–26:

TNIV	NIrV
21 But now apart from the law the righteousness of God has been made known, to which the Law and the Prophets testify. **22** This righteousness is given through faith in Jesus Christ to all who believe. There is no difference between Jew and Gentile, **23** for all have sinned and fall short of the glory of God, **24** and all are justified freely by his grace through the redemption that came by Christ Jesus. **25** God presented Christ as a sacrifice of atonement, through the shedding of his blood—to be received by faith. He did this to demonstrate his justice, because in his forbearance he had left the sins committed beforehand unpunished— **26** he did it to demonstrate his justice at the present time, so as to be just and the one who justifies those who have faith in Jesus.	**21** But now God has shown us how to become right with him. The Law and the Prophets give witness to this. It has nothing to do with obeying the law. **22** We are made right with God by putting our faith in Jesus Christ. That happens to all who believe. It is no different for the Jews than for anyone else. **23** Everyone has sinned. No one measures up to God's glory. **24** The free gift of God's grace makes all of us right with him. Christ Jesus paid the price to set us free. **25** God gave him as a sacrifice to pay for sins. So he forgives the sins of those who have faith in his blood. God did all of that to prove that he is fair. Because of his mercy he did not punish people for the sins they had committed before Jesus died for them. **26** God did that to prove in our own time that he is fair. He proved that he is right. He also made right with himself those who believe in Jesus.

4.8.6 New International Version (2011)

The *New International Version* of 2011 (NIV 2011) came out several years after The Committee on Bible Translation (CBT) had put out a call to seminaries and faculties of theology inviting suggestions for the proposed revision. It built on the earlier NIV (NT 1973; Bible, 1978, revised 1984) and the more extensive revision undertaken and published as the TNIV

(NT, 2002; Bible, 2005). From my own observations, the footnotes of the NIV 2011 are virtually identical with those of the TNIV.

In their preface the CBT explains its policy on the use of inclusive language (already a feature of the TNIV) and on the changing situation in the English language that earlier had used the masculine form of the third person pronoun to refer to men and women equally.

A comparison of the pattern of renderings used for Paul's δ-family in Galatians and Romans in the TNIV and NIV 2011 respectively reveals that only two occurrences were changed: whereas at Rom 3:25 and 3.26a TNIV reads "justice," the NIV 2011 reads "righteousness."

4.8.7 Tom Wright *The New Testament for Everyone* (2011)[13]

In the decade from 2001 to 2011, Tom Wright produced a series of popular commentaries on each New Testament writing, naming it the For Everyone series (*Matthew for Everyone*, etc.). It was published by SPCK in the United Kingdom, evidently with the encouragement of Simon Kingston and Joanna Moriaty of that publishing firm. Each commentary contained an English translation of the writing concerned. In 2011 SPCK gathered the translations from these commentaries and published them as *The New Testament for Everyone*. Attractively produced in hardback, the translation was liberally supplied with sectional headings and maps. In the USA it was published by HarperOne.

Our interest in this translation concerns how Wright handled Paul's δ-family in Galatians and Romans. In his preface, Wright acknowledges the challenge posed by this Greek word-family:

> ... the English word "righteousness" has been a technical term in theology for many years, and has often been used to translate the Greek *dikaiosyne*. But for many English speakers today it means *self*-righteousness: it's become a proud, "churchy" sort of word. So what are the alternatives? We simply haven't got them. We want a word that can pack "justice", "covenant faithfulness", and "right standing or relationship" all into the same hold ... There isn't such a word. So I have done my best to bring out the different flavor which *dikaiosyne* seems to carry in this or that passage.

Although Wright identifies "right standing or relationship" as one of the meanings δικαιοσύνη can bear, he makes no use of it in either Galatians

---

13. See also Moore, "N. T. Wright's Treatment."

or Romans. His renderings draw substantially on both the R-family and the J-family, but he also makes considerable use of "other means" in the proportions 35 R: 22 J: 20 O. Within the R-family the most common phrase is "in the right."

What characterizes Wright's renderings of this family, however, is the extensive use of "covenant"; it is found in association with words of the R-family, the J-family, and in other combinations such as "covenant membership" (Gal 3:21, 24); "covenant faithfulness" (Rom 10:3a); and "covenant status" (Rom 10:3b). In his translations of the 77 words of the δ-family in Galatians and Romans, Wright uses "covenant" no less than 29 times, twice in Galatians, 27 times in Romans! Yet Paul was no covenant theologian. He uses the word "covenant" only three times in Galatians (3:15, 17: 4:24), twice in Romans (9:4; 11:27), and *none* of these occurrences is directly linked to the apostle's expositions of "rectification."

Taking his renderings of this family as a whole, Wright uses such a wide range of expressions as to leave us incredulous that the apostle could have had such a plethora of meanings in mind.

Hab 2:4, quoted by Paul in both Galatians and Romans, is rendered inconsistently:

Gal 3:11: "the righteous shall live by faith."

Rom 1:17: "the just shall live by faith."

In Rom 4:5 God is characterized as "the one who declares the ungodly to be in the right." A straightforward reading of this statement leads to an understanding which is utterly opposed elsewhere in the Scriptures, Old and New Testament. It is impossible to believe that Paul intended it to be understood in that way.

Grafting his own eisegesis onto traditional approaches to translating the δ-family into English, Wright has produced an idiosyncratic translation of Paul's exposition of rectification by which his reader will hear what he has to say, but not what Paul intended to communicate.

4.8.8 Common English Bible

Completed in 2011, the *Common English Bible* (CEB) is a fresh translation sponsored by representatives from the following denominations: Presbyterian (USA), Episcopalian, United Methodist, Disciples of Christ, and United Church of Christ.

The translation was undertaken by one hundred and twenty biblical scholars from twenty-two faith traditions. Early drafts they produced were reviewed by seventy-seven reading groups from congregations across North America. As a consequence, over five hundred individuals were involved in producing the CEB. They were drawn from twenty-three faith communities.

The textual basis for the New Testament writings is Nestle-Aland *Novum Testamentum Graece* (^{27}1993).

The translators aspired to achieve a balance between "rigorous accuracy" when rendering the biblical texts with "an equally passionate commitment to clarity of expression in the target language."

The translators abandoned the long-standing practice in English biblical translation of avoiding the use of contractions altogether. While they continue to avoid them in certain situations (formal trials and royal interviews, much divine discourse, and poetic or liturgical discourse) they have made use of them particularly for direct speech.

In their renderings of words of the δ-family in Galatians and Romans, the CEB translators use the R-family in all but six of the sixty-four occurrences. Almost all of these involve "righteousness" or "righteous." For the verb δικαιοῦν they use "make righteous" (8x), "treat as righteous" (5x), although it is arguable that the referent is identical in all these instances. Hab 2:4 (cited Gal 3:11b and Rom 1:17) is rendered inconsistently as "righteous one" and "righteous person" respectively, even though we have here the same author using this text for a similar purpose in each case. At Rom 3:26a δικαιοσύνη is not represented at all, while at Rom 3:30 it is used twice for the single Greek occurrence. At Rom 2:26 an equivalent for δικαίωμα is entirely lacking.

While the extensive use of "righteousness" and "righteous" conveys Paul's doctrine in a rather wooden manner, nevertheless the CEB translators are to be commended for confining their renderings of the single Greek δ-family largely to a single English word-family, the R-family. By doing so they have brought their English renderings closer to the sense created by the words of the underlying Greek, where the family likeness is immediately apparent.

4.9 VERSIONS UTILIZING THE TWO-FAMILY APPROACH

Eight of the versions in the table of versions published after 1999 follow the traditional two-family approach to rending words of the δ-GR family (i.e., the HCSB, ESV, NET, TNIV, NABRE, NIV2011, Wright, and *The Voice*). The noun δικαιοσύνη is usually represented by "righteousness," occasionally by "justice"; the verb δικαιοῦν by "justify" (ESV, NABRE) or sometimes by both "justify" and "declare righteous" (HCSB, NET, TNIV, NIV2011); the adjective δίκαιος by "righteous" or "just."

Following this long-established tradition of English biblical translation has certain predictable consequences:

1. Paul's use of a single word-family, the δ-family, is quite lost on the English reader, since that family is represented in the main by two English word-families, the "right" family and the "just" family, as well as (in a few cases, and particularly for the noun δικαίωμα) by other means. Not only do these two English word-families have different roots, their meanings are not directly related.

2. Each of the main representatives of the "right" and "just" families, namely, "righteousness" and "justify, justification" respectively, is problematic. "Righteousness," while a word in current use, is used comparatively rarely; "justify, justification" do not have their everyday sense of "show/shown to be in the right," but are theological technical terms. This means that English versions employing them will either be misleading or unintelligible to their readers—unless a reader understands their theological significance. Worse, however, the core theological underpinning used to support the use of these English words as theological technical terms cannot be derived from the thought of the apostle himself!

In light of the fact that a number of twentieth-century renderings (e.g., Westcott, Williams, TEV, Barclay, Bruce) have shown that a one-family approach (using the "right" family) is viable and draws on everyday English rather than technical terms, the current situation is profoundly disappointing. It falls far short of such translation ideals as the following, expressed as far back as the 1960s:

> Unfortunately, the underlying theory of translation has not caught up with the development of skills; and in religious translating, despite consecrated talent and painstaking efforts, a comprehension

of the basic principles of translation and communication has lagged behind translating in the secular fields. One specialist in translating and interpreting for the aviation industry commented that in his work he did not dare to employ the principles often followed by translators of the Bible; "With us," he said, "complete intelligibility is a matter of life and death." Unfortunately, translators of religious materials have sometimes not been prompted by the same feeling of urgency to make sense...

Even the old question: Is this a correct translation? must be answered in terms of another question, namely: For whom? Correctness must be determined by the extent to which the average reader for which a translation is intended will be likely to understand it correctly.

Moreover, we are not concerned merely with the possibility of his understanding correctly, but with the overwhelming likelihood of it. In other words, we are not content merely to translate so that the average receptor is likely to understand the message; rather we aim to make certain that such a person is very unlikely to misunderstand it.[14]

Nida and Taber went on to illustrate from one of the passages that is crucial to the whole enterprise with which we are concerned and which is particularly apt for the group of translations under review, not to mention the long English translation tradition in which they stand:

When a high percentage of people misunderstand a rendering, it cannot be regarded as a legitimate translation. For example, in Romans 1:17 most traditional translations have "the righteousness of God is revealed from faith to faith," and most readers naturally assume that this is a reference to God's own personal righteousness. Most scholars are agreed, however, that this is not God's own righteousness, but the process by which God puts men right with himself (cf. Today's English Version [= Good News Bible]). It is the act of "justification" (to use a technical and generally misunderstood word) and not the character of righteousness. But a translation which insists on rendering the Greek literally as "the righteousness of God" is simply violating the meaning for the sake of preserving a formal grammatical correspondence.[15]

---

14. Nida and Taber, *Theory and Practice*, 1.
15. Ibid., 2.

This statement dates from as far back as 1969. How very differently subsequent English translations would read today if the critique of Nida and Taber had been taken to heart and their principles implemented!

4.10 RECTIFICATION IN THE ENGLISH BIBLE EARLY IN THE THIRD MILLENNIUM

When we take into account the situation at the beginning of the third millennium, with the widespread use of the NIV and of the very conservative revisions in the KJV tradition, in particular the NKJV, together with the more modest sales of the more scholarly editions (the NJB, NAB, REB, and NRSV) and the versions that have become available in the 1990s and the early part of the twenty-first century, it is clear that the relational approach to representing Paul's doctrine of rectification is in retreat when compared with the 1960s to 1980s when the GNB had a larger market share.[16] In spite of major strides made in English biblical translation during the twentieth century, it is indeed arguable that early in the third millennium the Bible reading public is little better off than was the case during the four centuries when the KJV and the Douay Bible dominated. For in the matter of how Paul's doctrine of rectification is communicated, the majority of translations purchased and in use suffer from precisely the same weaknesses that have dogged English biblical translation from its beginnings in the fourteenth century. The situation may be summed up as follows:

1. The long-standing tradition of expressing the most important family in Paul's expositions of rectification, the single δ-GR family, by *two* English word-families is proving very persistent—even though it has absolutely nothing to commend it. It characterizes both the more scholarly "standard" translations as well as the bulk of the more conservative or Fundamentalist versions which have a large share of the market. The consequence for those who use versions taking this approach is that Paul's message is typically either unintelligible or in serious danger of being misunderstood. What, for example, would the average reader make of "the righteousness of God," especially if they were unaware of it as a technical term? It hardly passes for idiomatic English, but if it conveys anything, it is likely to be the possessive sense of God's own attribute of righteousness, which commentators

---

16. Moore, "Doctrine of 'Justification.'"

generally reject. Similarly, for the theologically uninformed English reader who comes across "justify" in R-contexts, the natural tendency is for "vindicate" to be understood. This, however, is certainly not what Paul had in mind. For far too long Paul's doctrine of rectification in the English Bible has resembled a trumpet call whose intention is unclear (1 Cor 14:8)!

Discussing the translation principle that "Meaninglessness should be avoided in a text," Nida and Taber stated, "as a principle it is best at least to make sense in the text and put the scholarly caution in the margin, rather than to make nonsense in the text and offer the excuse in the margin."[17]

As some English versions have demonstrated, applying this principle to the translation of Paul's δ-GR family has the potential to transform the English reader's understanding of the doctrine the apostle held to be at the heart of the good news (Rom 1:16–17).

2. On the basis of our investigation, attempts to represent the core of Paul's meaning by words and concepts other than "right" must be deemed to have failed. The sixteenth-century attempt of the Rheims translators to replace "right" solely with "just" and cognates has rightly been abandoned in the more recent and more scholarly versions in the Roman Catholic tradition. The American Bible Society's attempt to replace "right" with "accept/acceptance" in the CEV, and that of the *God's Word* translators to use "approve/approval," encounter serious difficulties, not the least that in neither case have the translators demonstrated that the δ-GR family can have the meanings they impose. Crucial to the choice of a core meaning is the desirability, if at all possible, of bridging Paul's use of the δ-GR family for referring to God's restoration of a right relationship (embodied, for example in his phrase δικαιοσύνη θεοῦ) as well as to the moral righteousness which is to characterize the Christian life (illustrated by Paul's use of δικαιοσύνη in Romans 6). It is precisely this advantage that "right," in its various combinations, can offer.

3. The "relational" approach, developed during the twentieth century as an alternative to the two-family approach, majors on a single English word-family, the R-family, and regards rectification as the restoration of a right relationship. It has strong linguistic and lexical backing. Yet

---

17. Nida and Taber, *Theory and Practice*, 30.

although it has been available from as far back as 1937, and was heavily promoted through the GNB NT of 1966, the evidence suggests that today this approach is considerably less visible among English readers than it was in earlier decades.

Exegetical research supports the relational approach. Paul has left us clear evidence that the "rightness" he had in mind is a rightness in relationship to or with God. The evidence in favor of understanding Paul's view of rectification in relational terms is set out in the next chapter (see §5.5).

Once we accept this evidence and the arguments from communication theory that insist that a translation should be intelligible and give the least possible opportunity for misunderstanding, then the relational view of "justification" commends itself as the best option for the English language.

What, then, is the way forward? Following our examination of an extensive and representative range of English versions, the practical conclusions to be drawn may be stated succinctly as follows:

1. It is long past time to abandon the two-family approach to the translation of Paul's δ-GR family that has dominated English biblical translation since its inception in the fourteenth century. It has absolutely nothing to commend it.

2. The nearest English equivalent to the δ-family group is the R-family, with "right" at its core. This does not imply that a translator should never go outside the R-family. It does mean, however, that where the underlying Greek words clearly have the same referents, they should be translated consistently. Further, words of the δ-GR family in R-contexts or that convey moral righteousness, together with δικαίωσις, certainly should be translated by the R-family with "right" at its core.

3. Since Paul's own writings suggest that the "rightness" he has in mind is a rightness of relationship, this ought to be brought out in an English version. That this can be done has been amply demonstrated from twentieth-century versions that have taken this approach, from Charles B. Williams on.

4.11 CONSUMER CHOICE

As in many other areas in the Western world, readers of the English Bible early in the third millennium are faced with a very wide range of options.

Yet our survey has shown that there are many factors and many motivations contributing to the versions currently available. With the demise of the KJV as the dominant version, a wide variety of groups have aspired to capture the market. Some are widely representative of a range of denominations, others of just one! A majority are from the conservative or fundamentalist end of the spectrum, and it is their products that undoubtedly have the largest market share. From this situation, infinitely more complex than in earlier times, certain contributing factors emerge clearly:

1. Communication. There is no doubt that some versions appeal to the Christian public because they are very successful at communicating with their readers. Good communication is commendable, and is, indeed, essential. But it does not exempt the reviewer of a translation from evaluating whether what is being communicated is faithful to the message and intention of the original biblical author. That is the litmus test. "Warm fuzzies" in the reader are no substitute for an accurate understanding of the New Testament authors and their message.

2. Publication. It is a sad commentary on English Bible publication that the results of responsible biblical scholarship are all too often brushed aside simply because Bible publication is market-driven. Publishers are driven by the philosophy of what will sell. All too often their versions appeal to the lowest common denominator of the Christian reading public, appealing to gross ignorance and hyper-conservatism. By this means a vicious circle is set up and hyper-conservatism becomes self-perpetuating.

3. Promotion. Through promotional material, and by accepting positions on boards of Bible translation enterprises, reputable individual scholars lend their names to versions that (judging by the commentaries they produce) it is hard to believe they can conscientiously endorse. In a number of instances one is bound to wonder how extensively they have read and assessed the versions with which their names are associated!

4. Booksellers. Many Christian booksellers carry a restricted range of English versions. By restricting choice, they also restrict opportunity. Such booksellers are motivated not by the Christian precept of what

is best for their clientele, but by the profit motive. Those who are discount booksellers often trade on the widespread perception that if an item is cheap, it must be of divine origin.

Ironically, these factors provide a sad commentary on fallen human nature, when what we are discussing is a resource designed to address that very nature!

4.12 EVALUATION IS ESSENTIAL

It is evident that there is a need for English versions to be evaluated in relation to criteria such as the following:

1. What Greek text formed the basis for the translation?
2. Does the translation communicate in idiomatic and culturally sensitive English?
3. Does what is communicated accurately reflect the message of the Scriptures in their original languages, that is—as near as we can determine them—their authors' intentions?

But who is to undertake such evaluation? It would seem that the responsibility lies squarely with trained pastors and other Christian leaders, and behind them, their theological institutions. Abandoning such evaluation and the responsibility of making it widely known means leaving Bible sales solely to commercial enterprise and the market place and inevitably puts the truth in jeopardy.

4.13 CONCLUDING NOTE

In view of the situation sketched in this chapter, it is evident that there is a long way to go in gaining wide acceptance for presenting Paul's doctrine of rectification in a meaningful way to a person reading the Scriptures in English. This threefold conversation has demonstrated that fresh insights towards this end are to be gained from all three areas with which it has been concerned: (1) the New Testament; (2) historical theology; (3) the history of the English Bible. It is to be hoped that the scholar-translators who shape the English Bible in the third millennium will have the courage to face realistically the problem areas identified, and to remedy them. No one pretends that this is an easy task. It is, however, long overdue and only increases in urgency with the passage of time. To anyone who takes seriously the linguistic, communication, and translation insights gained over the past century or so, there is no viable alternative. Finally, for those who identify with the Apostle Paul in characterizing the essence of the good news as the revelation of δικαιοσύνη θεοῦ to faith (Rom 1:16-17), the importance and urgency of this task cannot be overstated.

5

An Anatomy of Paul's Use of the δ-Family

5.1 THE Δ-FAMILY

At the heart of Paul's doctrine of rectification (or "justification") is a family of words sharing the stem δικαι-. We will refer to them as the δ-family or δ-words. Our focus will be on Galatians and Romans, where Paul's fullest treatments of rectification are found. The usage of the δ-family in Galatians, Romans, and the New Testament as a whole is shown in the following table:

Paul's Use of the δ-Family in Galatians, Romans, and the NT

	GALATIANS	ROMANS	NT
The δ-GR Group (Words common to Galatians & Romans)	• δικαιοσύνη (4x) • δικαιοῦν (8x) • δίκαιος (1x)	• δικαιοσύνη (34x) • δικαιοῦν (15x) • δίκαιος (7x)	• δικαιοσύνη (92x) • δικαιοῦν (79x) • δίκαιος (39x)
The δ-R Group (Words occurring in Romans, but not in Galatians)		• δικαίωμα (5x) • δικαίωσις (2x) • δικαιοκρισία (1x)	• δικαίωμα (10x) • δικαίωσις (2x) • δικαιοκρισία (1x)

It will be observed that in Galatians only three of these words occur, while in Romans all six are found (although the additional three occur less frequently). It will be helpful to identify the words common to Galatians and Romans as the δ-GR group, those found only in Romans as the δ-R group.

In this monograph our interest focuses primarily on the δ-GR group.

5.2 WORDS OF THE Δ-GR GROUP ARE, BROADLY SPEAKING, USED IN TWO DISTINCT WAYS

Broadly speaking, these words are used in two distinct ways:

1. in a general, or "everyday" sense;
2. in a more specialized sense.

5.3 R-CONTEXTS

This distinction is not arbitrary, but is based on context. Paul's use of these words in a more specialized sense occurs in those contexts where he establishes his doctrine of rectification. We will designate them "R-contexts."

R-contexts can be identified not only by the presence of words of the δ-family, but also by the presence of at least one of a cluster of words, phrases, or concepts which include:

1. References to the Law (νόμος, ἔργα).
2. The good news.
3. Salvation.
4. χάρις and related concepts (ἀγάπη, ἀνοχή, ἀφιέναι, δωρεά, ἐλεεῖν, μακροθυμία, οἰκτίρειν, πλοῦτος, χρηστότης, with their cognates).
5. The δικαιοσύνη / θεοῦ combination.
6. The death and resurrection of Christ.
7. Faith (πίστις, πιστεύειν).
8. λογίζεσθαι.
9. Life (ζῆν, ζωή).
10. The universal availability of salvation (ἔθνη, Ἕλληνες).[1]

---

1. More detail is provided in Moore, *Rectification*, 1:78–85.

An Anatomy of Paul's Use of the δ-Family

We may illustrate the differences between (1) the use of δ-words in ordinary contexts, and (2) their use in R-contexts, by examining two passages in Romans.

1. In Rom 6:13, 16, 18, 19, 20 δικαιοσύνη is used in its usual sense of "righteousness," "what is right," a distinctly moral term. Here Paul spells out the implications of the new life the Christian has "under Christ Jesus" as God's slave. No longer are Christians to be slaves to sin; rather, they are to be slaves to what is right (Rom 6:18, 19), slaves to God (Rom 6:22).

2. On the other hand, Rom 1:16-17, is an R-context:

   > 16 For I'm not ashamed of the good news; after all, it is God's powerful means of bringing about salvation for every person who has come to faith, for the Jew in the first instance, and for the Greek. 17 For in the good news the way to a right relationship with God is revealed as a consequence of faith for a life of faith, just as it stands on record (Hab 2:4):
   >   It is the person who is in a right relationship
   >   as a consequence of faith, who will live. (USC)

   In it we find the following terms of those listed above:

1. The good news.
2. Salvation.
3. Faith.
4. Jew/non-Jew (Ἕλλην ["Greek"] here is used for ἔθνος ["non-Jew"]).
5. The δικαιοσύνη / θεοῦ combination.
6. Life.

Occurrences in R-contexts are most frequent in Galatians and Romans, but among the letters widely accepted as authentically Pauline, R-contexts are also found at Phil 3:4b-9, 1 Cor 6:11, and 2 Cor 5:21.

5.3.1 L-Contexts and F-Contexts as Subsets of R-Contexts

R-contexts may be further subdivided into two groups. These correspond with the two perceptions of how a person comes into a right relationship with God, described in §5.7 below. Contexts where the Law predominates may be referred to as L-contexts, while contexts where faith is in the ascendancy we will call F-contexts. Thus L-contexts and F-contexts are two subsets of R-contexts. While L-contexts point to a perceived way of coming into (or staying in) a right relationship with God that Paul rejects, F-contexts express the understanding of how a person comes into a right relationship with God that Paul endorses. Thus L-contexts present the negative expression of Paul's doctrine, F-contexts the positive expression.

5.4 THE RELATIONSHIP OF THE Δ-GR WORDS TO ONE ANOTHER IN R-CONTEXTS

When words of the δ-GR group are used in R-contexts, they have the same referent, that is, they refer to the same phenomenon, even though they function differently, according to whether they function as a noun, a verb, or an adjective. In such contexts, the verb δικαιοῦν refers to God's gracious act of bringing the ungodly, who have come to faith (in Christ) as a consequence of hearing the good news about Christ, into a right relationship. The noun δικαιοσύνη refers to the right relationship [with God] which comes to us as God's gift, not as something we can earn or deserve. In these contexts the adjective δίκαιος refers to being in a right relationship with God; the "righteous" person (ὁ δίκαιος) is the person who is in a right relationship [with God].

(For a diagram showing contexts in which the noun, verb, and adjective [or any two of them] occur together, see appendix C.)

5.5 THE RELATIONAL SENSE OF Δ-GR WORDS IN R-CONTEXTS

In our quest to identify precisely what Paul had in mind in his various uses of the δ-GR words, several lines of evidence converge to suggest that the apostle had personal relationship in view.

1. δικαιοσύνη θεοῦ. While Paul's use of the δικαιοσύνη / θεοῦ combination is varied (see appendix D), the anarthrous combination (2 Cor 5:21; Rom 1:17; 3:21-22) does seem to function as a "formula." By

understanding the δικαιοσύνη as (amoral) "rightness" (rather than "righteousness," with its moral connotation) and the θεοῦ as a genitive of source or of reference (respect), it may be understood as "a rightness from God" (cf. Rom 5:17), or "a rightness with reference to, or with respect to, God."[2] The "rightness" involved is clearly a rightness of *relationship*, that is, "a rightness of relationship from God" or "a right relationship with [respect to] God."

2. Three statements combine δ-GR words with a phrase drawing attention God's perspective. Two of these statements contain the verb (Gal 3:11; Rom 3:20), one the adjective (Rom 2:13). The associated phrase in two of these statements is παρὰ τῷ θεῷ (Gal 3:11; Rom 2:13), in the third, it is ἐνώπιον αὐτοῦ (Rom 3:20):

1. Gal 3:11: ὅτι δὲ ἐν νόμῳ οὐδεὶς δικαιοῦται παρὰ τῷ θεῷ δῆλον, ὅτι Ὁ δίκαιος ἐκ πίστεως ζήσεται.

    That no one is brought into a right relationship with God by means of the Law is self-evident, since (Hab 2:4):

    > It is the person who is in a right relationship
    > as a consequence of faith who will live. (USC)

2. Rom 2:13: οὐ γὰρ οἱ ἀκροαταὶ νόμου δίκαιοι παρὰ τῷ θεῷ, ἀλλ' οἱ ποιηταὶ νόμου δικαιωθήσονται.

    For it is not those who hear the Law who are in a right relationship with God, but those who keep the Law who will be brought into a right relationship. (USC)

3. Rom 3:20: διότι ἐξ ἔργων νόμου οὐ δικαιωθήσεται πᾶσα σὰρξ ἐνώπιον αὐτοῦ, διὰ γὰρ νόμου ἐπίγνωσις ἁμαρτίας.

    And as far as he is concerned, no human being will be brought into a right relationship as a consequence of doing what the Law requires, for it is through the Law that people come to know about sin. (USC)

Both phrases, παρὰ τῷ θεῷ and ἐνώπιον αὐτοῦ, belong to a considerable body of expressions in the Greek New Testament conveying the general sense of God's presence, including how things are seen from God's perspective. In the instances above, while each is

---

2. Wallace, *Greek Grammar*, 109–10; 127–28; cf. Robertson, *A Grammar*, 499; 781; LN 1:452–53, §34.46; Nida and Louw, *Lexical Semantics*, 19, 99.

expressed negatively, they convey God's approval of the person's status or standing.[3]

3. To this data we may add:

   1. Paul's use of the καταλλάσσειν/καταλλαγή ["reconcile, reconciliation"] word-group in Rom 5:1–11 and at 2 Cor 5:17–21, where in each case it interacts with words of the δ-family;
   2. Paul's use of προσλαμβάνεσθαι ("accept": Rom 14:3; 15:7b) where the believer is spoken of as being "accepted" by God and by Christ respectively.

All three areas: (1) God's granting of the gift of a right relationship, (2) being reconciled to God (from whom sin had alienated us), and (3) being accepted by God and Christ, belong to the sphere of personal relationships, and in expressing in English translation the first of these, God's rectifying activity, it is not only appropriate, but desirable, if not essential, that the notion of personal relationship finds expression.

5.6 THE MEANINGS OF THE Δ-GR WORDS

5.6.1 "Everyday" Uses/Senses

5.6.1.1 δικαιοσύνη

- righteousness, what is right. A distinctly *moral* word. In his *Republic*, Plato (c. 427–347 BCE) makes extensive use of this word.

5.6.1.2 δικαιοῦν

- vindicate, show to be in the right (e.g., Rom 3:4).

5.6.1.3 δίκαιος

- righteous (in a moral sense); ὁ δίκαιος: the righteous or upright person.

---

3. See further Moore, *Rectification*, Part One, §5.3.4 (1:127–33).

5.6.2 Specialized (Theological) Uses/Senses

5.6.2.1 δικαιοσύνη

- (amoral) rightness;
- right relationship: presented as a divine gift, not in the sense of the gift of moral righteousness, but of the gift of a right relationship (Rom 5:17).

There are three special combinations or associations Paul makes with δικαιοσύνη in R-contexts:

5.6.2.1.1 δικαιοσύνη θεοῦ

(see appendix D)

5.6.2.1.2 δικαιοσύνη AND νόμος

(see appendix E)

5.6.2.1.3 δικαιοσύνη AND πίστις

(see appendix F)

5.6.2.2 δικαιοῦν

- rectify; bring into a right relationship.

    Rom 4:5 provides the classic Pauline statement:

    > τῷ δὲ μὴ ἐργαζομένῳ, πιστεύοντι δὲ ἐπὶ τὸν δικαιοῦντα τὸν ἀσεβῆ, λογίζεται ἡ πίστις αὐτοῦ εἰς δικαιοσύνην,

    > However, for the person who doesn't do any work, but puts their faith in the one who brings the ungodly into a right relationship, that person's faith is regarded as the basis for a right relationship. (USC)

The GNB rendering of this verse provides a particularly bad example of irresponsible translation:

> But the person who depends on his faith, not on his deeds,

and who believes in the God who declares the guilty to be innocent,

> it is his faith that God takes into account in order to put him right with himself.

The phrase "depends on his faith" is unfortunate, but the phrase "the God who declares the guilty to be innocent" borders on the blasphemous, and runs counter to the whole tenor of the Scriptures. It has its origin in the Protestant notion that in "justification" God (as Judge) declares a person "not guilty" (cf. NIV2011: "God who justifies the ungodly") and justly deserves the criticism of being a "legal fiction."[4]

Although the verb of the δ-GR group (δικαιοῦν) is not the most frequently occurring word in that group (being second to δικαιοσύνη), there is a sense in which it provides the key to the meaning of these words in R-contexts.

In the realist view advocated in Roman Catholicism, the meaning of δικαιοῦν is understood to be "to make right." However, had Paul had this meaning in mind, it is difficult to believe he would have felt any need to urge his addressees to become slaves to δικαιοσύνη, "what is right" (Romans 6, especially Rom 6:16, 18, 19).

In the forensic view advocated by the majority of Protestants, δικαιοῦν is taken to mean "to declare righteous" (understood as the action of God as Judge). Applied to Rom 4:5 (a significant R-context) this would mean that God declares the ungodly to be righteous. It is impossible to believe that Paul had such a meaning in mind here. Apart from other considerations, there is a clear statement in the OT that God will not acquit the ungodly (Exod 23:7 MT: Keep far from a false charge; do not bring death on those who are innocent and in the right, for *I will not acquit the wrongdoer* (JPS), cf. Lxx: . . . καὶ οὐ δικαιώσεις τὸν ἀσεβῆ ἕνεκεν δώρων [you shall not acquit the impious person for the sake of bribes]). With good reason, such an interpretation has been dubbed a "legal fiction."

A third view, the one advocated here, is that in R-contexts δικαιοῦν refers to God's action of *rectifying* a person in the sense of bringing a person into a right relationship with himself. Applying this understanding to Rom 4:5, we would translate: "[the God] who brings the ungodly into a right relationship."

---

4. See Moore, "Romans 4.5 in TEV."

An Anatomy of Paul's Use of the δ-Family

5.6.2.3 δίκαιος

- ὁ δίκαιος is applied to the person who has received God's gift of a right relationship (which is how Paul understands Hab 2:4, quoted at both Gal 3:11 and Rom 1:17).

5.7 TWO PERCEPTIONS OF HOW A PERSON COMES INTO A RIGHT RELATIONSHIP WITH GOD

If anything stands out clearly in Paul's discussions of our topic, it is that there are two mutually exclusive perceptions of how a person comes into a right relationship with God. The apostle draws a contrast between these two perceptions or approaches in passage after passage: Gal 2:16; 3:2–3, 5; Rom 3:20, 22–5, 27–8, 30–1; 4:2-5; 9:30–33; 10:3–8; Phil 3:6–9 (see appendix I).

The first of these approaches consists in relying on keeping the Mosaic Law, or, as Paul likes to express it, "the works of the Law" (Gal 2:16, where this phrase occurs no less than three times). Whether this observance of the demands made by the Law is perceived to be a means of establishing a right relationship with God or of maintaining a right relationship with God (as the advocates of "covenantal nomism" insist) is immaterial.[5] The characteristic feature of this approach is a confidence in human ability to live up to the Law's demands (i.e., to God's demands) unaided. One of the critiques that Paul brings against this approach is that it encourages human pride or "boasting" (Rom 2:17; 4:2). Further, there are indications that he regarded this approach as hypothetical. It depended on keeping the Law in its entirety, but in his view human beings are incapable of doing so:

> Gal 3:10: Ὅσοι γὰρ ἐξ ἔργων νόμου εἰσὶν ὑπὸ κατάραν εἰσίν, γέγραπται γὰρ ⌜ὅτι⌝ Ἐπικατάρατος πᾶς ὃς οὐκ ⌜ἐμμένει⌝ πᾶσιν τοῖς γεγραμμένοις ἐν τῷ βιβλίῳ τοῦ νόμου τοῦ ποιῆσαι αὐτά.
>
> For those who take their stand on doing what the Law requires are under a curse, for it stands on record:

---

5. It could be argued, for example, that while Jews or Jewish Christians were simply *maintaining* their relationship with God, non-Jews needed to *establish* a right relationship with God. However, in the situation in the Galatian churches, where some were advocating circumcision, it would seem that a relationship with God had already been established through Paul's earlier evangelization there (whether we are thinking of Jewish Christians or Christians of non-Jewish background). In this case, circumcision would have been regarded as a means of *staying in* the covenant.

> Anyone who doesn't continue to do everything recorded in the Book of the Law is under a curse.

The second approach was related to the initiative God himself took in sending his Son into the world for the purpose of reconciling humankind to God. This was achieved by Christ's sacrificial death for humanity's sins. It is appropriated by faith, that is, by trusting in God or depending on him. It shuns all notions of being able to achieve anything that will ingratiate us to God, looking instead solely to God in his graciousness and mercy. Paul refers to this approach as "the righteousness of faith" or, as it can be translated, "the right relationship associated with faith."

5.8 THE Δ-R GROUP

As is recognized in most English translations, the meanings of the five occurrences of δικαίωμα in Romans are diverse, but within the orbits of the concepts of "right requirement" and "righteous act." The usage at Rom 5:16 seems to be more or less synonymous with the use of δικαίωσις at 5:18.[6]

The two occurrences of δικαίωσις occur in relative proximity to one another (Rom 4:25; 5:18). While some English translators have assigned them different meanings, it is more probable that they have the same meaning ("rectification") in each occurrence.

In the single instance of δικαιοκρισία ("righteous judgment," Rom 2:5) we have a word which has an unambiguously forensic meaning, that is, it is associated with the law-court. However, its forensic character arises not from the δικαιο- ("righteous") component, but from the -κρισία ("judgment") component.

5.9 PAUL'S USE OF THE OLD TESTAMENT TO SUPPORT HIS DOCTRINE OF RECTIFICATION

The study of the influence of prior concepts and practices on the development of religious phenomena is referred to as "the history of religions" (German: Religionsgeschichte). It is an approach which is both necessary and fraught with peril. It is necessary because it is clear that new religious concepts are not hatched in cultural vacuums, but draw on pre-existing ideas, at least in part. It is a dangerous approach because in New Testament

---

6. Moore, *Rectification*, 1:142.

studies we never know precisely what body of information the person whose ideological framework is being investigated was familiar with.

We may illustrate this issue from Paul's use of δικαιοσύνη θεοῦ (often translated "the righteousness of God"). While the apostle made limited use of this phrase, yet it is clearly of great significance for Paul. Further, the available evidence suggests that he may have been the first to use it, since there are no precise equivalents in the period prior to Paul.

Yet it is not uncommon to assume that the background of Pauline usage is that of Deutero-Isaiah and the Psalms.[7] Certainly in these Scriptures we do find numerous references to "my" righteousness and "your" righteousness and "his" righteousness, where in each case the pronouns refer to God's righteousness.[8] But even though these are close, we should not simply assume that they have the same referent. The reason for insisting on this linguistic precision can be illustrated by comparing the two occurrences of "God's righteousness" in Rom 3:21–22 with the two occurrences of "his righteousness" in Rom 3:25–26. Many exegetes (the present writer included) argue that "righteousness" has different referents in the two places, the first pair referring to God's saving righteousness, the second to God's personal attribute of righteousness.

The precision called for with the δικαιοσύνη/θεοῦ combination may be further illustrated from θεοῦ δικαιοσύνη (Rom 3:5). Like δικαιοσύνη θεοῦ later in the chapter (3:21-22), θεοῦ δικαιοσύνη is also anarthrous. The word order, however, is different. Is this significant, or are we just nitpicking? I believe it is significant. The δικαιοσύνη αὐτοῦ of Rom 3:25-26 clearly signifies δικαιοσύνη θεοῦ, though, as I and many others would argue, in the sense of God's own righteousness, his personal attribute of righteousness. I suggest that when Paul wished to speak of God's personal righteousness at Rom 3.5 (as the context demands) he deliberately inverted the order so that there could be no possible confusion with his "formula" δικαιοσύνη θεοῦ (1:17; 3:21-22). It also helps us understand why in 3:25-26 he used δικαιοσύνη αὐτοῦ rather than δικαιοσύνη θεοῦ.

Although there can be no doubt that references to righteousness in the Psalms played a significant role in the understanding of Paul's doctrine arrived at by Luther, there is no evidence that they were particularly influential for Paul's understanding. There are, in fact, only two Old Testament

---

7. E.g., Dunn, *Paul and the Mosaic Law*, 310–11; Stuhlmacher, *Revisiting*, 18–20.

8. E.g., Pss 5:8; 31:1; 36:6; 39:22 Lxx; 71:2, 15, 16; 89:14; 119:40; Isa 45:23; 46:13; 51:5, 8; 56:1; 59:17; 62:1. See further: Moore, *Rectification*, 1:182 n. 35.

passages that involve both a word of the δ-GR group and a word with the πιστ- stem (relating to faith) in the major Pauline writings on rectification, namely, Gen 15:6 and Hab 2:4:

> Gen 15:6: καὶ ἐπίστευσεν Αβραμ τῷ θεῷ, καὶ ἐλογίσθη αὐτῷ εἰς δικαιοσύνην.
> And Abram put his faith in God and it was considered as the right thing for him to do.

> Hab 2:4: ὁ δὲ δίκαιος ἐκ πίστεώς μου ζήσεται.
> But the person who is righteous as a consequence of faith . . . will live.

It is of interest that both of these are found in Galatians (3:6; 3:11) as well as Romans (4:3; 1:17), making it clear that they really were formative for the apostle's thought on rectification. They are, respectively, a representative of "the Law and of the Prophet[ic writings]s" which testify to δικαιοσύνη θεοῦ (Rom 3:21).

A third passage (Ps 143:2) is also common to both these letters, but it contains only a word of the δ-family, not the πιστ- stem, and in each case it is only alluded to, not quoted (see appendix H).

5.10 HOW PAUL'S Δ-GR GROUP HAS BEEN REPRESENTED IN ENGLISH BIBLICAL VERSIONS

The full Bible was not translated into English until the fourteenth century, during the Middle English period. From the very beginning, two English word-families were used to render the words of Paul's single word-family, the δ-family. We may designate them the R-family ("righteousness" and cognates) and the J-family ("justify" and cognates). Even in the Vulgate translation, on which the first English translations were based, Paul's δ-family was represented by a single Latin word-family (*iustitia* and cognates). Once the Reformers began to produce translations primarily for the laity of their day, for the New Testament writings they went back to the original language of composition, Greek. In his German translation, Martin Luther utilized only a single German word-family ("gerecht" and cognates). Although Tyndale informs us that he made a fresh start with his own translation work, he fell back on the two English word-families utilized from the beginning of the manuscript tradition.

An Anatomy of Paul's Use of the δ-Family

The significant factor to note is that although the words of the δ-GR group all have the same referent in R-contexts, these two English word-families have no obvious semantic connection. While "righteousness" and "righteous" have reference to a personal, moral quality, the usual meaning of "to justify" in English is "to vindicate," i.e., "to show (or demonstrate) to be in the right." As a consequence, the close etymological (and semantic!) connection evident in the original Greek (and in many languages of translation) between the noun, verb, and adjective of the δ-GR group, wherever two or more of them occur in any given passage, is frequently lost. The drawback of this approach for certain passages may be illustrated from Rom 3:26:

NASB	USC
... for the demonstration, I say, of His righteousness at the present time,	It was to demonstrate the rightness of his action at the present time,
that He might be just	so that he might be both in the right himself
and the justifier of the one who has faith in Jesus.	and the One who brings a person into a right relationship as a consequence of faith in Jesus.

(See also appendix J.)

5.11 THE CONCEPTS OF "RIGHTEOUS" AND "RIGHTEOUSNESS" IN ENGLISH

The major problem with the widespread Protestant notion of the imputation of Christ's righteousness to the believer (apart from the fact that Paul never mentions or implies it!) is that it actually has no meaning. It may be discussed at the conceptual level, but in reality it is actually meaningless.

To appreciate this, we need to reflect on what "righteousness" actually is. When the word is applied to an individual, it is usually intended to convey one of two possible concepts: either that the person concerned has a righteous disposition or a righteous character, which causes them to act in a right way, or it refers to a moral quality which is actually a label summing up past (known) behavior. The two are very closely related. The label (or judgment) "righteous" is a statement about the past; if on the basis of past behavior a person has been seen to act in a consistently righteous way, then we deduce that they have a righteous character. This then serves as a predictor for the future. Character references are predicated on such an assumption. The reason we have confidence to supply someone with a character reference is that we have seen how they have performed or behaved in the past. We then assume a certain stability in human character and commend a person to a prospective employer in the belief that the past pattern will continue into the future.

It will be patently obvious, however, that the qualities or character we describe as "righteous" are not transferable. We cannot write a character reference for a person on the basis of someone else's character. Similarly, the status of no. 1 tennis seed is attained solely by performance; it, too, is non-transferable. It has meaning only in terms of the particular individual associated with it.

The Scripture writers themselves support such an understanding. In the three-generational scenario depicted in Ezekiel 18, for example, it is made quite clear that each individual will be treated on the basis of their own moral standing. Paul has precisely the same outlook in Rom 2:1–16.

When the apostle does speak of imputing righteousness directly (only at Rom 4:6, 11) it is in the context of imputing faith as righteousness (modeled on Gen 15:6, cited at Rom 4:3). At no stage in his exposition of rectification does Paul suggest that the righteousness of one individual is transferable to another person or is able to be imputed to another. Neither does he make any such statement about the righteousness of Christ. In fact, as a concordance search will verify for anyone who takes the trouble to conduct it, the apostle never even mentions Christ's righteousness in his expositions of rectification. If the apostle did not find it necessary to mention "the righteousness of Christ," why is it considered necessary by so many to include it in a restatement of his doctrine?

These facts compel us to acknowledge that an understanding of Paul's doctrine as the imputation of the righteousness of another person (Christ) is actually meaningless, unable to correspond with reality, and certainly not in accordance with what the apostle himself taught.

5.12 THE ROLE OF RECTIFICATION IN PAUL'S THEOLOGY

Interpreters of Paul are divided over the way that the apostle's doctrine of rectification functions in relation to his overall theological understanding. While it was Luther's view that the doctrine of "justification" was at the very centre of Paul's thought, some of his followers have reached very different evaluations. For example, Albert Schweitzer (1875-1965) relegated "justification" to "the rim of the crater" rather than giving it central place; Joachim Jeremias (1900-79) argued that the apostle utilized this doctrine only in controversy with Judaizers; Krister Stendahl (1921-2008) held that Paul's main concern in expressing his doctrine of "justification" lay not so much with the doctrine *per se*, but with Jewish-Gentile relations. Consequently, for him Romans 9-11 is no mere excursus within Romans, but the very heart of that letter, a claim usually reserved for Rom 3:21-26.

A careful examination of the literary structure of each of the two letters in which Paul developed his doctrine of rectification most fully indicates that in each one rectification constitutes the central theme. In the earlier of the two, Galatians, Paul at once launches into a defense of the good news he proclaims, arguing that there is only one good news, that good news he had proclaimed among the Galatians, resulting in their conversion to Christ (Gal 1:6-9, 11-12). When, however, after a lengthy autobiographical explanation (Gal 1:13-2:14), he develops the actual content of that good news, it is by means of words of the δ-family as he expounds further his doctrine of rectification (Gal 2:16-3:29).

Similarly, in Romans, after the usual salutation and expression of thanksgiving for the addressees and his hope of visiting them in the near future, Paul states the leading motif of his letter (Rom 1:16-17):

> **16** Οὐ γὰρ ἐπαισχύνομαι τὸ εὐαγγέλιον, δύναμις γὰρ θεοῦ ἐστιν εἰς σωτηρίαν παντὶ τῷ πιστεύοντι, Ἰουδαίῳ τε πρῶτον καὶ Ἕλληνι·
> **17** δικαιοσύνη γὰρ θεοῦ ἐν αὐτῷ ἀποκαλύπτεται ἐκ πίστεως εἰς πίστιν, καθὼς γέγραπται·
> Ὁ δὲ δίκαιος ἐκ πίστεως ζήσεται.
>
> **16** For I'm not ashamed of the good news; after all, it is God's powerful means of bringing about salvation for every person who has come to faith, for the Jew in the first instance, and for the Greek.
> **17** For in the good news the way to a right relationship with God is

revealed as a consequence of faith for a life of faith, just as it stands on record:
> It is the person who is in a right relationship
> as a consequence of faith, who will live.

Paul immediately follows this statement with a lengthy section which functions to show that no human being—whether Jew or non-Jew—will emerge from God's tribunal with a verdict of "righteous" (Rom 1:18–3:20). He then sets forth God's own solution to this human dilemma, the sending forth of his Son into the world to be a reconciling sacrifice for humanity's sin (Rom 3:21–26). This passage is rich in δ-vocabulary, and is followed by three sections in which this vocabulary is also prominent: Paul's three corollaries of the doctrine of rectification (3:27–31), further explanation of the "righteousness of faith" illustrated from the case of Abraham (Romans 4), and further explanation concerning the role of Christ (Romans 5).

Romans 6–8 are concerned with how the rectified person is to become actually righteous (in a personal and moral sense). In the excursus treating the relationship between Jews and non-Jews (Romans 9–11) the apostle returns to the δ-family, using δικαιοσύνη no less than eleven times between Rom 9:30 and 10:10. In fact, words of the δ-family are used in every one of the first ten chapters of Romans and again in Romans 14 (though not all are used in R-contexts).

On the basis of this evidence we ought to treat any attempt to marginalize Paul's doctrine of rectification with great caution. It suggests rather that Luther, as so often, had gained an important insight, in this instance into the significance the doctrine of rectification held for Paul.

If δικαιοσύνη and cognates were significant for Paul's understanding of God's saving righteousness, δικαιοσύνη was also prominent for Paul's insistence that the ongoing Christian life is to be characterized by obedience to what is right (Romans 6). It seems very probable that Paul's use of the same vocabulary (albeit in different senses) has contributed to some of the confusion that still persists in the Roman Catholic view of "justification" over against the Protestant view.

Further, there seems no doubt that the Protestant practice of distinguishing "justification" from sanctification accurately represents Paul's understanding. To conflate God's initiating act of rectification and the ongoing process of sanctification (the Roman Catholic approach) is to expose one's view of rectification to the danger of one form of synergism or another.[9]

---

9. Bray and Gardner, "The Joint Declaration," 125–26.

On the other hand, those Protestants who have emphasized good works done in sanctification as evidence for the reality that God's rectifying act has actually taken place, seem to the present writer to have the healthiest view of the relationship between rectification and sanctification.

5.13 PAUL'S DOCTRINE OF RECTIFICATION: A CONCISE OVERVIEW

Although created by God, human beings are alienated from God by their evil behavior (sin). Sin has serious consequences and is universal in scope.

Humanity's alienation from God can be rectified only by dealing with human sin. In his role as the educator of his people Israel, God gave them the Mosaic Law. Although its primary function was to heighten awareness of sin, many came to regard it as the means of re-establishing a right relationship with God. Paul vehemently denies that Law fulfillment will achieve such a relationship.

However, God has taken the initiative in making provision for human beings to return to him. By sending his Son, Jesus Christ, into the world to be born as a human being, to exercise a proclaiming, teaching, and healing ministry, then to give his life as a reconciling sacrifice, God has addressed the issue of humanity's sin once and for all, past, present, and future. By raising Jesus from the dead and exalting him as Lord, God has powerfully demonstrated Jesus' divine Sonship.

Jesus' achievements constitute God's good news. It is in the context of the proclamation of that good news that faith arises—faith in Jesus Christ. It finds expression in calling on Jesus as Lord, and in heartfelt belief that God raised Jesus from the dead. When such faith arises, God is able to take the action of rectifying or bringing into a right relationship the person exercising such faith (i.e., of giving them the gift of a right relationship). With that rectification comes the full forgiveness of sins and the gift of God's Holy Spirit, as the means by which the rectified person can go on to become truly righteous in a moral sense (the process of sanctification). Through God's promise to Abraham (Gen 12:3; 22:18), the scope of the salvation or rectifying action God offers, is universal.

6

Applying These Insights to Paul's Letter to the Romans

IN THIS CHAPTER WE take the insights gained in chapter 5 and apply them to Paul's letter to God's people at Rome, written probably in 57 CE. The text of Romans is given in an English translation *Under the Southern Cross: The New Testament in Australian English*. It is displayed against a light gray background. In the translation, words of the δ-family are shown in bold. Their Greek form may be identified either from a Greek New Testament or from appendix B. Explanatory comments (in ordinary type) follow each passage.[1]

TO ROMANS

Paul's Letter to the Christians of Rome

1 Paul, Christ Jesus' slave, whose calling is that of apostle, who is set apart for God's good news **2** which he promised beforehand through his prophets in sacred writings; **3** it concerns his Son, who was descended from David on the human side, **4** while as to the Spirit of holiness, he was declared God's Son powerfully, as a consequence of rising from the dead: I am referring to Jesus Christ our Lord. **5** Through him we have received grace and apostleship for the obedience faith inspires among all the non-Jewish peoples, for his name's sake.

---

1. For a fuller discussion of the role played by the δ-family of words in the relevant passages, see Moore, *Rectification*, 1:26–75.

Applying These Insights to Paul's Letter to the Romans

> ⁶ You have a place among them and you yourselves are called by Jesus Christ; ⁷ I am referring to all of you in Rome who are dearly loved by God, who are called to be his holy people: grace and peace to you from God our Father and the Lord Jesus Christ.

This opening section of Paul's letter to the Christians of Rome reflects the usual practice when beginning a letter in the Greco-Roman world of the first century, having in order the three elements of (1) author, (2) addressees, and (3) greeting. In this instance the first element, announcing the author, is greatly expanded. Because Paul is an apostle, or missionary, of the good news, and the good news is focused on Jesus Christ, expansion of the author element is largely christological in character. It provides a brief summary of the identity, credentials, achievements, and mission of Jesus Christ as the Son of God. After identifying Paul, it begins by tying in the Christian message with the Scriptures of the Jewish Bible, which had been so significant for Paul in his upbringing as a Jew.

The addressees element is not introduced until 1:7, which also contains the Christianized form of the third greeting element: a blessing or benediction.

> ⁸ Let me begin by thanking my God for all of you, through Jesus Christ, because your faith is proclaimed throughout the world. ⁹ For God (whom I serve in my spirit in the good news about his Son) testifies for me how constantly you are in my thoughts ¹⁰ so that always, in all my prayers, I request that somehow there may be even just one occasion when, God willing, I shall have a successful journey and so come to you. ¹¹ For I am longing to see you, so that I might share some spiritual gift with you, resulting in your being strengthened. ¹² By that I mean that we might be mutually encouraged by each other's faith—both your faith and mine. ¹³ Brothers and sisters, I don't want you to be ignorant of the fact that I have often longed to come to you (but have been prevented up until now)

> so that I may have some fruit among you, just as I have among the rest of the non-Jewish peoples. **¹⁴** I owe a debt to Greeks as well as to uncivilized people, to wise people as well as to those who are lacking in intelligence. **¹⁵** That's why I want to proclaim the good news to you who are in Rome, as well.

As is the case in the majority of his letters, immediately after the formal salutation Paul expresses thanksgiving for the faith of his addressees (1:8). He assures them that they are constantly in his prayers (1:9-10); in particular, he prays that he might have the opportunity of visiting them and ministering among them (1:10-11). There is nothing paternalistic about Paul's attitude here; rather he expresses the expectation that such a visit would result in mutual encouragement (1:12). He explains that although his desire to visit them has been frustrated until now, it is of long standing (1:13), motivated by the obligation he feels to share the good news right across the human spectrum with all its racial, intellectual, and cultural variety (1:13-15).

> **¹⁶** For I'm not ashamed of the good news; after all, it is God's powerful means of bringing about salvation for every person who has come to faith, for the Jew in the first instance, and for the Greek. **¹⁷** For in the good news **the way to a right relationship** with God is revealed as a consequence of faith for a life of faith, just as it stands on record:
>
>> It is **the person who is in a right relationship** as a consequence of faith, who will live.

Mention of the good news, whose proclamation lies at the heart of Paul's apostolic ministry, leads into the statement of his *leitmotif* (leading theme) in 1:16-17. The good news is the powerful means God employs to mediate his salvation. That salvation is available to all who respond in faith, irrespective of their racial origin, irrespective of whether they belong to God's covenant people or not. For what is revealed through the good news

Applying These Insights to Paul's Letter to the Romans

is the way God has provided for coming into a right relationship with himself. It is a way characterized by faith from first to last, for not only is that relationship initiated by a person's faith response to the proclamation of the good news, but obedience in faith is the key—on the human side—to sustaining that relationship (cf. 1:5; 14:23; 16:26). Paul finds confirmation of his understanding of the good news in the statement of Habakkuk (Hab 2:4, cited Rom 1:17).

> **18** For God's anger is being revealed from heaven against all human godlessness and wrongdoing, when people suppress the truth by means of wrongdoing, **19** since what can be known about God is patently obvious to them; for God has made it obvious. **20** For ever since the world was created, it has been possible to perceive his invisible attributes, namely, his eternal power and deity. They are understood by means of what has been made. As a consequence, they have no excuse. **21** For, although they knew God, they didn't give him the glory he deserves as God, nor were they grateful. Instead, they became futile in their reasoning processes and their senseless hearts were darkened. **22** Claiming to be wise, in reality they became fools, **23** and exchanged the glory of the immortal God for images resembling a mortal human being, birds, four-footed animals, and reptiles.
>
> **24** That's why God abandoned them, in the lusts of their hearts, to impurity, for dishonouring their bodies among themselves; **25** they exchanged the truth about God for a lie and revered and worshipped the creature rather than the Creator, who is blessed for ever. Amen.
>
> **26** That's why God abandoned them to dishonourable passions; for not only did the females among them exchange their natural function for that which is contrary to nature, **27** but in the same way the males also gave up the natural function of the female and were inflamed in their longing for one another, males unashamedly operating with males and receiving in themselves the penalty that goes with their deviant ways.
>
> **28** And just as they didn't see fit to acknowledge God, God abandoned them to a worthless mind to engage in inappropriate behaviour. **29** They have been filled with every kind of wrong-doing,

evil, avarice, depravity; they are full of envy, murder, strife, deceit, craftiness; they are gossips, **30** slanderers, haters of God, violent, arrogant, boasters, taking the initiative in evil, disobedient to parents, **31** senseless, lacking any sense of loyalty, lacking family affection, not showing mercy. **32** Although they are well aware of God's **just decree**, that those who do such things deserve to die, they not only do these very things, but also approve of those who make a practice of them.

But why is there a need for "salvation" in the first place? In the lengthy section which follows (1:18–3:20) Paul explains the human dilemma with respect to God, the reason why human beings do not already automatically and naturally enjoy a right relationship with God. For the apostle the key lies in ungodly human behavior and wrongdoing (1:18). It is not that the reality of God is hidden from humankind. On the contrary, God has revealed himself through his creation (1:20). Rather it is human perversity that refuses to give God the honor due to him, while attributing divine qualities to gods of their own making (1:21–23). God responded to this situation by abandoning human beings to their own passions (1:24, 26, 28: note the threefold "abandoned"). While Paul's description of God's abandonment focused largely on homosexual practices (1:24, 26–27), from 1:29 the catalogue of vices widens to include an extensive range (1:29–31). Those who promote such behavior and such vices do so actively, intentionally, and with their full approval (1:32).

2 All of you, then, who set yourself up as judge, have no defence, for in standing in judgment over another person you condemn yourself, since you, the judge, are doing the very same things. **2** We are well aware that God's judgment aligns with reality when it falls on those who do such things. **3** You who stand in judgment over those who practise such things, yet do the same things yourself, do you imagine you will escape God's judgment? **4** Or are you despising the wealth of his kindness, forbearance, and patience, ignorant of the fact that God's kindness is leading you to a change of attitude? **5** Because of your obstinacy and unrepentant heart you are hoarding up anger for

Applying These Insights to Paul's Letter to the Romans

yourself on the day of anger when God's **righteous judgment** will be revealed, **⁶** when he 'will repay to each person what their deeds deserve.' **⁷** To those who are seeking glory, honour, and immortality by persisting in good deeds, he will give eternal life, **⁸** while for those who are motivated by selfish ambition and disobey the truth, who have been won over by wrongdoing, there will be anger and fury. **⁹** There will be trouble and distress for every human being who does what is wrong, first for the Jew, then for the Greek, **¹⁰** but for every person who does what is good there will be glory, honour, and peace, first for the Jew, then for the Greek. **¹¹** For God isn't taken in by superficial appearances.

Paul now addresses any person who sets themself up as judge of a fellow human being. The problem is that the self-appointed judge does precisely the same things he/she criticizes in others. Paul challenges such a person as to whether they are not despising the wealth of goodness, forbearance, and patience God is showing towards them (2:4). Judging others does not absolve a person of the need to give account to God for their own actions (2:5). God's judgment will be impartial; he is not fooled by those external factors human beings employ to present themselves to their fellow human beings in a favorable light (2:11), and his determinations will be based on *actual behavior* (2:7–10).

¹² Anyone who has sinned without the Law will also perish without the Law, and anyone who has sinned while under the Law will be judged by the Law. **¹³** For it is not those who hear the Law who are **in a right relationship** with God, but those who keep the Law who **will be brought into a right relationship**. **¹⁴** For whenever non-Jews, who don't have the Law, carry out the Law's requirements naturally, these people, though lacking the Law, provide the Law for themselves. **¹⁵** They demonstrate that the intention behind the Law is written in their hearts, their consciences also testifying among themselves, as their thoughts accuse or even come to their defence **¹⁶** on that occasion when God will judge the hidden affairs of human beings through Christ Jesus, in accordance with the good news I proclaim.

Paul now takes up an issue which divided society in his day into two categories, at least in the perception of those in each category. For the Jew, non-Jews lacked the special privileges Jews enjoyed in their covenant relationship with God, embodied particularly in the Law of Moses, but also in the prophetic and other writings making up the Jewish Scriptures. Yet Paul is anxious to point out that mere possession of this rich spiritual heritage was not enough; the ideals embodied in the Law did not automatically transfer into the life of the nation and into the lives of the individuals making it up. Paul even goes so far as to claim that if actual behavior is made the criterion, in some instances non-Jews actually outshine their Jewish contemporaries!

¹⁷ Suppose, however, you take the name of a Jew and rely on the Law and make God your boast **¹⁸** and claim to know what he desires and approve of what is excellent as a consequence of receiving instruction under the Law, **¹⁹** and have convinced yourself that you are a guide to the blind, a light for those in the dark, **²⁰** an instructor of the foolish, a teacher of the immature, who has knowledge and truth embodied in the Law. **²¹** Tell me, you who teach someone else, don't you teach yourself at the same time? You who proclaim publicly that people shouldn't steal, do you steal? **²²** You who say people shouldn't have have sex with someone else's partner, do you have sex with someone else's partner? You who detest idols, do you rob temples? **²³** You who express pride in being associated with the Law, do you dishonour God by breaking the Law? **²⁴** For, because of you, 'God's name is held in open contempt by non-Jews'—just as it stands on record.

It is indeed the failure of God's chosen people to implement the Mosaic ideals which creates the problem. Although Paul doesn't employ the term, it is essentially a problem of hypocrisy.

> **²⁵** For while circumcision is of value if you keep the Law, if you break the Law, your circumcision has reverted to the uncircumcised state. **²⁶** So if uncircumcised people keep those things the Law **quite rightly and properly requires**, won't their uncircumcised state be regarded as if it were circumcision? **²⁷** Then the person who in his natural state is uncircumcised, but keeps the Law, will stand in judgment over you who, although you have the Law in written form and have been circumcised, nevertheless break the Law. **²⁸** For a Jew isn't someone who merely has the appearance of being a Jew, nor is circumcision merely something seen in the flesh, **²⁹** but a Jew consists also in what is not seen, and circumcision is a matter of the heart, operating in the realm of the spirit, not merely in what is in written form. Such a person receives their affirmation not from human sources, but from God.

Still focusing on his own people, the Jews, Paul now isolates the primary rite they used to demarcate themselves from non-Jews: the rite of circumcision (cf. Eph 2:11). When it was instituted (Genesis 17), circumcision was to function as the sign and seal of the covenant between Abraham and his descendants (Gen 17:9–14; Rom 4:9–12). However, if it operates only at the level of a rite, an external ceremony, without being accompanied by that behavior that is appropriate to the covenant relationship it signifies, then circumcision is of no value whatever. Or, to put it another way, the non-Jew who lives up to the ideals of the covenant will be treated as if that person were circumcised (2:26–27).

> **3** Well then, what advantage does a Jew have? Or what value does circumcision have? **²** A great deal in every way. In the first place, the Jews were entrusted with the very oracles of God. **³** What if some of them proved unfaithful? Surely their unfaithfulness doesn't cancel God's faithfulness, does it? **⁴** Of course not. Instead, let God be true, even though every human being is a liar, just as it stands on record:
>
>> that you **may be shown to be in the right** by what you
>> say and may emerge victorious when you are tried in court.

> ⁵ Now if our wrongdoing establishes the fact that God is **in the right**, what are we to say? Surely not that God is unjust to be angry? (I am speaking from a human viewpoint.) ⁶ Of course not. Otherwise, how will God be capable of judging the world? ⁷ But (someone might argue) if God's truthfulness increases because I tell lies, and he gets the credit, why am I still being tried as a sinner? ⁸ And why not misrepresent us and say—as some people claim we say—'Let's make a practice of wrongdoing, so that good may come of it'? Their condemnation is just.

The way Paul has been arguing leads naturally to the questions with which this passage opens: What advantage does a Jew have? What is the point in being circumcised? (3:1). He maintains in the strongest possible terms that the Jew does have an advantage, pointing particularly to the possession of divine revelation, "the very oracles of God" (3:2). This leads Paul on immediately to a second issue, whose significance cannot be exaggerated: God's own personal attribute of (moral) righteousness, and the closely associated matter of his veracity. Drawing on both intricate argumentation taking the form of a diatribe and an appeal to the Scriptures of the Old Testament (Ps 50:6 Lxx), Paul upholds the uprightness of God's character and affirms the suitability of his qualifications to be judge of the universe (3:6). En route he alludes to detractors who misrepresent both him and his colleagues as those who advocate the practice of doing wrong so that good may follow (3:8).

> ⁹ What then? Are we any better off? Not at all. For we have already laid the charge that all people, both Jews and Greeks, are under sin, ¹⁰ just as it stands on record:
>> There isn't even one person who is **righteous**,
>> ¹¹ no-one who understands; there isn't anyone who actively searches for God.
>> ¹² All have turned aside, together they have become worthless; there isn't a person who does good, not even one.

> ¹³ Their throats are tombs that have been opened; they use their tongues to deceive; snake poison is under their lips;
> ¹⁴ their mouths are full of cursing and bitterness.
> ¹⁵ Their feet are quick to shed blood;
> ¹⁶ destruction and misery are in their paths,
> ¹⁷ and they don't know about the road to peace.
> ¹⁸ Respect for God has no place in their world-view.
>
> ¹⁹ Now we know that whatever the Law says is addressed to those who fall under the Law's jurisdiction, so that every mouth may be muzzled and the whole world may be held accountable to God. ²⁰ And as far as he is concerned, no human being **will be brought into a right relationship** as a consequence of doing what the Law requires, for it is through the Law that people come to know about sin.

Having discussed the situation of humankind as a whole (1:18–2:16) and of the Jew in particular (2:17–29) Paul is now ready to draw his argument to a conclusion. Reduced to its simplest terms, it is that no human being is able to stand before God's tribunal and come away with a verdict of "Not guilty." That conclusion applies no less to the Jew, with the Law and circumcision, than it does to the non-Jew. In fact, the way the Law functions in God's purpose is to bring about an awareness of sin (3:20). Paul supports his conclusion with a lengthy catena of quotations from the Old Testament Scriptures (3:10-18).

> ²¹ Now, however, quite apart from the Law, **the way to a right relationship** with God, attested to by the Law and the Prophetic Writings, has come to light, ²² **a right relationship** with God through faith in Jesus Christ for all who have faith. For there isn't any difference: ²³ since all have sinned and fall short of God's glory, ²⁴ they **are brought into a right relationship** freely, by his grace, through the liberation purchased by Christ Jesus. ²⁵ God put him on public display as a reconciling sacrifice though faith in his blood to demonstrate **the rightness of his action** in disregarding sins

committed previously [26]—due to God's clemency. It was to demonstrate **the rightness of his action** at the present time, so that he might be both **in the right** himself and the One who **brings a person into a right relationship** as a consequence of faith in Jesus.

Having sketched the dark backdrop of human sinfulness (1:18—3:20) Paul now introduces the solution God himself has provided for the human dilemma. God's solution is centered in his Son, Jesus Christ, whom he himself has sent into the world to be a reconciling sacrifice for human sin (3:24). In 3:21-22 he takes up the phrase δικαιοσύνη θεοῦ he had introduced in the statement of his *Leitmotif* in 1:17, in order to develop it more fully and to explain how it is at the heart of the message of good news he proclaims. The "rightness with respect to God" [δικαιοσύνη θεοῦ] that has now come to light with the coming of Christ is a "rightness with respect to God" which is through faith in Jesus Christ and which is open to *all* who come to faith (3:21-22). Such a divine provision is necessary since *all* fall short of God's glory (3:23) and the *only* way they can come into a right relationship with God is via the means God himself has graciously and freely provided in Christ and the act of liberation he has effected (3:24). Mindful of the concerns Paul expressed about God's personal uprightness and veracity expressed early in Romans 3, the apostle is now able to affirm that God has been able to effect a right relationship with those who have faith with full personal integrity. The *saving* righteousness of God (δικαιοσύνη θεοῦ, 3:21-22) is in complete accord with God's *own* (moral) righteousness (δικαιοσύνη ἀυτοῦ, 3:25-26), so that Paul can conclude that God is "in the right himself and the One who brings a person into a right relationship as a consequence of faith in Jesus" (3:26).

[27] Well then, where does boasting come in? It has no place. On what principle? The principle of works? Certainly not, but on the principle of faith. [28] For we maintain that a person **is brought into a right relationship** quite apart from doing what the Law requires. [29] Or is God only the God of Jews? Isn't he the God of non-Jews as well? Yes, of non-Jews as well. [30] After all, God is one, and just as he **will bring** a circumcised person **into a right**

relationship as a consequence of faith, so he will bring an uncircumcised person through faith. **31** Do we then repeal the Law through faith? Of course not. On the contrary, we uphold the Law.

Several corollaries follow the concise statement of Paul's view of rectification in 3:21–26. They number three to be exact, and may be restated in the following form:

1. All human boasting is entirely excluded on the grounds of faith and because "works of the Law" play no role whatever (3:27–28);
2. Faith is the one and only means by which people will be brought into a right relationship with God, whether they are Jews or non-Jews (3:29–30).
3. Far from rescinding the Law, Paul establishes it, or puts it on a firm footing (3:31).

4 Well then, what are we to say about the experience of Abraham, who, in human terms, is our ancestor? **2** For if Abraham **was brought into a right relationship** as a consequence of what he did, he has grounds for boasting, though not as far as God is concerned. **3** For what does the Scripture say?

> Abraham put his faith in God, and for him that was regarded as the basis for **a right relationship**.

Paul has just affirmed that he upholds the Law (3:31). But what does the Law mean for him? Since he follows up this statement by raising issues concerning Abraham, it seems probable he is has in mind Law as Torah here (cf. Gal 4:21–31). For the accounts of Abraham to which he alludes are found in the first of the five books making up the Torah, namely, Genesis. There it is made clear that Abraham entered into a right relationship with God. However, one particular statement in Genesis indicates clearly that the basis of Abraham's relationship with God was not what he did (which might well provide the basis for "boasting") but rather who he believed. This is clearly stated in Gen 15:6 (quoted by Paul in Rom 4:3). This text forms the basis for most of the discussion that follows in Romans 4 and leads the apostle to give it a general application later in the chapter (4:23–25).

> **4** Now for the working person wages are not considered to be a favour, but an obligation. **5** However, for the person who doesn't do any work, but puts their faith in the one who **brings** the ungodly **into a right relationship**, that person's faith is regarded as the basis for **a right relationship**.

Paul now introduces an illustration from everyday life: the person who works for wages. Once the work has been done, wages are seen as an obligation on the part of the employer. However, where no work has been done, yet a benefit is conferred, the only basis can be faith—just as was case with Abraham (4:3).

> **6** Just as David, too, speaks of how blessed the person is, whom God regards as being in **a right relationship** apart from what that person does:
>> **7** How blessed are those whose lawless acts are forgiven
>> and whose sins are covered over.
>> **8** How blessed is the man whose sin the Lord doesn't take
>> into account.

Paul now draws attention to another Old Testament example, that of David. In the opening lines of Psalm 31 Lxx (cited by Paul in Rom 4:7–8) David shows a consciousness of the sin he had committed, but above all he exults in the divine forgiveness he had experienced.

> **9** Well then, is this blessing for the circumcised person or for the person who isn't circumcised? After all, in the case of Abraham we maintain that faith was regarded as the basis for **a right**

Applying These Insights to Paul's Letter to the Romans

relationship. ¹⁰ Then in what circumstances was it so regarded? Was it in the circumcised state or in the uncircumcised state? It wasn't in the circumcised state, but in the uncircumcised state. ¹¹ And he received the symbol of circumcision as a seal of **the right relationship** associated with the faith he had while in the uncircumcised state. This enabled him to be the ancestor of all who have faith while in the uncircumcised state, so that they too might be regarded as **being in a right relationship**, ¹² as well as the ancestor of those circumcised who are not merely circumcised, but also follow in the footsteps of the faith our ancestor Abraham had while still in the uncircumcised state.

Paul goes on to explore the circumstances of Abraham's experience (as recorded in Gen 15:6). He points out that the patriarch was brought into a right relationship with God *when he was still in the uncircumcised state*. Only later was circumcision introduced as a sign and seal of what had already been granted because of Abraham's faith (Gen 17; Rom 4:11). The fact that his life embraced both the uncircumcised state (in which he was brought into a right relationship with God) as well as the later experience of circumcision, enables him to be the ancestor of both the uncircumcised person and the circumcised—provided each has faith. For it is *faith* that provides the spiritual bridge to Abraham.

¹³ For the promise made to Abraham and to his descendants, that he would inherit the world, wasn't based on the Law, but on **the right relationship** associated with faith. ¹⁴ For if the heirs are heirs as a consequence of Law, then there's no point in faith and the promise has been revoked. ¹⁵ For the Law brings about anger; but in situations where there is no Law, neither is there any breaking of the Law. ¹⁶ That's why it's a consequence of faith, so that it might be in accordance with grace, in order that the promise might be freely established for all his descendants, not just those coming from a situation of having the Law, but also those coming from a situation of having Abraham's faith. For Abraham is the ancestor of us all, ¹⁷ just as it stands on record, 'I have appointed you ancestor

of many nations,' in the presence of the God in whom he put his faith, who brings the dead to life and addresses things not yet in existence as if they already existed. **18** He it was who, in the face of hopelessness, exercised faith in hope, with the consequence that he became the ancestor of many nations in accordance with the statement, 'That is what your descendants will be like.' **19** He didn't become weak in faith when he thought about his own body, which had already died (being about a hundred years old) and the infertility of Sarah's womb. **20** He didn't doubt God's promise by way of unbelief, but was empowered by faith, giving glory to God, **21** being fully convinced that he who had made the promises was capable of carrying them out. **22** This is why 'for him that was regarded as the basis for **a right relationship.**'

23 The words 'for him that was regarded' weren't recorded solely for his benefit, **24** but also for ours, for whom it is about to be regarded, who have faith in the one who raised Jesus our Lord from among the dead. **25** He was handed over because of the offences we have committed and was raised so that **we might be brought into a right relationship**.

Paul is at pains to point out that Abraham's experience of being brought into a right relationship with God owed nothing to the Law, but was due solely to his faith (4:13). For while Law is closely associated with divine anger (4:15), faith is linked to grace (4:16) and promise (4:13, 14, 16, 20, 21). This in turn is due to God's wish that his salvation have the widest terms of reference possible, freely embracing non-Jew as well as Jew (4:16-17).

Paul undertakes a close examination of the circumstances of Abraham's life which led to his faith response and ultimately to its being recorded in the Torah (4:18-22).

In the concluding paragraph he applies Abraham's experience to the Christian experience of being brought into a right relationship with God (4:23-25). In the latter case it is not God as the maker of promises to Abraham regarding his posterity and the land they would ultimately come to possess, but God in his role as the one who raised Jesus, the Christian's Lord, from the dead (4:24-25). What motivated Jesus to submit himself to

Applying These Insights to Paul's Letter to the Romans

death was the need for the Christian's crimes to be dealt with, and the very reason for his rising from the dead was that the Christian might be brought into a right relationship with God (4:25).

> **5** So, **having been brought into a right relationship** as a consequence of faith, we are at peace with God through our Lord Jesus Christ. **²** It is through him, too, that we have gained access, by means of faith, into this favourable standing we presently enjoy, and we are overjoyed at the prospect of God's glory. **³** Not only that: we are also overjoyed in times of trouble, well aware that trouble produces perseverance, **⁴** perseverance produces character, character produces hope. **⁵** Such hope doesn't embarrass us, because God's love is poured into our hearts by the Holy Spirit who has been given to us.

Having treated faith-righteousness (as exemplified in Abraham) in Romans 4, in Romans 5 Paul returns to develop in greater detail the part played by Jesus Christ in the rectification of the Christian, which he had touched on only briefly earlier (3:21–26, especially 3:24). Three times in this chapter he refers to what has been achieved "through our Lord, Jesus Christ" (5:1, 11, 21). But as well as mentioning the positive outcomes (5:1–2) the apostle does not shy away from reference to the times of trouble a Christian faces and the role that trouble plays in the cycle of Christian growth (5:3–5). He reminds the Christians of Rome that God has given his children his Holy Spirit, and that the Spirit has a part to play in this growth (5:5).

> **⁶** For while we were still in a weakened condition, just at that very time, Christ died to benefit ungodly people. **⁷** Now it is hardly likely that anyone would die to benefit **a right-living person**, although someone may be prepared to die to benefit a good person; **⁸** but God demonstrates the love he personally has for us, in that while we were still *sinners*, Christ died to benefit us!

A true appreciation of the extent of God's love for humankind is possible only when one comes to a realization of the weak, helpless, and sinful condition which characterizes human beings. In the attempt to bring his message home, Paul uses a three-tiered analogy drawn from everyday human experience. He sketches a "hierarchy of morality" in which goodness is the highest virtue, righteousness is next, and well below, at the very base (or below ground level?) is sinfulness (5:7–8). Here again, while the emphasis falls on God's love for us, it is Christ who died in order to benefit us (5:8).

> **⁹** Now, then, that **we have been brought into a right relationship** by means of his blood, all the more will we be saved from anger through him. **¹⁰** For if while we were enemies we were reconciled to God through the *death* of his Son, how much more, now that we are reconciled, will we be saved through his *life*! **¹¹** Not only so, but our pride is in God, through our Lord, Jesus Christ, through whom we have now obtained reconciliation.

Paul now employs a series of *a minori ad maius* arguments (reasoning that if the lesser case holds true, then how much more the greater case does). If in the past, when we were sinners, we were brought into a right relationship through Christ's blood, how much more, now that we are in this right relationship, will we be saved from God's anger in the future? If God did so much for us when we were his enemies, how much more will he do for us now that we have been reconciled to him! If Christ achieved all this through his *death*, what will he do for us now that he is *risen and alive*?

> **¹²** That's why, just as sin entered the world through one person and death entered through sin, so also death came over all people: because all sinned. **¹³** For sin was in the world even before the Law was given, but sin isn't charged to a person's account when there is no Law. **¹⁴** Nevertheless, death reigned from Adam until Moses—even over those who had sinned in a way that didn't resemble Adam's trespass.

In explaining how sin entered into the world of humankind, Paul draws on the Adam narrative (Genesis 3) to locate sin's entry via a single person. (He takes no account of Eve!) In doing so he is leading up to the point later in this passage (5:15) where he will introduce a comparison and

Applying These Insights to Paul's Letter to the Romans

contrast between Adam, representing humankind characterized by sin, and Jesus Christ as the head of a new humanity, a humanity in right relationship with God.

In this passage death, as the consequence of sin, also entered through the one person, Adam. While Paul affirms that death affected all people, the reason Paul gives should be noted carefully: all sinned (5:12). In other words, the death each person experiences is due to the sin they personally have committed. The presence of death in the world is attributable in the first place to Adam, but the death that comes over all people is a consequence of their own sin.

Paul also makes the point that sin's presence in the world pre-dated the giving of the Law (5:13). This implies that death, too, was present during that period—in fact, it "reigned" (5:14).

> Now Adam serves as a model of the person who was to come after him. **15** However, his offence also provides a contrast with the free gift:
> For if many died through one person's offence, how much more will God's grace and the gift motivated by grace, given through the one person Jesus Christ, abound for many.
> **16** Further, the gift doesn't resemble the case of the one person who sinned:
> For while judgment was the consequence of one offence and resulted in punishment, the free gift consequent upon many offences resulted in **a rectifying of the situation**.
> **17** For if death reigned through one person by means of that one person's offence, how much more will those who receive the abundance of grace and the gift of **a right relationship**, reign through the one person Jesus Christ!
> **18** So then, just as one person's offence impacted on all people, leading to punishment, so also one person's **right act** impacted on all people, leading to **a right relationship** characterized by life.
> **19** For just as many were constituted sinners through one person's disobedience, so also many will be brought into **a right relationship** through the obedience of one.
> **20** Law slipped in so as to increase the offences; however, where sin increased, grace increased out of all proportion, **21** in order that,

just as sin reigned by means of death, so also grace might reign through **a right relationship**, resulting in eternal life through Jesus Christ our Lord.

At Rom 5:14b Paul introduces Adam as a "type," or antitype, of Jesus Christ. For it soon becomes obvious that the contrasts outweigh the similarities (5:16). In fact Paul goes on to provide seven pairs of contrasts between Adam and Jesus Christ with a little introductory or explanatory material between some of them.[2]

The δ-family is particularly prominent here: three occurrences are drawn from the δ-GR group (δικαιοσύνη, 5:17,21; δίκαιος, 5:19), three from the δ-R group (δικαίωμα, 5:16,18; δικαίωσις, 5:18).

With the close of Romans 5 and his description of the part played by Jesus Christ in it, the apostle has concluded his exposition of the doctrine of rectification. Subsequently he turns to the issue of how the believer, now that he/she is in a right relationship with God, is to become righteous in reality, righteous in an actual, ethical sense.

6 Well then, what are we to say to all this? 'Let's go on sinning, so that God's gracious dealings with us may increase'? **2** Of course not! How can a person who has died as far as sin is concerned still go on living under its influence? **3** Surely you aren't ignorant of the fact that anyone who has been baptized into Christ Jesus has been baptized into Christ's death, are you? **4** Consequently, through baptism we were entombed with him in the realm of death, so that just as Christ was raised up from among the dead through the Father's glory, so we too would be able to live in the newness life brings. **5** For it follows that if we have been fused with something like his death, we will also be fused with something like his resurrection. **6** We are well aware that our old being has been crucified with him, so that sin's body might be rendered ineffective, that we might no longer be slaves to sin. **7** For a person who has died **has been released** from sin. **8** Yet if we died with Christ we believe we will also

---

2. Rom 5:15a, 16a, 20a; see further Moore, *Rectification*, 1:286.

with him, ⁹ well aware that Christ, having been raised from among the dead, will never die again—death no longer has mastery over him! ¹⁰ For in that he died, he died to sin once and for all, but in that he is alive, he is alive to God. ¹¹ On this basis, you are to consider yourself to be dead as far as sin is concerned, but alive through Christ Jesus as far as God is concerned.

At this point Paul begins to address the issue of how a Christian becomes righteous in a personal, moral sense. It will occupy Romans 6–8.

The issue arises out of a statement made a little earlier by Paul: "where sin increased, grace increased out of all proportion" (5:20). Picking it up at the beginning of Romans 6, he puts into the mouth of his diatribe partner the interjection: "Let's go on sinning, so that God's gracious dealings with us may increase."

In denying that this outlook is appropriate for a Christian, Paul refers to the baptismal rite as a picture of the believer's identification with Christ in his death (6:2, 3, 5, 6, 7, 8, 10, 11), burial (6:4), and resurrection (6:4, 5, 8, 9, 10, 11).

¹² So don't allow sin to reign in your mortal bodies so that you obey your bodies' desires, ¹³ neither present the various parts of your bodies to sin as agents of wrongdoing; instead, present yourselves to God as those who have come back from among the dead and the various parts of your bodies to God as agents of **what is right**. ¹⁴ For sin is not to have mastery over you, for you aren't under Law, but under grace.

¹⁵ What then? Are we to sin because we aren't under Law but under grace? Certainly not! ¹⁶ Aren't you aware that when you present yourselves to something as obedient slaves, you are slaves to what you obey, whether it's sin, that results in death, or obedience, that results in **what is right?** ¹⁷ But, thank God, when you were sin's slaves you became obedient from your hearts to the program of teaching to which you were handed over; ¹⁸ having been set free from sin, you became slaves to **what is right!** ¹⁹ I am using

everyday language because of your human limitations. For just as you presented the various parts of your bodies as slaves to impurity and lawlessness, with lawlessness as the consequence, so now present the various parts of your bodies as slaves to **what is right**, with holiness as the consequence. [20] For when you were slaves to sin, you were free with respect to **what is right**. [21] However, what benefit did you have at that time? You are now ashamed of those things, for they end up in death. [22] But now that you've been set free from sin and have become slaves to God, the produce you gain is holiness, and the final outcome is eternal life. [23] For the wages sin pays is death, but the gift God freely gives is eternal life through Christ Jesus, our Lord.

Paul's addressees are urged to sever their connection with sin and to present the various parts of their bodies to God, on the grounds that as they are now under grace, sin need no longer exercise its former mastery over them.

He soon adopts imagery drawn from his everyday world (cf. 6:19a), the image of slavery, sustaining it until virtually the end of Romans 6 (6:16–23). The basic stance Paul adopts is that all human beings are slaves. They do, however, have a choice as to who their master is to be. They can serve sin (6:16, 17, 19, 20) or they can be slaves to God (6:22) and to "what is right" (6:16, 18, 19). Paul urges his addressees to consider what returns they got from slavery to sin and points them to the outcome of becoming slaves to what is right (6:20–23).

7 Or can it be that you are ignorant, my friends—for I'm addressing people who are familiar with the Law—that the Law has jurisdiction over a person only while they are still alive? [2] For a married woman is bound by Law only as long as her husband is alive; if her husband dies, she is freed from the Law as it relates to her husband. [3] So then it follows that if she has a relationship with another man while her husband is still alive, she will be called an adulteress; but if her husband dies, she is released from the Law, so that she is not an adulteress if she has a relationship with another man. **4** Consequently, my friends, through Christ's body you too have died to the Law, so that you may have a relationship with another person, with him who was raised from among the dead, so that you may be productive for God. **5** For when we operated only at the human level, the sinful desires which were aroused by the Law in the various parts of our bodies, resulted in produce for death; **6** but now that we have died to what held us in its grip and have been released from the Law, we serve as slaves in the newness characteristic of the Spirit, and not in the oldness characteristic of the written code.

As he continues to explore how a moral transformation is effected in the Christian, Paul considers what contribution the Law may have. He commences with an intricate analogy based on a married woman who is widowed (7:2-4). He concludes that through Christ's body the Christian has died to the Law, freed to serve as slaves in the newness of the Holy Spirit (7:4,6).

7 Then how should we express it? Is the Law sinful? Certainly not! On the contrary, I wouldn't have known about sin if it hadn't been for the Law. For I wouldn't have known about desiring what others have, except that the Law used to say, 'You are not to desire what others have.' **8** But sin, seizing its opportunity through the commandment, produced in me every form of desiring what others have; for, in the absence of Law, sin is dead. **9** There was a time when I was alive apart from the Law, but when the commandment came along, sin came back to life; **10** I died, and found that the very commandment, which was meant to bring life, resulted in death. **11** For sin, seizing its opportunity through the commandment, deceived me, and, through the commandment, put me to death. **12** Consequently, the Law is holy and the commandment is holy, **right**, and good. **13** Then did something good become the means of my death? Certainly not! On the contrary, sin—in order that it might be exposed as sin—used what is good to cause my death, so that through the commandment sin might become sinful in the extreme.

Once again Paul attributes to the Law the role of exposing sin for what it is (7:7). Yet sin is able to manipulate the Law so that it proves to be death to Paul (7:11,13). The apostle continues to uphold the Law as something holy, right and good (7:12), but in the end it is no match for sin. The end result is that sin is exposed for what it is—sinful in the extreme (7:13). Given Paul's Jewish upbringing, it is difficult to know precisely how to understand 7:9: "There was a time when I was alive apart from the Law."

> **14** Now we are well aware that whereas the Law is spiritual, I am merely human, sold out to sin. **15** I don't understand my own actions: for I don't do what I want to, but rather it is what I hate that I do. **16** If I end up doing what I don't want, I am in agreement with the Law, that it is good. **17** In these circumstances it is no longer I who bring it about, but sin, which has taken up residence in me. **18** For I know all too well that nothing good resides in me, that is, in my human nature. For while the desire for something good is present in me, the means of carrying it out is not. **19** For it isn't the good I want to do that I end up doing, rather it's the evil I don't want that I put into practice. **20** Now if I do what I don't really want to do, it is no longer I who carry it out, but sin residing in me. **21** So then I experience the principle that when I want to do what is good, evil is present in me. **22** For while I agree with God's Law deep within, **23** I observe another principle operating in the various parts of my body: it fights against the principle at work in my mind and takes me prisoner through the principle of sin which is in the various parts of my body. **24** Wretched person that I am! Who will rescue me from the body of this death? **25** Thanks be to God, he will—through Jesus Christ our Lord. So then, I myself am a slave to God's Law in my mind, but in my human nature I am a slave to the principle of sin.

While Paul is able to affirm the Law in very positive terms, he is aware that he himself is "merely human, sold out to sin" (7:14). Rom 7:14–25 constitutes a penetrating insight into human nature, specifically, human nature as it is experienced by a Christian. Paul captures authentically the gap between aspiration and practice in the Christian life (7:15, 16, 18b, 19, 20). Twice he affirms that it is sin that brings about the mismatch of aspiration and deed (7:17, 20). And through the sense of defeat there rings another note, a note of confidence that God, through Christ, will ultimately overcome (7:25).

> **8** It follows, then, that there is now no punishment for those who are under Christ Jesus. **²** For the Spirit-principle, the principle of life through Christ Jesus, has set you free from the principle of sin and death. **³** For what the Law was incapable of doing (in that it was weak through human nature) God achieved by sending his own Son in the likeness of sinful human nature and as a sin-offering. He condemned sin in human nature, **⁴** in order that what the Law **quite rightly and properly requires**, might be fulfilled in those of us who live not by conforming to human nature, but by conforming to the Spirit. **⁵** For those who conform to human nature think merely at the human level, but those who conform to the Spirit think about matters relating to the Spirit. **⁶** The mind-set associated with human nature means death, whereas the mind-set associated with the Spirit means life and peace, **⁷** because the mind-set associated with human nature is hostile towards God, for it doesn't submit to God's Law, nor is it capable of doing so. **⁸** Consequently, those who are under the control of human nature aren't able to please God.

Paul pauses to affirm the release from fear of punishment that those who embrace the life offered through Christ experience (8:1). He then depicts two mutually exclusive principles, one characterized by sin and death, the other by the Holy Spirit and the life which comes through Christ Jesus (8:2). He goes on to explain how God, by sending his Son to take on human form, has achieved what the Law was unable to achieve: the condemnation of sin in human nature, thus opening the way to fulfillment of the Law. However, such fulfillment is possible only through the indwelling Spirit of God. For as Paul has just affirmed (8:2), it is the principle of the Holy Spirit that overcomes the principle of sin and death. The contrasting nature of these two principles, and how human nature, left to its own devices, sides with the principle of sin and death, is brought out in 8:5–8.

> ⁹ You, however, aren't under the control of human nature, but are under the control of the Spirit—if God's Spirit resides in you. Now if any person doesn't have Christ's Spirit, that person doesn't belong to Christ. ¹⁰ But if Christ is in you people, while your bodies are dead (because of sin), your spirits are life (because of **a right relationship**). ¹¹ If the Spirit of the one who raised Jesus from among the dead resides in you, he who raised Christ from among the dead will bring your mortal bodies to life through his Spirit, who resides within you.

Here Paul insists that the Christian is not locked in to a life that operates at the merely human level, with its natural accompaniments, sin and death. Because God has given his children his Holy Spirit (8:9b), life under the control of the Spirit is now possible (8:9a). For the presence of the Holy Spirit in the Christian offers benefits not only for the present, but also for the future: the resident Spirit is the basis for the Christian's future resurrection (8:11).

> ¹² So then it follows, brothers and sisters, that we are under obligation, not to our human nature, to live by conforming to our human nature ¹³ —for if you live in conformity to your human nature, you will soon die—but if by means of the Spirit you put the deeds of the body to death, you will live. ¹⁴ For it is those who are led by God's Spirit who are God's sons and daughters. ¹⁵ For you didn't receive a spirit of slavery again, resulting in fear, but you received a spirit of adoption as sons and daughters, by which we cry out 'Abba', that is, 'Father.' ¹⁶ The Spirit himself testifies together with our spirits that we are God's children. ¹⁷ Yet if we are children, we are also heirs, that is, God's heirs, as well as joint-heirs with Christ—provided that we suffer with him, so that we may also be glorified with him.

The lesson to be drawn from the situation Paul has sketched is that the Christian is under obligation, not to human nature, but to the indwelling

Applying These Insights to Paul's Letter to the Romans

Holy Spirit (8:12–13). Paul depicts the scenario as a contrast between slavery and freedom—the slavery of conforming to our own passions or the freedom which is rooted in being God's children, analogous to sons coming of age and therefore coming into all the privileges of full sonship (8:14–15). The Christian has the inward testimony that this is so from the Spirit residing within (8:16). And to be God's children means to enjoy the full range of privileges that entails—as well as the suffering that identification with Christ inevitably brings (8:17).

18 For I consider that the sufferings of the present time don't bear comparison with the glory yet to be revealed to us. **19** For the creation is looking forward with eager expectation to God's children being revealed. **20** For the creation was subjected to frustration, not willingly, but on account of the one who subjected it in hope, **21** because even the creation itself will be set free from its enslavement to decay, in order to have the glorious freedom characteristic of God's children. **22** For, as we are well aware, the whole creation has been groaning together and suffering the agony of labour pains until now; **23** but more than that, we ourselves, who have the initial evidence of the Spirit, also groan inwardly as we eagerly look forward to our adoption, the liberation of our bodies. **24** For it is in hope that we are saved. A hope that is already a reality is no hope at all, for who hopes for something that is already a reality? **25** But if we are hoping for something that is not yet a reality, we look forward to it eagerly and persistently. **26** Furthermore, the Spirit comes to our aid at the point at which we are most vulnerable, for we don't really know what we should be praying for in the way we ought, but the Spirit himself intercedes intensely with groans which can't be put into words, **27** and he who searches hearts is well aware of how the Spirit is thinking, because he intercedes on behalf of God's people as God wishes. **28** We know that all things work together for good to those who love God, who are called in accordance with his purpose, **29** because those whom he knew in advance he also predetermined to conform to his Son's image, so that his Son might be the eldest of a large family. **30** Now those he

> predetermined, he also called, and those he called, he also **brought into a right relationship**, while those he **brought into a right relationship** he glorified as well.

Having mentioned suffering, Paul takes it up briefly to put it in the perspective of what God has in the future, not only for his children, but also for the entire creation (8:19–22). That divine plan is the basis for Christian hope (8:23–25), and the evidence for it is experienced through the ministry of God's Spirit in the present, especially in the Christian's aspiration to communicate with God (8:26–27). It is simply further evidence of the love God has for his children, who, on the basis of his advanced knowledge, he has chosen in advance, called, brought into a right relationship, and glorified (8:28–30). Yet the glory experienced to date is only a foretaste of the glory yet to be revealed (8:18).

³¹ Well then, what conclusions are we to draw from all this?
If *God* is for us, who can be against us?
³² He who didn't spare his own Son, but handed him over on behalf of us all, how could he fail to also make everything freely available with him?
³³ Who will lay charges against those whom *God* has chosen?
Will it be *God*, who **brings people into a right relationship**?
³⁴ Who is it who punishes?
Is it Christ Jesus who died—or rather who was raised!—who is also on God's right, and who intercedes on our behalf?
³⁵ What can separate us from Christ's love? Can trouble or anguish or persecution or hunger or insufficient clothing or danger or sword?
³⁶ Just as it stands on record:

> Because of you, we are being put to death throughout the day; we are regarded as sheep destined for slaughter.

³⁷ On the contrary, in all such matters we have decisive victory through him who loved us. ³⁸ For I am convinced that neither death nor life, neither angels nor authorities, neither present situations

nor future situations, nor powers, **³⁹** nor height, nor depth, nor any other created thing, is able to separate us from God's love expressed through Christ Jesus our Lord.

A consideration of the matters Paul has taken up leads inevitably to one conclusion: that the quality that dominates in God's dealings with humankind is his love; God is *for* us (8:31)! It is seen in all that God has done for us through his Son, Jesus Christ (8:32–34). It is a bond so strong there is absolutely nothing that can intervene between the human being and his or her God (8:38–39), not even the sufferings to which Paul had earlier alluded (8:35–36, cf. 8:17–18). It is here, in the confidence the Christian may have in his/her God, that the assurance of salvation is to be rooted.

9 With my conscience testifying to me through the Holy Spirit, I am speaking the truth under Christ and am not telling lies **²** when I say that there is immense sorrow and unremitting anguish in my heart. **³** For I could even wish that I myself might be accursed, cut off from Christ, on behalf of my brothers and sisters, who, biologically speaking, are my relatives. **⁴** They are Israelites, to whom belong the adoption, as well as the glory, the covenants, the legislation, the divine service, and the promises. **⁵** The patriarchs belong to them, and, biologically speaking, the Messiah came from them. May he, who is God over all, be blessed for ever, Amen!

Having completed his exposition of rectification (3:21—5:21) and his explanation and exhortations on how the Christian becomes righteous in a moral sense (Rom 6–8), Paul now takes up some of the other corollaries mentioned in Rom 3:27–31. In Romans 9–11 he has a particular interest in the relationship between Jews and non-Jews in the overall purposes of God. At the commencement of each of the three sections (which were later recognized in the form of chapter divisions) he makes a statement about his personal relationship to his own people, Israel (9:1–5; 10:1–3; 11:1–2). In the passage above he affirms the privileges and all the advantages associated with Israel's special role as God's people (9:4–5).

> **⁶** Not that what God has communicated has failed. For it isn't necessarily all who have descended from Israel who constitute Israel. **⁷** After all, it is not *all* Abraham's descendants who are his children, but 'it is your descendants through Isaac who will take your name.' **⁸** That is, it isn't the children who are naturally born who are God's children, but the children associated with the promise who are regarded as descendants. **⁹** After all, these are the terms of the promise: 'I will come at this time and Sarah will have a son.'
> **¹⁰** Not only was that the case, but it was also the case with Rebecca, as a consequence of her going to bed with one man, our ancestor Isaac. **¹¹** For before her children had been born or had done anything at all (whether good or bad), in order that God's purpose might proceed in accordance with what he had determined, **¹²** not because of what they had done, but because of the one who calls, she was told, 'the elder will be a slave to the younger,' **¹³** just as it stands on record, 'I loved Jacob, but I hated Esau.'

Paul is conscious that for some of his addressees there may appear to be a credibility gap between God's revelation, vouchsafed to Israel, and the way things have turned out for that nation. Drawing on the narrative material of the Torah, he illustrates from the cases of Isaac (born to Sarah, 9:6-9) and Jacob (born to Rebecca, 9:10-13). He points out that mere physical descent from Israel (i.e., Jacob) does not automatically confer membership in [God's nation of] Israel (9:6-9). It is rather a case of divine promise (9:8-9), of divine purpose (9:11) and of divine calling (9:12). It does not rest on what a person has done (9:12), but on divine preference (9:13).

> **¹⁴** How, then, shall we express it? Surely there isn't injustice on God's part, is there? Certainly not! **¹⁵** After all, he says to Moses, 'I will have mercy on the person on whom I have mercy and I will show compassion to the person to whom I show compassion.' **¹⁶** It follows, then, that it isn't a case of what a person wants, or of the effort they put in, but of God having mercy. **¹⁷** For this is how the text of Scripture addresses Pharaoh: 'It was for this very purpose that I raised you up, that I might demonstrate my power in you and

Applying These Insights to Paul's Letter to the Romans

so that my name might be proclaimed throughout the earth.' **18** It follows, then, that he has mercy on whoever he wants, but he also hardens whoever he wants.

19 One of you will say to me, 'Why then does he still find fault? For who is in a position to resist what he wants?' **20** But then who are you, a mere mortal, to answer back to *God*? Surely what is being shaped won't say to the person shaping it, 'What did you make me like this for?' will it? **21** Or doesn't the potter who owns the clay have the right to make from the same lump one utensil for a noble purpose, another for a menial purpose? **22** What if God, wishing to demonstrate his anger and to make known his power, tolerated with a great deal of patience utensils of anger destined for destruction, **23** so that he might also make known the wealth of his glory for utensils of mercy which he had prepared in advance for glory?

Paul's discussion of God's elective purposes, as worked out through the patriarchs, raises a further issue: Has God been entirely fair in the way he has acted? (9:14). Arguing for the legitimacy of divine prerogative, Paul again draws on the Torah to cite the case of Pharaoh (9:15–18). He concludes that the key to this issue once again is not human performance (9:16), but divine mercy (9:15, 16, 18).

Anticipating a further difficulty in the minds of his addressees ("Why then does he still find fault? For who is in a position to resist his wishes?" 9:19) Paul takes up the illustration of potter and clay to reinforce his argument for divine prerogative. As well as reaffirming divine mercy (as the key to understanding utensils prepared for glory, 9:23) he also advances divine patience as the key to understanding "utensils of anger" (9:22), such as Pharaoh.

24 He also called us not only from among Jews but also from among non-Jews, **25** just as he says in Hosea:

> I will call those who are not my people, 'My people,'
> and I will call her, who is not loved, 'beloved';
> **26** and it will come about that in the place where

> they were told, 'You are not my people,'
> there they will be called
> 'children of the living God.'
>
> **²⁷** But Isaiah cries out in relation to Israel:
>
> Even if Israel's children were as numerous
> as the sand of the seashore,
> only the remnant will be saved.
> **²⁸** For the Lord will execute his sentence on earth
> in full and decisively.
>
> **²⁹** And just as Isaiah had said earlier:
>
> If the Lord of massive military forces hadn't left us a line of descent,
> we would have become like Sodom and would have been like Gomorrah.

A series of Old Testament quotations follows, in which Paul takes up the scope of God's saving purposes. The quotation from Hosea makes it clear that non-Jewish people are included in God's call, while the two quotations from Isaiah reinforce what he had said earlier, that mere physical descent from Israel does not automatically confer membership in the nation of Israel as God's chosen people (9:6–7). Indeed, only a "remnant" of Israel is to be saved (9:27).

> **³⁰** What, then, are we to say? That non-Jews, who didn't pursue **a right relationship**, obtained **a right relationship**, **a right relationship** based on faith, **³¹** while Israel, pursuing a Law designed to establish **a right relationship**, didn't attain to the Law. **³²** Why not? Because their pursuit of it was based, not on faith, but as if it depended on human behaviour. They stumbled over the stumbling-stone, **³³** just as it stands on record:

Applying These Insights to Paul's Letter to the Romans

> Look! I am laying in Zion a stumbling-stone
> and a rock causing offense;
> yet the person who puts their faith in him
> will never have cause to be ashamed.

Analyzing the situation, Paul concludes that the clue to the inclusion of non-Jews, and the failure of Israel to attain to the Law God had given them, lay in the differing approaches they took to obtaining righteousness, i.e., a right relationship with God. While Israel relied on its behavioral response to the Law, non-Jews exercised faith. As Paul had stated as far back as his first and second corollaries (3:27–30) faith is the only means by which one can experience God's rectifying act.

10 Brothers and sisters, my heart's desire and request to God on their behalf is for their salvation. ² For I testify concerning them that they have zeal for God, but it isn't an informed zeal. ³ So, being ignorant of the **right relationship** God provides, and endeavouring to establish **a right relationship** on their own terms, they failed to submit to the **right relationship** God provides. ⁴ For Christ fulfils the purpose of the Law, resulting in **a right relationship** for everyone who has faith.

The contrast between these two different approaches towards being brought into a right relationship with God is now spelt out in more detail. Israel is to be commended for its zeal, but its failure is to be explained in terms of its ignorance of the right relationship which God alone can provide, and which is available only though faith. We cannot obtain it by setting our own terms (10:3). Further, to have faith in Christ is to have faith in the one who is the goal of the Law (10:4).

⁵ For concerning the **right relationship** based on the Law, Moses writes as follows: 'The person who has achieved these things will live by means of them.' ⁶ But the **right relationship** based

> on faith speaks in this way: 'Don't say in your heart, "Who will ascend to heaven?"'—that is, to bring Christ down— **⁷** 'or, "Who will descend to the deep?"'—that is, to bring Christ back from among the dead. **⁸** Then what does it say? 'The message is near you; it is on your lips and in your heart'—that is, it is the message about faith which we proclaim. **⁹** For if you acknowledge the Lord Jesus with your lips and believe in your heart that God raised him from among the dead, you will be saved. **¹⁰** For by means of the heart there is faith, resulting in **a right relationship**, by means of the lips there is acknowledgment, resulting in salvation. **¹¹** For the Scripture text says, 'No-one who puts their faith in him will ever have cause to be ashamed.' **¹²** For there is no difference between Jew and Greek, for the same Lord is Lord over *all*, being rich to all who call on him; **¹³** for, 'Everyone who calls on the Lord's name will be saved.'

The contrast between the approach to a right relationship advocated by Moses and that advocated in the good news continues. Moses' approach is based on personal achievement (10:5), but the right relationship based on faith is proclaimed through the good news (10:8). The person who responds to that good news accepts inwardly that God raised Christ from the dead, and confesses openly that Jesus is Lord (10:9–10). Paul supports his argumentation in the first place from the texts in Deuteronomy that involve Moses (Deut 30:12–14), but also from the prophets Isaiah and Joel. Again they point to the universality of the salvation the Lord offers (10:11–13).

> **¹⁴** How then can they call on someone in whom they have not believed? How can they believe in someone of whom they have never heard? But how can they hear unless there is public proclamation? **¹⁵** But then how can people make public proclamation unless they've been sent? Just as it stands on record, 'How beautiful are the feet of those who bring the good news of good events!'

In a series of rhetorical questions Paul then elucidates the "mechanics" of how "righteousness by faith" or "the right relationship associated

Applying These Insights to Paul's Letter to the Romans

with faith," comes about. Ultimately the whole process is anchored in God himself, as the one who sends his servants out (10:15).

> **16** However, not everyone has obeyed the good news. For Isaiah says, 'Lord, who has believed what we report?'
> **17** So then faith is the consequence of listening, and listening occurs through the message about Christ.
> **18** But let me ask: Didn't they have the opportunity of listening? They certainly did:
>
>> Their sound has gone out into all the earth,
>> their communications have reached even the extremities
>> of the inhabited world.
>
> **19** But let me ask: Surely it wasn't the case that Israel didn't know, was it? First Moses says:
>
>> I will arouse you to jealousy with those who aren't even
>> a nation, I will arouse you to anger with a stupid nation.
>
> **20** then Isaiah is so bold as to say:
>
>> I was found by those who weren't even looking for me;
>> I appeared to those who weren't even asking for me.
>
> **21** By contrast, he says to Israel:
>
>> All day long I have implored—with outstretched hands—
>> a disobedient and obstinate people.

The proclamation of the good news is one thing; how people respond to it is another matter. Paul takes up this issue here. First, he locates the origin of saving faith in people who are listening to the good news being proclaimed (10:17). Second, he draws on another series of OT quotations to demonstrate both that Israel has passed up opportunities to respond positively to God, and that non-Jewish people have become involved in the salvation God offers (10:18–21).

11 Let me ask, then: Surely God hasn't rejected his own people, has he? Certainly not! For I, too, am an Israelite, descended from Abraham, belonging to Benjamin's tribe. **²** God hasn't rejected his own people, whom he knew about in advance. Why, aren't you aware of what the Scripture text says through Elijah, how he appeals to God against Israel?

> **³** Lord, they have killed your prophets; they have demolished your altars; only I am left, and they are trying to take my life as well.

⁴ But what was the divine response?

> I have reserved for myself seven thousand men who haven't bowed their knees to Baal.

⁵ So too, then, at the present time a remnant has come into being, chosen by grace. **⁶** However, if it is by grace, it no longer depends on human behaviour, otherwise grace would no longer be grace. **⁷** Then what conclusion are we to draw? That Israel failed to obtain what it was searching for. While those who were chosen obtained it, the rest were hardened, **⁸** just as it stands on record:

> God rendered them semi-conscious, with eyes unable to see and ears unable to hear right to this very day.

⁹ And David says:

> May their table become a snare and a trap, their downfall and their retribution; **¹⁰** May their eyes become dark, so that they can't see, and their backs be permanently bent.

Paul's earlier statements and proof texts could suggest that God has rejected his own people (11:1); here he is anxious to dispel such a notion. He points first to the case of Elijah (11:2b–4), before developing the notion of a remnant, a remnant chosen by grace (11:5). Once again any idea of human behavior as the basis for God's choice, is excluded (11:6). While this concept of an elect remnant operates within Israel, it also carries the

Applying These Insights to Paul's Letter to the Romans

implication that Israel as a whole, or that part of Israel that falls outside the elect, failed in its quest (11:7–10).

> **11** Then let me ask: Surely they haven't gone so wrong as to suffer a complete demise, have they? Certainly not! Rather, through the offence they committed, salvation has come to non-Jews, so as to arouse them to jealousy. **12** Now if the offence they committed enriched the world and their demise enriched the non-Jews, how much greater impact will they have when they fulfil their destiny?
>
> **13** However, to you who are not Jews, let me say this: As I am an apostle sent to non-Jews, I place a high value on the service I bring, **14** hoping somehow to arouse to jealousy those who are my own flesh and blood and save some of them. **15** For if their rejection meant reconciliation for the world, what will their acceptance mean but life from the dead? **16** For it follows that if the initial produce is holy, then the whole lump is, and if the root is holy, so too are the branches.

Even when Israel is at its lowest point, however, it serves God's purposes. For Israel's present demise has only served to bring salvation to non-Jewish peoples, and this in turn is designed to arouse them to jealousy (11:11). Paul employs the device of *a minori ad maius* (from the lesser to the greater) to argue that if Israel brings such benefits when at its lowest point, then the benefits it will bring when it is fulfilling its destiny will be all the greater (11:12, 15)! He reinforces this argumentation by appealing to the analogies of the firstfruits and the main crop, and to the root and the branches: if the part is holy, then so is the whole (11:16).

> **17** But what if some of the branches were broken off and you, a wild olive, were grafted into them and came to have a share in the nutrition provided by the olive tree's root-system? **18** Don't boast at the expense of the branches. But even if you do boast, it isn't you who sustains the root, but the root that sustains you. **19** Then, you will argue, 'Branches were broken off, so that I could be grafted in.' **20** Quite so; they were broken off because of their unbelief, but

> you stand only by virtue of your faith. Don't get a swelled head, but be concerned, **²¹** for if God didn't spare the tree's own natural branches, surely he won't spare you.
>
> **²²** Notice then both God's kindness and his severity: in the case of those who fell, it is severity; in your case it is kindness—provided you persist in his kindness, otherwise you too will be cut off. **²³** Furthermore, if those of whom we have been speaking don't persist in a state of unbelief, they will be grafted back in—for God has the ability to graft them in again. **²⁴** For if you could be cut out of your natural environment, that of a wild olive tree, and, contrary to nature, be grafted into a cultivated olive tree, it follows that it is a great deal easier for those people whose natural environment it was, to be grafted back into their own olive tree.

Taking up the root and branches analogy, Paul now applies it to the specific example of an olive tree and the practice of grafting. In his analogy Israel is likened to a cultivated olive tree, non-Jews to a wild olive tree. It is directed primarily to non-Jews and to any sense of undeserved pride, boasting, or triumphalism they may feel in relation to Israel (11:18–24). For if God is capable of removing natural branches to graft in wild branches, it would be no problem to him to graft cultivated branches back in to their original tree (11:24).

> **²⁵** Brothers and sisters, I don't want you to be ignorant about this mystery, otherwise you will seem wise in your own estimation; for a partial hardening has come about for Israel until the full complement of non-Jews comes in. **²⁶** In this way all Israel will be saved, just as it stands on record:
>
>> The Deliverer will emerge from Zion; he will deflect ungodliness from Jacob. **²⁷** And this is the covenant I will enter into with them when I take away their sins.
>
> **²⁸** From the perspective of the good news, they are enemies as far as you are concerned, but from the perspective of election, they are dearly loved because of their ancestors. **²⁹** For God doesn't

Applying These Insights to Paul's Letter to the Romans

change his mind about the gifts he gives people or the vocation to which he calls them. **30** For just as you were once disobedient to God, but now have been treated with mercy during their disobedience, **31** so also these people now have disobeyed, so that they themselves may now be treated with mercy. **32** For God has subsumed all people under the category of disobedience, so that he may have mercy on them all.

Paul endeavors to express the mystery of the partial hardening that had befallen the Israel of Paul's day (11:25). The key points are that ultimately all Israel will be saved (11:26), that all humanity has been subsumed under the category of disobedience (11:32) and that the key divine attribute involved is mercy (11:30–32).

> **33** What depth of riches and wisdom and knowledge God has!
> His decisions lie beyond discovery,
> and his paths beyond tracking down.
> **34** For who has known what the Lord was thinking?
> Or who has become his consultant?
> **35** Or who has taken the initiative by first giving him a gift
> so as to have the favour repaid to them?
> **36** Because everything originates with him,
> comes about through him,
> and exists for him.
> To him be the glory for ever! Amen.

The apostle concludes this significant excursus, in which he has treated several of the corollaries expressed in 3:27–31, with a paean in praise of the God who initiated the good news (11:33–36).

> **12** So, on the basis of God's mercies, brothers and sisters, I urge you to present your bodies to God as a living sacrifice, dedicated and pleasing to him, your logical act of worship. **²** Don't conform to contemporary society, but be transformed by the renewal of your minds, so that you may discern what God desires: what is good, pleasing to him, and perfect.

His theological exposition completed, Paul now turns to exhortation and to the day to day applications appropriate to being in a right relationship with God. He calls first for a dedication of one's body to God, through which a renewed mind is able to transform a person and align their life with what God desires.

> **³** For by the grace given to me I am telling every one of you not to think more highly of yourself than you ought to think, but to think in a balanced way, each taking into account the measure of faith God has imparted. **⁴** For just as we have many components in one body, but all the components differ in function, **⁵** so we who are many are one body under Christ, but individually components of one another. **⁶** We each have different gifts, depending on the grace given to us: if it is prophecy, let it be in proportion to our faith; **⁷** if it is serving others, in our service; if we are a person who teaches, in our teaching; **⁸** if we are a motivator, let's motivate; if we make donations, let's do so generously, from sincere motives; if we exercise a ministry of care, let's do so expeditiously; if we have a ministry of compassion, let's go about it gladly.

In a Christian fellowship there is a diversity of gifts. Here the apostle urges each of his addressees not to put too high an estimate on how valuable they personally are (12:3), but to exercise their particular gift to the full and in a way that brings the maximum benefit to others (12:4–8).

Applying These Insights to Paul's Letter to the Romans

⁹ Love is to be absolutely genuine. Detest what is evil, adhere to what is good. ¹⁰ Have the kind of affection for one another that brothers and sisters do; outdo one another in showing respect. ¹¹ Don't be slack in zeal, maintain your spiritual fervour, be the Lord's slave. ¹² Be joyful in hope, patient in trouble, persistent in prayer. ¹³ Share what you have, to meet the needs of God's people; pursue hospitality. ¹⁴ Wish those who persecute you all the best; wish them all the best, don't wish them harm. ¹⁵ Be glad with those who are glad, cry with those who are crying. ¹⁶ Adopt the same attitude to all other people: don't adopt an attitude of superiority, but get about with humble people. Don't think you are wiser than you really are. ¹⁷ Don't pay back wrong with wrong, but think carefully about what all people regard as good. ¹⁸ If at all possible, to the extent that it depends on you, be at peace with everyone. ¹⁹ Don't take revenge, dear friends, but give anger its place, for it stands on record, 'Revenge is my prerogative, I'll do the paying back,' says the Lord. ²⁰ On the contrary, 'If your enemy is hungry, give him something to eat, if he is thirsty, give him a drink, for by doing so you will heap live coals on his head.'

²¹ Don't be defeated by what is wrong, but defeat what is wrong with what is good.

Moving to those attributes and aspects of lifestyle which are available to every Christian, Paul takes up a range of issues, offering advice as to how best to implement them.

13 Every person is to submit to the higher authorities. For there is no authority apart from those who come under God, and those in existence have been established by God. ² Consequently, anyone resisting them, is resisting the authority set in place on God's orders, and those who have resisted will bring condemnation on themselves. ³ For rulers aren't a threat to good activities, but to evil activities. Do you wish to be in the situation where you have no fear of the authority? Do good, and you will earn its praise, ⁴ for in that case it is God's agent to you for good. However, if you do what is wrong,

> then be afraid, for it doesn't bear the sword for nothing, but is the agent of God's anger, punishing the person who does wrong. **⁵** That's why it is essential to submit, not only because of anger, but also for conscience's sake.
>
> **⁶** That's also the reason you should pay taxes; for the authorities are God's servants busily engaged in his service. **⁷** Discharge your obligations to everyone, paying tax to the person to whom tax is due; customs duties to whom customs duties are due; respect to the person who deserves respect; honour to the person who deserves to be honoured.

Beginning with the Christian's obligation to submit to authorities in the political and governmental sphere (13:1), Paul moves on to the implications this has for paying taxes, and from there to other "debts" Christians owe within the society about them.

> **⁸** Don't owe anyone anything—except to love one another. For anyone who loves the other person, has fulfilled the Law. **⁹** For the commandments 'You are not to have sex with someone else's partner, you are not to murder, you are not to steal, you are not to desire what others have,' as well as any other commandment there happens to be, are encapsulated in this: 'You are to love your neighbour as you love yourself.' **¹⁰** Love doesn't treat a neighbour badly, that's why love is the fulfilment of the Law.

One such standing debt is the obligation to love one another, for in practicing love, a Christian fulfills the Law (13:8, 10). Paul points out that those of the Ten Commandments that are concerned with our duties towards our neighbors, may be subsumed under the commandment to love one another (13:9–10).

Applying These Insights to Paul's Letter to the Romans

¹¹ Further, regarding the times we live in, you are to be aware that it is already time for us to be aroused from sleep, for our salvation is nearer now than it was when we first came to faith. ¹² The night is almost over, day is about to break. So let us discard the activities associated with darkness, and get dressed in the armour of light. ¹³ Let's go about life in an orderly way, as is appropriate to daytime, not in wild parties and drinking bouts, not in promiscuity and sexual excesses of various kinds, not in quarreling and jealousy. ¹⁴ Rather, get dressed in the Lord Jesus Christ and don't provide your human nature with opportunities to indulge its desires.

Using the analogy of daylight and nighttime, of being awake and sleeping, the apostle urges his addressees to behave in ways appropriate to their Christian standing and to the advanced hour in which they lived.

14 Accept the person who is weak in the Christian faith, but not for the purpose of arguing over matters on which there is a variety of opinion. ² For while one person believes it is all right to eat anything, a person who is weak in the faith is a vegetarian. ³ The person who eats anything is not to despise the person who doesn't, nor is the person who abstains from eating some things to pass judgment on a person who does; after all, *God* has accepted that person! ⁴ Who do you think you are, you who pass judgment on someone else's domestic servant? It is with respect to their own master that a person stands or falls, and stand they will, for their master is perfectly capable of making them stand.

⁵ Again, while one person makes a distinction between one day and another, another person treats every day the same; each person is to be fully convinced in their own mind. ⁶ The person who regards a day as special regards it as special before the Lord; now whoever eats meat does so before the Lord, for they give thanks to God, while the person who abstains from meat, does so before the Lord and also gives thanks to God.

Paul's Concept of Justification

In any Christian community there will always be a variety of opinions on a range of behavioral issues. By way of illustration, Paul identifies three such issues in 14:1—15:13 and offers some general principles. The three issues are: (1) Should one eat meat, or be a vegetarian? (14:2, 3, 6, 15, 17, 20, 21, 23); (2) Should one observe special days in the Christian calendar, or treat all days as the same? (14:5, 6). (3) Should one drink wine, or not? (14:17, 21). A number of principles emerge from Paul's hortatory exposition. In the passage above we find the following: (1) variety of opinion is not to lead to arguments (14:1); (2) no Christian is to despise (14:3, 10) or judge (14:3, 10, 13) a fellow-Christian; (3) God has accepted our fellow Christians, however much their opinions may differ from our opinions (14:3); (4) a fellow-Christian, as God's servant, is answerable to their master—God—alone, not to us (14:4)! (5) each person is to be fully persuaded in their own mind (14:5, 23).

> **7** For none of us lives in isolation and no-one dies in isolation. **8** For if we live, it is for the Lord that we live, and if we die it is for the Lord that we die. So whether we live or die, we belong to the Lord. **9** Why, it was for this very purpose that Christ died and became alive, that he might be lord over both those who have died and those who are alive.

The common proverb, "No person is an island" captures exactly the point Paul wishes to make here. He goes on to make Christ in his death and resurrection a paradigm for the Christian life, so that whether dead or alive, whether in death or in life, we belong to Christ. His lordship extends equally to both situations (14:9).

> **10** But as for you, why do you pass judgment on your fellow-Christian? And as for you, why do you despise your fellow-Christian? For we are all to stand before God's tribunal, **11** for it stands on record:

Applying These Insights to Paul's Letter to the Romans

> As surely as I live, says the Lord, every knee will bend in homage before me, and every tongue give praise to God.
>
> **¹²** It follows, then, that each one of us will personally give account to God.

To discourage the judging and despising of our fellow Christians, Paul gives his addressees a solemn reminder of their own accountability to God.

> **¹³** So let us no longer pass judgment on one another. Instead, let us resolve not to put anything objectionable or anything causing offence in a fellow-Christian's path. **¹⁴** Under the Lord Jesus, I am well aware and have been convinced, that nothing is impure in itself; it is impure only in the mind of the person who reckons it so. **¹⁵** For if your fellow-Christian is upset over food, you are no longer living your life based on love; don't allow your food to destroy that person, on behalf of whom Christ died. **¹⁶** So don't let what you people regard as good be spoken of as evil. **¹⁷** For God's kingdom isn't a matter of eating and drinking, but of **what is right**, and of peace and of joy through the Holy Spirit. **¹⁸** For a person who serves Christ as a slave in this matter not only pleases God, but has human approval as well.

Further general principles that emerge here are: (6) we are to resolve not to offend a fellow-Christian by promoting our own preferences in matters of indifference (14:13); (7) no food is impure *per se*; its impurity is only in the mind of the person who holds it to be so (14:14); (8) we are to live our lives based on love (14:15); (9) we are not to allow our preferences on matters of indifference to destroy another person, for whom Christ died (14:15); (10) God's kingdom consists not of external matters of indifference, but of spiritual qualities, qualities brought about by the Holy Spirit (14:17); (11) a person who implements these principles has human as well as divine approval (14:18).

> **19** So then, let us pursue those things that promote peace and are constructive for one another. **20** Do not—for the sake of food!—destroy God's work! All things are pure, but for the person for whom eating meat is objectionable, it is wrong. **21** It is better not to eat meat or drink wine or do anything else that your fellow-Christian finds objectionable. **22** As for you personally, keep your faith a matter between yourself and God. Blessed indeed are those who don't condemn themselves by what they approve. **23** But anyone who has doubts already stands condemned if they eat, because their eating isn't motivated by faith, and everything not motivated by faith is a sin.

It follows that Christians are to shape their behavior and lifestyle by consideration of the needs of others. As to personal convictions, these are strictly between the individual and God. The overarching principle for all of life is that "everything which is not motivated by faith is a sin." (14:23).

> **15** We who are strong have an obligation to put up with the weaknesses of those who are not strong and not merely to please ourselves. **2** Each of us is to do what pleases our neighbour for good, with a view to what is constructive. **3** For even the Messiah didn't please himself, but just as it stands on record, 'The insults of those insulting you have fallen on me.' **4** For those things that were written down in advance were recorded in order to teach us, so that through the endurance and the encouragement the Scriptures provide, we might have hope. **5** May the God of endurance and encouragement grant that you may be like-minded among yourselves in a way that is appropriate to Christ Jesus, **6** so that, sharing a common purpose, you may glorify the God and Father of our Lord Jesus Christ, united in what you say.

Christians coming from a position of strength are not simply to indulge themselves in these matters, but are to follow the example of the Messiah, who did not please himself. Taking that stance was costly for him. It

Applying These Insights to Paul's Letter to the Romans

meant bearing the brunt of the insults directed towards God (15:3, citing Ps 68:10 Lxx). Having quoted from the Jewish Scriptures, Paul takes the opportunity of pointing out their relevance, even though they were committed to writing in an age long since past. They function to provide us with endurance and encouragement, for the simple reason that behind them lies the God of endurance and encouragement (15:4–6).

> ⁷ Accept one another, therefore, just as Christ also accepted you—for the glory of God! ⁸ For let me point out that Christ has become a servant to those who are circumcised for the sake of God's truth, so that the promises given to the ancestors might be kept, ⁹ that is, that non-Jewish people might glorify God because of his mercy, just as it stands on record:
>
>> For this reason I will acknowledge you among non-Jewish people and I will sing praise to your name.
>
> ¹⁰ And again it says:
>
>> Be glad, you non-Jewish people, with his people.
>
> ¹¹ And again:
>
>> Praise the Lord, all you non-Jewish people and let all the peoples praise him.
>
> ¹² And again, Isaiah says:
>
>> There will be a root from Jesse, and he who rises up to rule non-Jewish people;
>> in him non-Jewish people will place their hopes.
>
> ¹³ May God, the very source of hope, fill you with all joy and peace as you lead the life of faith, so that you may abound in hope, through the power of the Holy Spirit.

As he brings this section (14:1—15:13) to a close, Paul reiterates his exhortation to the addressees to accept one another in the way that God/Christ had accepted them (15:7, cf. 14:1, 3). In serving God's covenant people, Christ did so in order that the promises to the patriarchs might be fulfilled, in particular the promise that non-Jewish peoples would also benefit from God's mercy (15:8–9). The apostle follows this statement with a catena of four quotations from the OT Scriptures in support of the inclusion of non-Jews in God's saving purposes.

> **14** As far as I personally am concerned, my brothers and sisters, I am convinced that you yourselves are full of goodness, filled with all knowledge, and are quite capable of admonishing one another. **15** But I've been bold enough to write to you, partly as a reminder to you (because of the grace given to me by God) **16** so that I might be a servant of Christ Jesus to non-Jewish people, engaged in the priestly service of God's good news, so that the offering of non-Jewish people may prove acceptable, having been consecrated by the Holy Spirit.
>
> **17** That is why I can boast—under Christ Jesus—in matters relating to God. **18** For I wouldn't dare to say anything about those things Christ did not bring about through me for obedience by non-Jewish people by what I did and said, **19** by the ability to work miraculous signs and amazing deeds, by the power of God's Spirit, so that I have fully proclaimed the good news about Christ in a circuit extending from Jerusalem to Illyricum. **20** In doing so, I made it my policy to proclaim the good news only where the name of Christ wasn't already known, so that I might not build on someone else's foundation, **21** but just as it stands on record:
>
> > Those to whom the announcement about him
> > has not been made will see,
> > and those who have not heard will understand.

At this point Paul returns to personalia reminiscent of those in 1:8–15, including his plans for a future visit to the Christians of Rome (15:22–24, 28–32). He expresses his confidence in the Roman Christians (15:14) and provides details of his calling and ministry as an apostle to non-Jews—its geographical spread, its accompanying miracles, its pioneering orientation.

> ²² That's also the reason I have so frequently been prevented from coming to you; ²³ now, however, I no longer have a role in these regions, but a desire (going back many years) to visit you, as I travel to Spain. ²⁴ For I hope to see you as I pass through and to be assisted on my way there by you, provided I may first enjoy your company, at least for a while. ²⁵ But at present I am on my way to Jerusalem, serving God's people. ²⁶ For it has pleased Macedonia and Achaia to contribute something to the poor among God's people in Jerusalem. ²⁷ For they were pleased to do so, and are indeed their debtors; for if non-Jewish people have a share in their spiritual benefits, they are under obligation to serve them in the material sphere as well. ²⁸ So once I have completed this task, and safely delivered this contribution to them, through you I will depart for Spain. ²⁹ Now I know that when I come to you I will come with Christ's full blessing.

In connection with his proposed visit to Rome Paul mentions also his plans for a Spanish mission, and expresses the hope that his Roman friends will assist in launching him on this (15:24). In the meantime, however, he is bound for Jerusalem to deliver to the poor among the Christians there a collection taken up by the churches of mainland Greece (Macedonia and Achaia) (15:25–28).

> ³⁰ I urge you, brothers and sisters, through our Lord Jesus Christ and through the Spirit's love, to join me in the contest by your prayers to God on my behalf, ³¹ asking that I may be rescued from those in Judea who don't have faith and that the service I'm providing to Jerusalem may be acceptable to God's people, ³² so that I may come to you joyfully, by God's will, and relax in your company.
> ³³ May the God of peace be with all of you. Amen.

Thinking of his imminent trip to Judea and Jerusalem, the apostle solicits prayer from the Roman Christians, well aware of the opposition it will engender and the dangers it will entail.

> **16** I commend Phoebe to you; she is our sister as well as a deacon of the congregation at Cenchreae. ² I do this so that under the Lord you will give her the kind of welcome that is fitting for God's people and provide for her in whatever matter she needs you. For she herself has been of great assistance to many—including to me personally.

Phoebe, a deacon in the church of Cenchreae, not far from Corinth, is to visit Rome, so Paul here provides her with a commendation to the church there. It is quite possible that it was she who conveyed Paul's letter to the Christians of Rome.

> ³ Greet Prisca and Aquila, my fellow-workers in Christ Jesus, ⁴ who put their own necks at risk for my life. It's not only I who am grateful to them, but also all the non-Jewish congregations ⁵ —not to mention the congregation that meets in their home! Greet my dear friend Epaenetus, who is the first convert to Christ from the Roman Province of Asia. ⁶ Greet Mary, who has worked so hard for you. ⁷ Greet Andronicus and Junia, my fellow-countrymen, who were in prison when I was; they are outstanding among the apostles and became Christians before I did. ⁸ Greet Ampliatus, my dear friend in the Lord. ⁹ Greet Urbanus, our fellow-worker under Christ and my dear friend Stachys. ¹⁰ Greet Apelles, who has proved faithful to Christ. Greet those from Aristobulus's household ¹¹ Greet my fellow-countryman Herodian. Greet those from Narcissus's household who are under the Lord. ¹² Greet Tryphaena and Tryphosa, women who have worked hard for the Lord. Greet my dear friend Persis; she has done extensive hard work for the Lord. ¹³ Greet Rufus, a choice person under the Lord, and his mother, who is mother to me as well! ¹⁴ Greet Asyncritus, Phlegon, Hermes,

Applying These Insights to Paul's Letter to the Romans

Patrobas, Hermas, and the Christians with them. **¹⁵** Greet Philologus and Julia, Nereus and his sister, and Olympas, and all God's people with them. **¹⁶** Greet one another with a holy kiss. All Christ's congregations send you their greetings.

There is now a lengthy catalogue of people in the Roman church to whom Paul sends greetings. As well as these "greetings to," at the conclusion he places "greetings from" all Christ's congregations.

¹⁷ I urge you, dear friends, to watch out for those who foster divisions and cause people to go wrong—acting contrary to the teaching you learned. Avoid them, **¹⁸** for such people aren't slaves to our master, Christ, but to their own appetites, and by means of smooth talk and flattery they deceive the hearts of the unwary. **¹⁹** For your obedience is common knowledge, so that I am very glad about you. However, I want you to be wise as to what is good, but innocent as to what is evil. **²⁰** Then the God of peace will soon crush Satan under your feet. May the grace of our Lord Jesus Christ be with you.

Before concluding, Paul warns his addressees of the danger posed by those who create trouble for God's people by fostering quarrels among them and causing them to go wrong. Paul analyses the situation and motives of such people, and provides a profile of them (15:17–18). Again Paul expresses his confidence in the addressees and in a good outcome in relation to the troublemakers (15:19–20).

²¹ Timothy, my fellow-worker, sends you his greetings, as do Lucius, Jason, and Sosipater, my fellow-countrymen. **²²** I Tertius, who wrote this letter down, send you greetings in the Lord. **²³** Gaius, who is host to me and to the whole congregation, sends you greetings. Erastus, the city treasurer, sends you his greetings, as does brother Quartus.

Further greetings are sent from those with Paul. In particular we may note Timothy, Tertius (Paul's amanuensis, who wrote down his letter to Romans), Gaius, in whose home Paul stayed while in Corinth, and in whose house the Corinthian church used to have its meetings, and a prominent citizen of that city and church, Erastus.

> **25** To him who is able to put you on a solid footing, as it says in the good news I announce and the proclamation about Jesus Christ, in accordance with the revelation of the secret kept silent since time immemorial, **26** but now brought to light through the Prophetic Writings and, in accordance with the command of the eternal God, made known to all the non-Jewish peoples for the obedience faith inspires— **27** to the only God, the wise God, be glory for ever, through Jesus Christ. Amen.

Paul concludes with a doxology in which he mentions the good news that has been the subject of his earlier theological exposition; the writings of the prophets, which point to the events recounted in the good news; the non-Jews, to whom he is apostle; and faith, the response that finds acceptance with God as the essential precondition for God's rectifying act. Above all, as the focus of Paul's doxology, are God himself and his Son Jesus Christ, through whom God's saving purposes have been turned into a reality.

7

Conclusions

EVER SINCE THE TRANSLATION of the whole Bible into English during the fourteenth century, the majority of English translators have shown a preference for rendering Paul's single Greek word-family, the δ-family (δικαιοσύνη and cognates), by two English word-families, the R-family ("righteousness" and cognates) and the J-family ("justify" and cognates). This situation persists in the "standard" translations of the present day.

In the fourteenth century the prevailing interpretation of "justification" in the Western church was the realist view. "Justification" involved God making a person righteous (in a moral sense) as a lifelong process. Often the initial act on God's part was referred to as the "first justification," while the "second justification" referred to the continuing process by which a Christian pilgrim was made increasingly righteous *de facto*.[1]

However, with the Reformation of the sixteenth century a second view was initiated by Luther and shaped under the influence of Melanchthon. As a consequence of the latter's influence, it became customary for Protestants to explain "justification" in terms of the imputation of Christ's righteousness to the believer. It was a position taken over by Calvin, so that it was held in common by both major Protestant streams, the Lutheran and the Calvinistic or Reformed. This view explained God's act of "justification" in *forensic* rather than realist terms. God's role was envisaged as that of a *judge*, who *pronounced* a person righteous. Since, according to Paul's foundational text, Rom 4:5, God's action in rectification is effected on the *ungodly*, if we understand δικαιοῦν in that context as meaning "declare righteous" then

---

1. The "first justification" in the Catholic view corresponds roughly with the Protestant concept of "justification," while the "second justification" approximates to the Protestant concept of "sanctification."

without question God's veracity is clearly impugned, since the ungodly clearly are not "righteous" (understood in its usual moral sense).

Beginning in the nineteenth century, some within the Protestant tradition expressed dissatisfaction with the forensic understanding of the classical Protestant view. A third view began to emerge, which gained considerable strength in the twentieth century. It understood rectification primarily in terms of God's restoration of a *right relationship*, although early advocates often combined this insight with a forensic understanding. This "relational" view has had representatives right across the denominational spectrum. It was adopted, in whole or in part, for a number of English translations and was widely disseminated through the *Good News Bible* whose influence peaked probably in the 1970s and 1980s. This approach was also supported by the lexicons and other translators' aids produced by the Bible societies. Yet by the turn of the twenty-first century none of the mainstream translations was making use of the relational approach. The two English word-families approach they persisted in using put Paul's doctrine of rectification in danger either of being completely unintelligible or of being seriously misunderstood by the average reader of English.

THE NEED FOR A PARADIGM SHIFT

If this broad sketch, which endeavors to sum up the material in the preceding chapters, accurately depicts the situation, then it is clear that there is an urgent need for a paradigm shift with respect to the aspect of Paul's thinking under discussion. This paradigm shift is called for in the three areas that affect Paul's doctrine of rectification and the way it is presented.

7.1 In the Fundamental Concept

Even in the present day it is not uncommon for discussions of the doctrine of rectification to be expressed in the "either-or" categories that date back almost five hundred years to the Reformation period. Either the doctrine is to be understood in *realist* terms (as in the Roman Catholic view) in which the emphasis is on the transformation of a person's character by the infusion or implantation of "righteousness" (in the sense of a righteous character) to the Christian, or it is to be understood in *forensic* terms as the divine judicial verdict which inaugurates the Christian life (as in the classical Protestant view). In the latter case it is usual to explain that this divine judgment is able to take place without impugning God's integrity because of the imputation of Christ's righteousness to the believer. Unfortunately for those who hold this view, Paul stated no such thing, and did not find it necessary even to mention the righteousness of Christ in his expositions of rectification. In both general theological writing and in ecumenical dialogue this five-hundred-year-old impasse creates the impression of being rather tired. It seems incapable of any real reconciliation, as any honest appraisal of the ecumenical dialogues in more recent times is bound to admit.

The key to the difference in these two explanations lies in the verb δικαιοῦν. In the realist understanding δικαιοῦν means "to make righteous," in the forensic view, "to declare righteous." The problem is that the verb is relatively rare outside the New Testament. In terms of the surviving literary evidence, both meanings just given are at best dubious. A careful study of Pauline usage does, however, establish that in R-contexts, i.e., the contexts in which Paul establishes his doctrine of rectification, there is a very close connection between the three words of the δ-family most commonly used by Paul, namely the δ-GR group (δικαιοσύνη, δικαιοῦν, δίκαιος). It becomes clear that in R-contexts, the differences between them operate at the level of *grammatical function* only, not at the level of *meaning*. Thus they share *a common referent*, to which they relate as noun, verb, and adjective respectively. The implication of this analysis for the verb, δικαιοῦν, is that in Pauline usage in R-contexts it means "rectify," "set right," "bring into a right relationship."

Such a conclusion establishes a third way of understanding the doctrine Paul wished to express when he used words of the δ-family in the semi-technical sense characteristic of his writing, especially in his letter to the congregations in Galatia and in his letter to the Christians at Rome. It may be described as the *relational* view. On the basis of the Pauline evidence it aligns with the standard Protestant view in understanding God's rectifying act as that act which inaugurates the Christian life in an individual. It is possible because of the response of faith ("the obedience of faith," Rom 1:5; 16:26) in the context of the proclamation of the good news (Rom 10:17). That good news focuses on Jesus Christ in his death as a reconciling sacrifice for human sin and on his resurrection as the divine declaration that Jesus is the Son of God (Rom 1:4, cf. 4:25). Jesus Christ, especially in his death and resurrection is, of course, also faith's focus. While God's rectifying act brings a person—an ungodly person who exercises faith (Rom 4:5;

5:6)—into a right relationship, the transformation of that person's character into a genuinely righteous character occurs in the process of "sanctification" which follows God's rectifying act (Rom 6:19). It calls for the believer's submission to God and to "what is right" [δικαιοσύνη] (Rom 6:13, 16, 18, 19). While a person's relationship with God does not depend on their sanctification (but ever only on God's rectifying act), in terms of the assurance of salvation the evidence of a life that is being transformed is a significant factor, as the Reformers and the Puritans never tired of pointing out.

In the relational understanding of rectification, then, the verb δικαιοῦν means "to right," "to rectify," "to bring into a right relationship." From the point of view of the person whom God brings into a right relationship, it is *amoral*. It is possible only because the sacrificial, reconciling work of Jesus Christ in his death has effectively dealt with human sin and because God has recognized Christ's work by raising his Son from the dead. It is conditional upon the obedience of faith, a faith that is in Jesus Christ as the one who has died and been raised to make reconciliation and a right relationship possible.

Corresponding to the verb, the noun δικαιοσύνη refers to (amoral) "rightness," a rightness of relationship, or simply, "a right relationship." Paul regards this as a gift (Rom 5:17), not as a divine judgement. It is motivated by God's grace, by God's love, by God's mercy; hence its gift-like character.

The apostle's use of the δικαιοσύνη/θεοῦ combination calls for special comment. He employs it both with the article and without. In the former instances, the article is attached either to both words in the combination, or to only one. His use of the anarthrous form δικαιοσύνη θεοῦ conveys the impression of a fixed formula and is very likely to have originated with Paul himself. It appears to refer to "rightness with respect to God" or "[a] rightness of [relationship with] God." On the other hand, the various forms taken by the δικαιοσύνη/θεοῦ combination, when Paul uses the article with it, indicate looser usage, although understanding the θεοῦ element as a genitive of *source* seems to give the best sense in each instance.[2]

Corresponding to both verb and noun, the adjective δίκαιος, when applied to a person who has been the object of God's action of δικαιοῦν, that is, who has received God's gift of δικαιοσύνη, refers to a person who has been brought into a right relationship (Rom 1:17).

The meanings just given may be referred to as *semi-technical meanings* made use of by Paul. They are extensions of the everyday meanings of these

---

2. Moore, *Rectification*, 1:105–26; see also appendix D.

Conclusions

three words, special applications that emerge because of the associations Paul gives them (such as the combination δικαιοσύνη/θεοῦ or the combination δικαιοσύνη/πίστεως) and because of their use in R-contexts.[3] In writing to the Christians of Rome, whom as a community Paul had never met, the apostle was bound to use vocabulary they would understand, even if he extended the range (and thereby the meaning) of that vocabulary in the way just described.

It is important to recognize that Paul used these words of the δ-GR family in two broad senses, with both the semi-technical meanings just described, but also in their ordinary everyday usage. This is especially the case in Romans, whereas in Galatians all, or nearly all instances (depending on how we interpret Gal 5:5) are in the semi-technical sense.[4]

Consequently, we find δικαιοσύνη used to refer to both the divine gift of "right relationship" (Rom 5:17) and to moral righteousness (Romans 6). Thus Paul was able to use the one word δικαιοσύνη to embrace two rather different concepts. Without doubt this fact has been a major contributor to the confusion about precisely what rectification refers to, right up to the present day—as the recent ecumenical dialogues confirm.

Finally, passages identified in Paul's expositions of rectification as R-contexts deserve comment. We have observed that R-contexts are made up of two subsets, L-contexts and F-contexts, according to whether the Law or faith dominates. While Paul's δ-vocabulary spans both, in L-contexts the perceived means of coming into a right relationship with God is by fulfilling the works of the Law. It involves an element of judgment, and so such passages are forensic in character. On the other hand, in F-contexts the perceived means of coming into a right relationship is through faith in the provision God has made for this through Jesus Christ. These passages are not forensic in character, but emphasize that entering into a right relationship comes to us as God's gift. They come into the category of social relationships rather than the law-court. In this sense Paul's δ-vocabulary is to be understood quite literally rather than figuratively; instead of pronouncing a verdict like a judge, he actually brings us into a right relationship with himself, he really does give us a right relationship!

---

3. Ibid., 1:86–105.

4. It must be borne in mind, however, that the Galatian congregations to whom Paul was writing knew him personally and no doubt were familiar with the way he used the δ-family, or at least the δ-GR group.

7.2 In the Descriptor for the Doctrine

In the English language the common term for describing the Pauline doctrine which depends upon, and focuses on, words of the δ-family is "justification." As such it is a theological technical term, a fact which is acknowledged by the standard English dictionaries. Of course the word "justification" does have other meanings in English. Here too the clue to the meaning of the noun lies in the verb "justify." In their most common non-theological usage "justify, justification" are closely synonymous with "vindicate, vindication." Further, it is worth noting that even though many in the Protestant tradition—with its *forensic* understanding—may not realize it, "justify" is not a term of the law-courts at all; the judge's role is not to "justify" ("vindicate") anybody, but simply to pronounce one of two verdicts in relation to a charge that has been brought against an accused person: "guilty," or "not guilty." A closer equivalent for those wishing to convey a forensic understanding would be the cluster "acquit, acquittal," but, curiously, these are in fact relatively rare in English versions.

However, our primary concern is with what the apostle meant to convey by the verb δικαιοῦν. As we have seen, a number of considerations discourage the view that he had a forensic scenario in mind. When God devised a way to bring humankind into a right relationship with himself, he stepped in to rectify the human plight, to "set it right," to "fix it up" in more popular parlance. Some years ago one of my students, then in the second half of her thirties, maintained that she had hardly ever heard "rectify" used in English. Since then I have taken particular note of its use in the mass media, and can now report that it is relatively common and is used in such a way that its everyday use fits very well with Paul's use of the verb δικαιοῦν. God's action can then be substantivized as "rectification," and there is a small but significant number of scholars who prefer to use such vocabulary to describe the Pauline doctrine.[5] By the substitution of three letters, "rec-" for "jus-," it is possible to turn a meaningless or misleading phrase (*jus*-tification) that has plagued theological enterprise in English for far too long into a meaningful descriptor (*rec*-tification). Entrenched practice and vested interests are inadequate grounds on which to retain the term "justification," and in the third millennium, with the communication stakes ever increasing, we who have a concern for the good news and the Christian message should gladly embrace such a change.

---

5. Moore, *Rectification*, 1:1 n. 4.

CONCLUSIONS

7.3 In the Expression of the Doctrine in Scripture Translation

In the Roman Catholic tradition, with its realist understanding of rectification, the traditional preference in English translations and in theological exposition has been for the J-family, with δικαιοσύνη (or, more precisely, its Latin equivalent, *iustitia*) normally rendered "justice" (rather than the Protestant equivalent, "righteousness"). The only gain the Rheims translators made by this approach was to render Paul's single Greek word-family by a single English word-family ("justice, justify, just"). Their preference for the J-family arose from the circumstance that in the Vulgate (on which their translation was based) Paul's vocabulary took the form of the single word-family *iustitia, iustificare, iustus*. It has to be said, however, that in idiomatic English "justice" has never been as effective as "righteousness" in the theological contexts being referred to. Even the attempt of the NJB revisers of the JB to address the problem by introducing the qualifier "saving" in the phrase "saving justice" (where the JB frequently had "righteousness") can hardly be regarded as successful, for this hybrid phrase does not sit well as a meaningful term in English. In their NT revision of 1987 the American Catholic revisers of the NAB moved from an extensive use of the J-family to a mix of the R-family and the J-family which closely resembles the traditional Protestant approach.

Protestants have traditionally used the two English word-families approach initiated in the Lollard and other Middle English versions of the fourteenth century and continued in the sixteenth century by Tyndale. Since the two most prominent words "righteousness" and "justify" have no obvious etymological or semantic connection, the English reader who is unaware of the situation is unlikely to realize that in the original Greek they represent a single word-family. The point of such a comment is that things do not have to be this way. As a number of twentieth-century English translators have demonstrated, it is possible to use a single English word-family (the R-family is preferred) to convey Paul's meaning much more effectively.

Attention has already been drawn in a previous section to the fact that in their non-theological uses "justify, justification" have as near synonyms "'vindicate, vindication." Consequently, when Rom 4:5 is so translated as to speak of the God who "justifies the ungodly" (as it frequently is!) the

English reader who comes to it unaware of the theological use of the verb is most likely to understand it as speaking of the God who vindicates the ungodly. Nothing could be further from Paul's intention, or, for that matter, the intention of the biblical writers across the board. For this reason the use of the J-family here can be described with some precision as thoroughly misleading. In a world in which communication and communication theory have been studied academically, such an approach is quite unacceptable, especially when there are more viable alternatives. Yet five of the "standard" translations today take precisely this approach for Rom 4:5 (NJB, REB, NRSV, NABRE, NIV2011).

Comments similar to those on δικαιοῦν can be made about the misleading phrase "the righteousness of God" which persists even in most of the "standard" translations (REB, NRSV, NABRE, NIV2011). A natural reading of this in English can only take the phrase as a reference to God's personal quality of (moral) righteousness. Yet 1600 years ago Augustine made it clear that this was not what Paul had in mind in the places where he used δικαιοσύνη θεοῦ. Notwithstanding the fact that the majority of scholars today accept Augustine's insight, it has made little impact on English translation practice, especially in the "standard" translations!

In considering specifically how Paul's doctrine is best conveyed in English, and particularly in English biblical translations of Paul's writings, it is clearly desirable to use a single English word-family, just as the apostle used a single Greek word-family for his key terms. That this is possible in English no less than it is in Latin or in German or in a host of other languages has been amply demonstrated in a number of twentieth-century English versions. Further, it is clear that the R-family ("right," "righteousness") is the most appropriate word-family; alternative approaches (such as those used in the CEV and in *God's Word*) cannot be deemed to have been successful. The necessity for the approach being advocated does not lie merely in improving current translational practice; on the contrary, it is essential if the long-standing problems of sheer unintelligibility and seriously misleading renderings are to be avoided. This is not a case of bandaging the finger, but of urgent, life-saving, heart surgery.

While there is a good case for totally abandoning the word "justification" for Paul's doctrine and replacing it with "rectification," in the matter of English translation the word "rectification" has very limited value, and I would be inclined not to use it at all (see the USC translation of Romans in chapter 6 of the present work). While it fits very well for δικαίωσις, that noun occurs only twice in Romans (its only occurrences in the NT).[6] "Rectify" suits the verb δικαιοῦν well enough, but we face a problem with the noun δικαιοσύνη, the most common word of the δ-family in Paul's writings. Here "rectitude" fits uses outside R-contexts in a formal sense, but its very restricted use in English and the connotative baggage it tends to carry, deem it unsuitable for an idiomatic English translation on the functional equivalence model. More seriously, especially in regard to R-contexts, δικαιοσύνη indicates a *quality* or a *relationship*, not the result of an action on God's part (as is the case with δικαίωσις). For the ordinary uses of δικαιοσύνη, "righteousness" admittedly carries its own connotative baggage, but as a term conveying a moral quality it is, in the writer's view, still the best single word option in English. Moving away from a single word option, "what is right" is idiomatic and fits these uses very well.

---

6. If it seems undesirable to adopt as the standard term for a doctrine a translation equivalent that occurs only twice in Paul's writings, this is precisely what has been done for "justification." In the King James Version "justification" occurs just three times, two accounted for by δικαίωσις (Rom 4:25; 5:18), the third by δικαίωμα (Rom 5:16).

Appendix A
Glossary

δ-family   The family of words used by Paul to establish his doctrine of rectification. The doctrine takes its name from this word-family. Common to Galatians and Romans are: δικαιοσύνη, δικαιοῦν, and δίκαιος. Found in Romans only are: δικαίωμα, δικαίωσις, and δικαιοκρισία.

δ-GR group   Words of the δ-family common to both Galatians and Romans, comprised of the noun δικαιοσύνη, the verb δικαιοῦν, and the adjective δίκαιος.

δ-R group   Words of the δ-family found only in Romans, comprised of the nouns δικαίωμα (5x), δικαίωσις (2x), and δικαιοκρισία (1x).

F-contexts   R-contexts in which the focus is on faith, the approach to rectification Paul wished to endorse.

J-family   A family of English words used to translate words of the δ-family. It is comprised of: justice, justify, just, justification.

L-contexts   R-contexts in which the Law is the focus. It is the approach to rectification which Paul opposed.

R-contexts   Contexts in which Paul establishes his doctrine of rectification. Such contexts are established by the presence of

Appendix A

a word or words of the δ-family plus words and concepts drawn from a cluster of terms associated with R-contexts.

R-family — A family of English words used to translate words of the δ-family. Traditionally, it is comprised of right, righteous, righteousness, but by extension expressions like rightness, right relationship, have sometimes been used.

Appendix B
All Occurrences of the δ-Family in Galatians and Romans (In Order)

1. GALATIANS

δίκαιος	δικαιοσύνη	δικαιοῦν
		2:16 [3x]
	2:21	2:17
	3:6	
		3:8a
		3:11a
3:11b		
	3:21	
		3:24
		5:4
	5:5	
(1)	(4)	(8)
		[13]

Appendix B

2. ROMANS

δικαιοκρισία	δίκαιος	δικαιοσύνη	δικαιοῦν	δικαίωμα	δικαίωσις
		1:17a			
	1:17b				
				1:32	
2:5					
		2:13a			
			2:13b		
				2:26	
			3:4		
		3:5			
	3:10				
			3:20		
		3:21			
		3:22			
			3:24		
		3:25			
		3:26a			
	3:26b				
			3:26c		
			3:28		
			3:30		
			4:2		
		4:3			
			4:5a		
		4:5b			
		4:6			
		4:9			
		4:11 [2x]			
		4:13			
		4:22			
					4:25

Appendix B

δικαιοκρισία	δίκαιος	δικαιοσύνη	δικαιοῦν	δικαίωμα	δικαίωσις
			5:1		
	5:7				
			5:9		
				5:16	
		5:17			
				5:18a	
					5:18b
	5:19				
		5:21			
			6:7		
		6:13			
		6:16			
		6:18			
		6:19			
		6:20			
7:12					
				8:4	
		8:10			
			8:30 [2x]		
			8:33		
		9:30 [3x]			
		9:31			
		10:3 [3x]			
		10:4			
		10:5			
		10:6			
		10:10			
		14:17			
(1)	(7)	(34)	(15)	(5)	(2)

[64]

TOTAL = 77

Appendix C

The Relationships among the δ-GR Words in R-Contexts

(Greek Text)

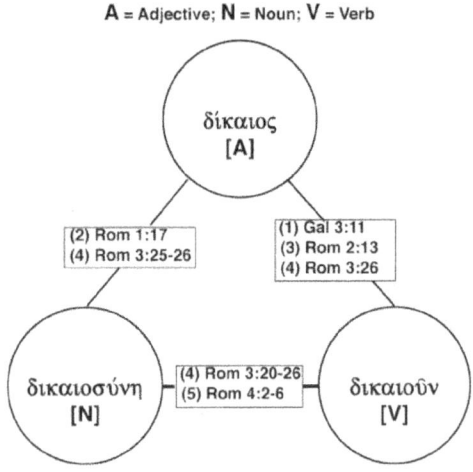

1. **Gal 3:11**: ὅτι δὲ ἐν νόμῳ οὐδεὶς **δικαιοῦται** παρὰ τῷ θεῷ δῆλον, ὅτι Ὁ **δίκαιος** ἐκ πίστεως ζήσεται... (Hab 2:4)

2. **Rom 1:17**: **δικαιοσύνη** γὰρ θεοῦ ἐν αὐτῷ [τῷ εὐαγγελίῳ] ἀποκαλύπτεται ἐκ πίστεως εἰς πίστιν, καθὼς γέγραπται· Ὁ δὲ **δίκαιος** ἐκ πίστεως ζήσεται. (Hab 2:4)

3. **Rom 2:13**: οὐ γὰρ οἱ ἀκροαταὶ νόμου **δίκαιοι** παρὰ τῷ θεῷ, ἀλλ᾽ οἱ ποιηταὶ νόμου **δικαιωθήσονται**.

4. **Rom 3:20–26**: [20] διότι ἐξ ἔργων νόμου οὐ **δικαιωθήσεται** πᾶσα σὰρξ ἐνώπιον αὐτοῦ, διὰ γὰρ νόμου ἐπίγνωσις ἁμαρτίας.

Appendix C

²¹ Νυνὶ δὲ χωρὶς νόμου **δικαιοσύνη** θεοῦ πεφανέρωται, μαρτυρουμένη ὑπὸ τοῦ νόμου καὶ τῶν προφητῶν, ²² **δικαιοσύνη** δὲ θεοῦ διὰ πίστεως Ἰησοῦ Χριστοῦ, εἰς πάντας τοὺς πιστεύοντας, οὐ γάρ ἐστιν διαστολή. ²³ πάντες γὰρ ἥμαρτον καὶ ὑστεροῦνται τῆς δόξης τοῦ θεοῦ, ²⁴ **δικαιούμενοι** δωρεὰν τῇ αὐτοῦ χάριτι διὰ τῆς ἀπολυτρώσεως τῆς ἐν Χριστῷ Ἰησοῦ· ²⁵ ὃν προέθετο ὁ θεὸς ἱλαστήριον διὰ πίστεως ἐν τῷ αὐτοῦ αἵματι εἰς ἔνδειξιν τῆς **δικαιοσύνης** αὐτοῦ διὰ τὴν πάρεσιν τῶν προγεγονότων ἁμαρτημάτων ²⁶ ἐν τῇ ἀνοχῇ τοῦ θεοῦ, πρὸς τὴν ἔνδειξιν τῆς **δικαιοσύνης** αὐτοῦ ἐν τῷ νῦν καιρῷ, εἰς τὸ εἶναι αὐτὸν **δίκαιον** καὶ **δικαιοῦντα** τὸν ἐκ πίστεως Ἰησοῦ.

5. **Rom 4:2–6:** ² εἰ γὰρ Ἀβραὰμ ἐξ ἔργων **ἐδικαιώθη**, ἔχει καύχημα· ἀλλ᾽ οὐ πρὸς θεόν, ³ τί γὰρ ἡ γραφὴ λέγει; Ἐπίστευσεν δὲ Ἀβραὰμ τῷ θεῷ καὶ ἐλογίσθη αὐτῷ εἰς **δικαιοσύνην**. (Gen 15:6) ⁴ τῷ δὲ ἐργαζομένῳ ὁ μισθὸς οὐ λογίζεται κατὰ χάριν ἀλλὰ κατὰ ὀφείλημα· ⁵ τῷ δὲ μὴ ἐργαζομένῳ, πιστεύοντι δὲ ἐπὶ τὸν **δικαιοῦντα** τὸν ἀσεβῆ, λογίζεται ἡ πίστις αὐτοῦ εἰς **δικαιοσύνην**, ⁶ καθάπερ καὶ Δαυὶδ λέγει τὸν μακαρισμὸν τοῦ ἀνθρώπου ᾧ ὁ θεὸς λογίζεται **δικαιοσύνην** χωρὶς ἔργων· (quotes Psalm 32:1-2, on forgiveness, in 4:7–8).

Appendix C

The Relationships among the δ-GR Words in R-Contexts

(English Translation)

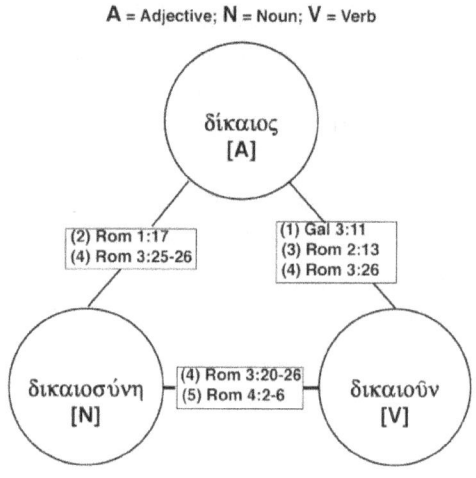

1. **Gal 3:11:** That no-one **is brought into a right relationship [V]** with God by means of the Law is self-evident, since:

   It is **the person who is in a right relationship [A]** as a consequence of faith who will live. (Hab 2:4)

2. **Rom 1:17:** For in the good news **the way to a right relationship [N]** with God is revealed as a consequence of faith for a life of faith, just as it stands on record:

   It is **the person who is in a right relationship [A]** as a consequence of faith, who will live. (Hab 2:4)

Appendix C

3. **Rom 2:13**: For it is not those who hear the Law who are **in a right relationship** [A] with God, but those who keep the Law who **will be brought into a right relationship** [V].

4. **Rom 3:20–26**: [20] And as far as he is concerned, no human being **will be brought into a right relationship** [V] as a consequence of doing what the Law requires, for it is through the Law that people come to know about sin.

   [21] Now, however, quite apart from the Law, **the way to a right relationship** [N] with God, attested to by the Law and the prophetic writings, has come to light, [22] **a right relationship** [N] with God through faith in Jesus Christ for all who have faith. For there isn't any difference: [23] since all have sinned and fall short of God's glory, [24] **they are brought into a right relationship** [V] freely, by his grace, through the liberation purchased by Christ Jesus. [25] God put him on public display as a reconciling sacrifice though faith in his blood to demonstrate **the rightness of his action** [N] in disregarding sins committed previously [26] —due to God's clemency. It was to demonstrate **the rightness of his action** [N] at the present time, so that he might be both **in the right** [A] himself and the One who **brings a person into a right relationship** [V] as a consequence of faith in Jesus.

5. **Rom 4:2–6**: [2] For if Abraham **was brought into a right relationship** [V] as a consequence of what he did, he has grounds for boasting, though not as far as God is concerned. [3] For what does the Scripture say?

   > Abraham put his faith in God, and for him that was regarded as the basis for **a right relationship** [N]. (Gen 15:6)

   [4] Now for the working person wages are not considered to be a favour, but an obligation. [5] However, for the person who doesn't do any work, but puts their faith in the one who **brings** the ungodly **into a right relationship** [V], that person's faith is regarded as the basis for **a right relationship** [N]. [6] Just as David, too, speaks of how blessed the person is, whom God regards as **being in a right relationship** [N] apart from what that person does … (quotes Psalm 32:1–2, on forgiveness, in 4:7–8.)

Appendix D

All Occurrences of the δικαιοσύνη / θεοῦ Combination in the Pauline Corpus

2 Cor 5:21: τὸν μὴ γνόντα ἁμαρτίαν ὑπὲρ ἡμῶν ἁμαρτίαν ἐποίησεν, ἵνα ἡμεῖς γενώμεθα **δικαιοσύνη θεοῦ** ἐν αὐτῷ.

Even though Christ had no personal experience of sinning, God made him a sin offering on our behalf, so that we might come into a right relationship with God through him.

Rom 1:17: [16] Οὐ γὰρ ἐπαισχύνομαι τὸ εὐαγγέλιον, δύναμις γὰρ θεοῦ ἐστιν εἰς σωτηρίαν παντὶ τῷ πιστεύοντι, Ἰουδαίῳ τε πρῶτον καὶ Ἕλληνι· [17] δικαιοσύνη γὰρ θεοῦ ἐν αὐτῷ ἀποκαλύπτεται ἐκ πίστεως εἰς πίστιν, καθὼς γέγραπται· Ὁ δὲ δίκαιος ἐκ πίστεως ζήσεται.

[16] For I'm not ashamed of the good news; after all, it is God's powerful means of bringing about salvation for every person who has come to faith, for the Jew in the first instance, and for the Greek. [17] For in the good news the way to a right relationship with God is revealed as a consequence of faith for a life of faith, just as it stands on record:

> It is the person who is in a right relationship as a consequence of faith, who will live.

Rom 3:5: εἰ δὲ ἡ ἀδικία ἡμῶν θεοῦ δικαιοσύνην συνίστησιν, τί ἐροῦμεν; μὴ ἄδικος ὁ θεὸς ὁ ἐπιφέρων τὴν ὀργήν; κατὰ ἄνθρωπον λέγω.

Now if our wrongdoing establishes the fact that God is in the right, what are we to say? Surely not that God is unjust to be angry? (I am speaking from a human viewpoint.)

Appendix D

Rom 3:21: Νυνὶ δὲ χωρὶς νόμου δικαιοσύνη θεοῦ πεφανέρωται, μαρτυρουμένη ὑπὸ τοῦ νόμου καὶ τῶν προφητῶν,

Now, however, quite apart from the Law, the way to a right relationship with God, attested to by the Law and the prophetic writings, has come to light,

Rom 3:22: δικαιοσύνη δὲ θεοῦ διὰ πίστεως Ἰησοῦ Χριστοῦ, εἰς πάντας τοὺς πιστεύοντας. οὐ γάρ ἐστιν διαστολή . . .

a right relationship with God through faith in Jesus Christ for all who have faith. For there isn't any difference . . .

Rom 10:3a: ἀγνοοῦντες γὰρ τὴν τοῦ θεοῦ δικαιοσύνην, καὶ τὴν ἰδίαν δικαιοσύνην ζητοῦντες στῆσαι . . .

So, being ignorant of the right relationship God provides, and endeavouring to establish a right relationship on their own terms, . . .

Rom 10:3c: τῇ δικαιοσύνῃ τοῦ θεοῦ οὐχ ὑπετάγησαν.

. . . they failed to submit to the right relationship God provides.

Phil 3:9: . . . εὑρεθῶ ἐν αὐτῷ, μὴ ἔχων ἐμὴν δικαιοσύνην τὴν ἐκ νόμου ἀλλὰ τὴν διὰ πίστεως Χριστοῦ, τὴν ἐκ θεοῦ δικαιοσύνην ἐπὶ τῇ πίστει,

that I might be found under him, not having my own righteousness, which originates with the Law, but that which is through faith in Christ, the right relationship that originates with God, based on faith.

Appendix E
Law-Righteousness

Acknowledging that there are two contrasting perceptions of how a person comes into a right relationship with God, Paul represents one of them by making a close link between the [Mosaic] Law and righteousness.

Rom 10:3: ἀγνοοῦντες γὰρ τὴν τοῦ θεοῦ δικαιοσύνην, καὶ τὴν ἰδίαν δικαιοσύνην ζητοῦντες στῆσαι τῇ δικαιοσύνῃ τοῦ θεοῦ οὐχ ὑπετάγησαν.

So, being ignorant of the right relationship God provides, and endeavouring to establish a right relationship on their own terms, they failed to submit to the right relationship God provides.

Rom 10:5: Μωϋσῆς γὰρ γράφει ὅτι τὴν δικαιοσύνην τὴν ἐκ τοῦ νόμου ὁ ποιήσας ἄνθρωπος ζήσεται ἐν αὐτῇ. (citing Lev 18:5.)

For concerning the right relationship based on the Law, Moses writes as follows: 'The person who has achieved these things will live by means of them.'

Appendix F
Faith-Righteousness

In Paul's Letter to the Roman Christians, faith and believing are brought into a very close connection with righteousness in the following six places:

Rom 1:16-17: ¹⁶ Οὐ γὰρ ἐπαισχύνομαι τὸ εὐαγγέλιον, δύναμις γὰρ θεοῦ ἐστιν εἰς σωτηρίαν παντὶ τῷ πιστεύοντι, Ἰουδαίῳ τε πρῶτον καὶ Ἕλληνι· ¹⁷ δικαιοσύνη γὰρ θεοῦ ἐν αὐτῷ ἀποκαλύπτεται ἐκ πίστεως εἰς πίστιν, καθὼς γέγραπται· Ὁ δὲ δίκαιος ἐκ πίστεως ζήσεται.

¹⁶ For I'm not ashamed of the good news; after all, it is God's powerful means of bringing about salvation for every person who has come to faith, for the Jew in the first instance, and for the Greek. ¹⁷ For in the good news the way to a right relationship with God is revealed as a consequence of faith for a life of faith, just as it stands on record:

> It is the person who is in a right relationship as a consequence of faith, who will live.

Rom 4:3: τί γὰρ ἡ γραφὴ λέγει; Ἐπίστευσεν δὲ Ἀβραὰμ τῷ θεῷ καὶ ἐλογίσθη αὐτῷ εἰς δικαιοσύνην.

For what does the Scripture say?

> Abraham put his faith in God, and for him that was regarded as the basis for a right relationship.

Rom 4:11a: καὶ σημεῖον ἔλαβεν περιτομῆς, σφραγῖδα τῆς δικαιοσύνης τῆς πίστεως τῆς ἐν τῇ ἀκροβυστίᾳ, εἰς τὸ εἶναι αὐτὸν πατέρα πάντων τῶν πιστευόντων δι' ἀκροβυστίας, εἰς τὸ λογισθῆναι αὐτοῖς τὴν δικαιοσύνην . . .

Appendix F

And he received the symbol of circumcision as a seal of the right relationship associated with the faith he had while in the uncircumcised state. This enabled him to be the ancestor of all who have faith while in the uncircumcised state, so that they too might be regarded as being in a right relationship . . .

Rom 4:13: Οὐ γὰρ διὰ νόμου ἡ ἐπαγγελία τῷ Ἀβραὰμ ἢ τῷ σπέρματι αὐτοῦ, τὸ κληρονόμον αὐτὸν ⌜εἶναι κόσμου, ἀλλὰ διὰ δικαιοσύνης πίστεως·

For the promise made to Abraham and to his descendants, that he would inherit the world, wasn't based on the Law, but on the right relationship associated with faith.

Rom 9:30c: Τί οὖν ἐροῦμεν; ὅτι ἔθνη τὰ μὴ διώκοντα δικαιοσύνην κατέλαβεν δικαιοσύνην, δικαιοσύνην δὲ τὴν ἐκ πίστεως . . .

What, then, are we to say? That non-Jews, who didn't pursue a right relationship, obtained a right relationship, a right relationship based on faith . . .

Rom 10:6: ἡ δὲ ἐκ πίστεως δικαιοσύνη οὕτως λέγει· Μὴ εἴπῃς ἐν τῇ καρδίᾳ σου· Τίς ἀναβήσεται εἰς τὸν οὐρανόν; τοῦτ᾽ ἔστιν Χριστὸν καταγαγεῖν·

⁶ But the right relationship based on faith speaks in this way: 'Don't say in your heart, "Who will ascend to heaven?" ' —that is, to bring Christ down— ⁷ 'or, "Who will descend to the deep?" ' —that is, to bring Christ back from among the dead. ⁸ Then what does it say? 'The message is near you; it is on your lips and in your heart'—that is, it is the message about faith which we proclaim.

Appendix G
Paul's Use of λογίζεσθαι in Galatians and Romans

In Protestant discussions of "justification," the notion of "imputation" has a prominent place, particularly the imputation of Christ's righteousness to the believer. Paul knows nothing of the latter notion. In R-contexts he never speaks of Christ's righteousness as such, let alone claiming it is imputed to the believer. He does, however, use the underlying Greek word, λογίζεσθαι, which may be rendered in English as "impute" (as well as a range of other meanings, including "think," "consider," "reckon"). While in Galatians the apostle uses λογίζεσθαι only once, in the quotation from Gen 15:6 (Gal 3:6), in Romans he employs it nineteen times. It is not used in any of the other passages where Paul refers to his doctrine of rectification (such as 2 Cor 5:21 or Phil 3:9).

The following table sets out the nineteen uses in Romans, providing a translation or paraphrase and / or comments on each.

No.	Ref.	Translation or Paraphrase/Comments
1	2:3	Of the hypocrite: Do you **suppose** you'll escape God's judgment?
2	2:26	Lack of circumcision **is treated as the equivalent of** circumcision, as long as faith is present.
3	3:28	We **consider** a person to be set right by faith, apart from observing works of the Law.

Appendix G

No.	Ref.	Translation or Paraphrase/Comments
4	4:3	'Abraham believed God, and it was **credited** to him as righteousness.' [citing Gen 15:6].
5	4:4	In the case of the working person, wages are not **considered** a favour, but an obligation.
6	4:5	... to the one who does not work but trusts God who brings the ungodly into a right relationship, that person's faith is **credited** as righteousness. [Gen 15:6 is generalized to the ungodly person who has faith.]
7	4:6	David says the same thing when he speaks of the blessedness of those to whom God **credits** righteousness apart from works: [David speaks of the man whom God **considers** to be in right standing apart from works.]
8	4:8	the Lord does not **take** sin **into account** [citing Ps 32:1-2].
9	4:9	Abraham's faith was **credited** to him as righteousness [alluding to Gen 15:6].
10	4:10	It was **credited** to Abraham before he was circumcised [alluding to Gen 15:6].
11	4:11	And he received the sign of circumcision, a seal of the righteousness that he had by faith while he was still uncircumcised. So then, he is the father of all who believe but have not been circumcised, in order that righteousness might be **credited** to them. [Abraham is the model for all who have faith, giving Gen 15:6 general application]

Appendix G

No.	Ref.	Translation or Paraphrase/Comments
12	4:22	Explanation as to why God **considered** Abraham to be in a right relationship [alluding to Gen 15:6].
13	4:23	The words "it was **credited** to him" [Gen 15:6] were written not for him alone . . .
14	4:24	. . . but also for us, to whom God **will credit** righteousness—for us who believe in him who raised Jesus our Lord from the dead.
15	6:11	Christians are to **consider** themselves dead in relation to sin.
16	8:18	Paul **considers** that the coming glory far outweighs present sufferings.
17	8:36	. . . it is written: "For your sake we face death all day long; we **are considered** as sheep to be slaughtered." [citing Ps 44:22].
18	9:8	. . . it is not the natural children who are God's children, but it is the children of the promise who **are regarded** as Abraham's offspring.
19	14:14	Whoever **considers** something to be unclean, to that person it is unclean.

OBSERVATIONS:

1. Of the instances in the table above, only the occurrences of λογίζεσθαι in nos 4–14 (pertaining to Romans 4) are concerned with God's action in Paul's doctrine of rectification.

Appendix G

2. Three of the above occurrences are due to OT quotations (nos 4, 8, 17). Gen 15:6 (no. 4) also directly influenced a further seven occurrences (nos 6, 9, 10, 11, 12, 13, 14).

3. While God λογίζεται . . . δικαιοσύνην ["considers (in) right relationship] (nos 7, 11, 14), the context makes it clear that personal faith is the basis for his action. Nowhere does Paul speak of Christ's righteousness being "credited" or "imputed" to the believer.

4. Λογίζεσθαι is used in a negative sense (no. 8) to indicate that God does not take sin into account (cf. Jer 31:34, cited Heb 8:12).

Appendix H
The Allusions to Psalm 143:2 in Galatians 2:16 and Romans 3:20

Ps 143:2 καὶ μὴ εἰσέλθης εἰς κρίσιν μετὰ τοῦ δούλου σου ὅτι οὐ δικαιωθήσεται ἐνώπιον σου πᾶς ζῶν.

and do not enter into judgment with your slave, since no living thing will be shown to be in the right in your view.

Gal 2:16 εἰδότες δὲ ὅτι οὐ δικαιοῦται ἄνθρωπος ἐξ ἔργων νόμου ἐὰν μὴ διὰ πίστεως Ἰησοῦ Χριστοῦ, καὶ ἡμεῖς εἰς Χριστὸν Ἰησοῦν ἐπιστεύσαμεν, ἵνα δικαιωθῶμεν ἐκ πίστεως Χριστοῦ καὶ οὐκ ἐξ ἔργων νόμου, ὅτι ἐξ ἔργων νόμου οὐ δικαιωθήσεται πᾶσα σάρξ.

[We] are well aware that no-one is brought into a right relationship [with God] as a consequence of doing what the Law requires, but only through faith in Jesus Christ. So it was that we put our faith in Christ, in order that we might be brought into a right relationship as a consequence of faith in Christ, and not by doing what the Law requires, since no human being will be brought into a right relationship by doing what the Law requires.

Rom 3:20 [19] Οἴδαμεν δὲ ὅτι ὅσα ὁ νόμος λέγει τοῖς ἐν τῷ νόμῳ λαλεῖ, ἵνα πᾶν στόμα φραγῇ καὶ ὑπόδικος γένηται πᾶς ὁ κόσμος τῷ θεῷ· [20] διότι ἐξ ἔργων νόμου οὐ δικαιωθήσεται πᾶσα σὰρξ ἐνώπιον αὐτοῦ, διὰ γὰρ νόμου ἐπίγνωσις ἁμαρτίας.

[19] Now we know that whatever the Law says is addressed to those who fall under the Law's jurisdiction, so that every

mouth may be muzzled and the whole world may be held accountable to God. **20** And as far as he is concerned, no human being will be brought into a right relationship as a consequence of doing what the Law requires, for it is through the Law that people come to know about sin.

Appendix I
Two Perceived Approaches to Establishing a Right Relationship with God in Paul's Letters

Law	Reference	Faith
the relationship is *achieved* by working		the relationship is *granted as a gift* through faith
15 We who are Jews by birth and not sinners of non-Jewish origin **16** are well aware that no-one is brought into a right relationship [with God] as a consequence of doing what the Law requires,	Gal 2:16	
		but only through faith in Jesus Christ, and we put our faith in Christ, so that we might be brought into a right relationship as a consequence of faith in Christ
and not as a consequence of doing what the Law requires, since no human being will be brought into a right relationship as a consequence of doing what the Law requires.		

Appendix I

Law	Reference	Faith
[2] Did you receive the Spirit as a consequence of doing what the Law requires,	Gal 3:2–3	
		or as a consequence of the faith associated with listening? [3] Having begun with the Spirit,
are you so stupid as to now be concluding on the merely human plane?		
	Gal 3:5	Well then, does he who supplies the Spirit to you and who works miracles among you do so
as a consequence of your doing what the Law requires,		or as a consequence of the faith associated with listening?
[20] Now as far as he [God] is concerned, no human being will be brought into a right relationship as a consequence of doing what the Law requires, for it is through the Law that people come to know about sin.	Rom 3:20, 22–25	

Appendix I

Law	Reference	Faith
		22 ... For there is no difference: **23** since *all* have sinned and miss out on God's glory, **24** they are brought into a right relationship freely, by his grace, through the redemption which is in Christ Jesus. **25** God put him on public display as a reconciling sacrifice though faith in his blood ...
27 Well then, where does boasting come in? It has no place. On what principle? The principle of works?	Rom 3:27–28	
		Certainly not, but on the principle of faith. **28** For we argue that a person is brought into a right relationship quite apart from doing what the Law requires.
2 For if Abraham was brought into a right relationship as a consequence of what he did, he has grounds for boasting, though not as far as God is concerned.	Rom 4:2–5	
		3 For what does the Scripture say? Abraham put his faith in God, and that was regarded as the basis for his right relationship.'

Appendix I

Law	Reference	Faith
4 Now for the working person wages are not considered to be a favour, but an obligation.		**5** However, for the person who doesn't do any work but who puts their faith in the one who brings the ungodly into a right relationship, that person's faith is regarded as the basis for a right relationship.
	Rom 9:30–33	**30** Then what are we to say? That non-Jews, who did not pursue a right relationship, obtained a right relationship, a right relationship based on faith,
31 while Israel, pursuing a Law designed to establish a right relationship, did not attain to the Law. **32** Why not? Because their pursuit of it was based, not on faith, but as if it depended on human behaviour. They stumbled over the stumbling-stone **33** just as it stands on record:		
Take note! I am laying in Zion a stumbling-stone and a rock causing offense,		yet the person who puts their faith in him will not be disappointed.
3 ... being ignorant of the right relationship God provides, and endeavouring to establish a right relationship on their own terms, they [Israel] failed to submit to ...	Rom 10:3–8	

Appendix I

Law	Reference	Faith
		... the right relationship God provides. **4** For Christ is the goal of the Law, leading to a right relationship for every person who has faith. For Christ fulfils the purpose of the Law, so that everyone who has faith is in a right relationship.
5 For concerning the right relationship based on the Law, Moses writes as follows: 'The person who has achieved these things will live by means of them.'		
		6 But the right relationship based on faith speaks in this way: 'Do not say in your heart, "Who will ascend to heaven?"'—that is, to bring Christ down— **7** 'or, "Who will descend to the deep?"'—that is, to bring Christ back from among the dead. **8** Then what does it say? 'The message is near you; it is on your lips and in your heart'—that is, it is the message about faith which we proclaim publicly.

Appendix I

Law	Reference	Faith
⁶ ... as to righteousness based on the Law, [I was] faultless. **⁷** But whatever was gain for me personally, I consider to be forfeited because of the Messiah. **⁸** More than this, I consider *everything* to be forfeited because it is so much better to know Christ Jesus my Lord, on whose account I have forfeited everything and regard it as dung,	Phil 3:6–9	
		so that I might gain Christ **⁹** and be found under him,
not having my own righteousness, which results from the Law,		but the right relationship which is through faith in Christ, the right relationship which originates with God, based on faith.

Appendix J

Three Approaches to Englishing Paul's δ-Family Illustrated from Romans 3:21–26.

NJB (1985)	NIV (2011)	USC (2014)
21 God's saving justice was witnessed by the Law and the Prophets, but now it has been revealed altogether apart from law:	**21** But now apart from the law the righteousness of God has been made known, to which the Law and the Prophets testify.	**21** Now, however, quite apart from the Law, the way to a right relationship with God, attested to by the Law and the Prophetic Writings, has come to light,
22 God's saving justice given through faith in Jesus Christ to all who believe.	**22** This righteousness is given through faith in Jesus Christ to all who believe.	**22** a right relationship with God through faith in Jesus Christ for all who have faith.
23 No distinction is made: all have sinned and lack God's glory,	There is no difference between Jew and Gentile, **23** for all have sinned and fall short of the glory of God,	For there isn't any difference: **23** since all have sinned and fall short of God's glory,
24 and all are justified by the free gift of his grace through being set free in Christ Jesus.	**24** and all are justified freely by his grace through the redemption that came by Christ Jesus.	**24** they are brought into a right relationship freely, by his grace, through the liberation purchased by Christ Jesus.

Appendix J

NJB (1985)	NIV (2011)	USC (2014)
[25] God appointed him as a sacrifice for reconciliation, through faith, by the shedding of his blood, and so showed his justness; first for the past, when sins went unpunished because he held his hand;	[25] God presented Christ as a sacrifice of atonement, through the shedding of his blood—to be received by faith. He did this to demonstrate his righteousness, because in his forbearance he had left the sins committed beforehand unpunished—	[25] God put him on public display as a reconciling sacrifice though faith in his blood to demonstrate the rightness of his action in disregarding sins committed previously [26] —due to God's clemency.
[26] and now again for the present age, to show how he is just and justifies everyone who has faith in Jesus.	[26] he did it to demonstrate his righteousness at the present time, so as to be just and the one who justifies those who have faith in Jesus.	It was to demonstrate the rightness of his action at the present time, so that he might be both in the right himself and the One who brings a person into a right relationship as a consequence of faith in Jesus.

Select Bibliography

The Amplified Bible containing the Amplified Old Testament and the Amplified New Testament. Grand Rapids: Zondervan, 1965.

Anderson, Hugh George, et al., eds. *Justification by Faith: Lutherans and Catholics in Dialogue VII.* Minneapolis: Augsburg, 1985.

Augustine of Hippo. *Saint Augustin: Anti-Pelagian Writings.* Edited by Philip Schaff. Select Library of the Nicene and Post-Nicene Fathers of the Christian Church, First Series, vol. 5. Grand Rapids: Eerdmans, 1971.

Aune, David E., ed. *Rereading Paul Together: Protestant and Catholic Perspectives on Justification.* Grand Rapids: Baker Academic, 2006.

Barclay, William. *The New Testament: A New Translation.* London: Collins/Fontana, 1976.

Barnes, Robert. "Onely fayth iustifieth befor God." In *The whole workes of W. Tyndall, Iohn Frith, and Doct. Barnes, three worthy martyrs, and principall teachers of this Church of England, collected and compiled in one Tome togither beyng before scattered, & now in print here exhibited to the Church.* To the prayse of God, and profite of all good Christian Readers. London: John Daye, 1573. [This tract was originally appended to "A supplication unto the most gracious prince, King Henry VIII. by Robert Barnes, D.D."]

Barth, Karl. *Church Dogmatics.* 4 vols. Edinburgh: T. & T. Clark, 1936-69.

Bauer, Walter. *A Greek-English Lexicon of the New Testament and other early Christian literature.* ed. Frederick William Danker. Chicago: University of Chicago, ^{3}2000. [BDAG] Based on Walter Bauer's *Griechisch-deutsches Wörterbuch zu den Schriften des Neuen Testaments und der frühchristlichen Literatur.* ed. Kurt Aland and Barbara Aland, ^{6}1988, and on previous English editions by W. F. Arndt, F. W. Gingrich, and F. W. Danker.

Beilby, James K., and Paul Rhodes Eddy, eds. *Justification: Five Views.* Spectrum Multiview. Downers Grove, IL: InterVarsity Academic, 2011.

Bird, Michael F. *The Saving Righteousness of God: Studies on Paul, Justification, and the New Perspective.* Paternoster Biblical Monographs. Eugene, OR: Wipf & Stock, 2007.

———, and Preston M. Sprinkle, eds. *The Faith of Jesus Christ: Exegetical, Biblical, and Theological Studies.* Peabody, MA: Hendrickson, 2009.

Bray, Gerald, and Paul Gardner. "The Joint Declaration on the Doctrine of Justification." *Churchman* 115 (2001) 110–27.

Bruce, Frederick Fyvie. *An Expanded Paraphrase of the Epistles of Paul.* Exeter: Paternoster, 1965.

Burgess, Joseph A., and Marc Kolden, eds. *By Faith Alone: Essays on Justification in Honor of Gerhard O. Forde.* Grand Rapids: Eerdmans, 2004.

Select Bibliography

Byrne, Brendan. *Romans*. Sacra Pagina 6. Collegeville, MN: Liturgical, 1996.

The Cambridge History of the Bible. Cambridge: Cambridge University Press. vol. 1: From the beginnings to Jerome, ed. P. R. Ackroyd and C. F. Evans, 1970; vol. 2: The West from the Fathers to the Reformation, ed. G. W. H. Lampe, 1969; vol. 3: The West from the Reformation to the present Day, ed. S. L. Greenslade, 1963.

Carson, Donald A., ed. *Right with God: Justification in the Bible and the World*. Grand Rapids: Baker, 1992.

———. "The Vindication of Imputation: On Fields of Discourse and Semantic Fields." In *Justification: What's at Stake in the Current Debates?*, edited by Mark Husbands and Daniel J. Treier, 46–78. Downers Grove, IL: InterVarsity, 2004.

———, Peter T. O'Brien, and Mark A. Seifrid, eds. *Justification and Variegated Nomism*. 2 vols. Grand Rapids: Baker, 2001, 2004.

Cassirer, Heinrich Walter. *God's New Covenant: A New Testament Translation by Heinz W. Cassirer*. Grand Rapids: Eerdmans, 1989.

The Catholic Study Bible: The New American Bible, Including the Revised New Testament, Translated from the Original Languages with Critical Use of All the Ancient Sources. Edited by Donald Senior. New York: Oxford University Press, 1990.

Chamberlin, William J. *Catalogue of English Bible Translations: A Classified Bibliography of Versions and Editions Including Books, Parts, and Old and New Testament Apocrypha and Apocryphal Books*. New York: Greenwood, 1991.

Clifford, Alan C. "The Gospel and Justification." *EvQ* 57 (1985) 247–67.

Common English Bible. Nashville: Common English Bible, 2011.

Coverdale, Miles. *Remains of Myles Coverdale*. Parker Society. Cambridge: Cambridge University Press, 1846.

———. *Writings and Translations of Myles Coverdale*. Parker Society. Cambridge: Cambridge University Press, 1844.

Crabtree, Arthur B. *The Restored Relationship: A Study in Justification and Reconciliation*. W. T. Whitley Lectures for 1961. London: Carey Kingsgate, 1963.

Cranfield, Charles E. B. *A Critical and Exegetical Commentary on the Epistle to the Romans*. 2 vols. International Critical Commentary. Edinburgh: T. & T. Clark, 1975, 1979.

Cranmer, Thomas. *The Works of Thomas Cranmer*. Vol. 2. Edited by John Edmund Cox. New York: Johnson Reprint Corporation, 1968.

Daniell, David. *Tyndale's Old Testament, being the Pentateuch of 1530, Joshua to 2 Chronicles of 1537, and Jonah. In a modern-spelling edition*. New Haven: Yale University Press, 1992.

———. *William Tyndale: A Biography*. New Haven: Yale University Press, 1994.

Dunn, James D. G. "In Search of Common Ground." In *Paul and the Mosaic Law*, edited by James D. G. Dunn, 309–34. Tübingen: J. C. B. Mohr [Paul Siebeck], 1996.

———. *The New Perspective on Paul*. Rev. ed. Grand Rapids: Eerdmans, 2008.

———. "Once more, ΠΙΣΤΙΣ ΧΡΙΣΤΟΥ." In *Society of Biblical Literature 1991 Seminar Papers*, edited by Eugene H. Lovering, 730–44. Atlanta: Scholars, 1991.

———, ed. *Paul and the Mosaic Law*. WUNT 89. Tübingen: J. C. B. Mohr [Paul Siebeck], 1996.

Edwards, Jonathan. "Justification by Faith Alone." In *The Works of Jonathan Edwards: With an Essay on His Genius and Writings*, edited by Henry Rogers et al., 1:622–54. London: William Ball, 1839.

Select Bibliography

Erasmus, Desiderius. *Novum Instrumentum. Basel 1516.* Faksimile-Neudruck mit einer historischen, textkritischen und bibliographischen Einleitung von Heinz Holeczek Hrsg. Stuttgart-Bad Cannstatt: Frommann-Holzboog, 1986.

Fenton, Ferrar, ed. *The Holy Bible in Modern English: Containing the Complete Sacred Scriptures of the Old and New Testaments Translated into English Direct from the Original Hebrew, Chaldee and Greek.* Merimac, MA: Destiny, 1966.

Finney, Charles Grandison. *Finney's Systematic Theology.* Minneapolis: Bethany Fellowship, 1976.

Fitzmyer, Joseph A. *Romans: A New Translation with Introduction and Commentary.* AB 33. New York: Doubleday, 1993.

Forshall, Josiah, and Frederic Madden, eds. *The Holy Bible, Containing the Old and New Testaments, with the Apocryphal Books, in the Earliest English versions made from the Latin Vulgate by John Wycliffe and His Followers.* 4 vols. Oxford: Oxford University Press, 1850.

The Geneva Bible. A facsimile of the 1560 edition. With an introduction by Lloyd E. Berry. Madison: University of Wisconsin Press, 1969.

Good News Bible: The Bible in Today's English Version. New York: ABS, 1976.

Good News for Modern Man: The New Testament in Today's English Version. Sydney: Collins, 1966/69.

Goodspeed, Edgar Johnson, trans. *The Bible. An American Translation . . . The New Testament.* Chicago: University of Chicago Press, 1931.

Gundry, Robert Horton. "Grace, Works, and Staying Saved in Paul." *Biblica* 66 (1985) 1–38.

———. "The Nonimputation of Christ's Righteousness." In *Justification: What's at Stake in the Current Debates?*, edited by Mark Husbands and Daniel J. Trier, 17–45. Downers Grove, IL: InterVarsity, 2004.

Hart, Trevor A., ed. *The Dictionary of Historical Theology.* Grand Rapids: Eerdmans, 2000.

Herbert, A. S., ed. *Historical Catalogue of Printed Editions of the English Bible 1525—1961.* Revised and expanded from the editions of T. H. Darlow and H. F. Moule, 1903. London: The British and Foreign Bible Society, 1968.

The Holman Christian Standard Bible. Nashville: Holman, 2004.

The Holy Bible: American Standard Version. New York: Thomas Nelson, 1901.

The Holy Bible. An exact reprint in Roman type, page for page, of the Authorized Version published in the year 1611, with an introduction by Alfred W. Pollard. Oxford: Oxford University Press, 1985.

The Holy Bible containing the Old and New Testaments. [Revised Version.] With marginal references. Oxford: Oxford University Press, 1898.

The Holy Bible containing the Old and New Testaments with the Apocryphal/Deuterocanonical Books: New Revised Standard Version. Nashville: Thomas Nelson, 1990.

The Holy Bible: English Standard Version. Wheaton, IL: Crossway, 2001.

The Holy Bible: The NET Bible (New English Translation). Biblical Studies Press, 2001.

The Holy Bible: New Century Version. Dallas: Word, 1991.

Holy Bible: New International Reader's Version (NIrV). Grand Rapids: Zonderkidz, 2005.

The Holy Bible: New International Version. The New Testament. London: Hodder & Stoughton, 1974.

The Holy Bible: New International Version. Grand Rapids: Zondervan, 1978.

The Holy Bible: New International Version. Grand Rapids: Zondervan, 1984.

Holy Bible: New International Version. Grand Rapids: Zondervan, 2011.

Select Bibliography

The Holy Bible: Revised Standard Version. Comfort ed. New York: William Collins, 1952.

Holy Bible: Today's New International Version. Colorado Springs: International Bible Society, 2005.

[*The*] *Holy Bible, translated from the Latin Vulgat diligently compared with the Hebrew, Greek, and other editions in divers languages.* The Old Testament first published by the English College at Doway, A.D. 1609 and the New Testament [of our Lord and Saviour Jesus Christ, translated from the Latin Vulgat: diligently compared with the original Greek and] first published by the English Collegeat Rhemes, A.D. 1582. With annotations, references, and an historical and chronological index. Newly revised and corrected according to the Clementin Edition of the Scriptures. 6th ed. Dublin: James Reilly, 1794.

Husbands, Mark, and Daniel J. Treier, eds. *Justification: What's at Stake in the Current Debate?* Downers Grove, IL: InterVarsity, 2004.

The Jerusalem Bible. Standard ed. London: Darton, Longman & Todd, 1966.

The Joint Declaration on the Doctrine of Justification in Confessional Lutheran Perspective. St. Louis: The Lutheran Church—Missouri Synod, 1999.

JPS Hebrew-English Tanakh: The Traditional Hebrew Text and the New JPS Translation. 2nd ed. Philadelphia: Jewish Publication Society, 1999.

Jüngel, Eberhard. *Justification: The Heart of the Christian Faith: A Theological Study with an Ecumenical Purpose.* Edinburgh: T. & T. Clark, 2001.

Knox, Ronald A., trans. *The Holy Bible: A Translation from the Latin Vulgate in the Light of the Hebrew and Greek Originals.* School ed. London: Burns & Oates, 1957.

Küng, Hans. *Justification: The Doctrine of Karl Barth and a Catholic Reflection.* Philadelphia: Westminster, 1981.

Lane, Anthony N. S. *Justification by Faith in Catholic-Protestant Dialogue: An Evangelical Assessment.* Edinburgh: T. & T. Clark, 2002.

The Living Bible. Paraphrased by Kenneth Nathaniel Taylor. Wheaton, IL: Tyndale, 1971.

Louw, Johannes P., and Eugene A. Nida, eds. *Greek-English Lexicon of the New Testament Based on Semantic Domains.* 2 vols. New York: United Bible Societies, 1988.

Luther, Martin. *Die gantze Heilige Schrifft Deudsch.* 2 vols., and introductory vol. Munich: Roger & Bernhard, 1972.

———. *Luther's Works.* Edited by Jaroslav Pelikan and Helmut T. Lehmann. American ed. 55 vols. Philadelphia: Muhlenberg, 1955-1986.

———. *Septembertestament, 1522.* r.i. Stuttgart: Deutsche Bibelgesellschaft, 1982.

Mattes, Mark C. *The Role of Justification in Contemporary Theology.* Grand Rapids: Eerdmans, 2004.

Matthew, Thomas. *The Byble, which is all the holy Scripture: In whych are contayned the Olde and Newe Testament truly and purely translated into English by Thomas Matthew.* Antwerp?: printed for R. Grafton & E. Whitchurch of London, 1537. [Microfilm: English Books before 1640; 1A, Reel 99 = DMH no.34].

McGrath, Alister Edgar. *Iustitia Dei: A History of the Christian Doctrine of Justification.* 2 vols. Cambridge: Cambridge University Press, 1986.

———. *Justification By Faith: What It Means for Us Today.* Grand Rapids: Zondervan, 1988.

Melanchthon, Philip. "Apology of the Augsburg Confession (1531)." In *Book of Concord: The Confessions of the Evangelical Lutheran Church*, edited and translated by Theodore Gerhardt Tappert, 97-285. Philadelphia: Fortress, 1959.

Select Bibliography

———. *Melanchthon on Christian Doctrine: Loci Communes, 1555*. Translated by Clyde L. Manschreck. New York: Oxford University Press, 1965.

Meyer, Heinrich August Wilhelm. *Critical and Exegetical Handbook to the Epistle to the Romans*. Translated by John C. Moore et al. Critical and Exegetical Commentary on the New Testament 5. New York: Funk & Wagnalls, 1884.

Moffatt, James. *A New Translation of the Bible Containing the Old and New Testaments*. [Also titled: *The Bible. A New Translation*.] Concordance ed. New York: Harper & Row, 1935.

Moo, Douglas J. *The Epistle to the Romans*. NICNT. Grand Rapids: Eerdmans, 1996.

Moore, Richard Kingsley. "2 Cor 5,21: The Interpretative Key to Paul's Use of δικαιοσύνη θεοῦ?" In *The Corinthian Correspondence*, edited by R. Bieringer, 707–15. BETL 125. Leuven: Peeters, 1996.

———. "ΔΙΚΑΙΟΣΥΝΗ and Cognates in Paul: The Semantic Gulf between Two Major Lexicons (Bauer-Arndt-Gingrich-Danker and Louw-Nida)." *Colloquium* 30 (1998) 27–43.

———. "The Doctrine of 'Justification' in the English Bible at the Close of the Twentieth Century." *The Bible Translator* 45 (1994) 101–16.

———. "Issues Involved in the Interpretation of δικαιοσύνη θεοῦ in the Pauline Corpus." *Colloquium* 23 (1991) 59–70.

———. "'Justification' in NIrV and NIV 2011: Two Very Different Approaches from the Same Stable." *The Bible Translator* 64 (2013) 241–53.

———. "N. T. Wright's Treatment of 'Justification' in *The New Testament for Everyone*." *Expository Times* 125 (2014) 483–86.

———. *Rectification ('Justification') in Paul, in Historical Perspective, and in the English Bible: God's Gift of Right Relationship*. Vol. 1, *Paul's Doctrine of Rectification*; vol. 2, *The Doctrine of Rectification in Its Historical Development*; vol. 3, *Paul's Doctrine of Rectification in English Versions of the New Testament*. Lewiston, NY: Edwin Mellen, 2002–2003.

———. *Right with God: Paul and His English Translators: An Examination of the Meaning of δικαιοσύνη, δικαιοῦν and δίκαιος in the Epistles of Paul the Apostle to the Churches of Galatia and to the Church at Rome, and of Their Rendering in English Translations of These Scriptures*. 2 vols. PhD diss. Brisbane: University of Queensland, 1978.

———. "Romans 4.5 in TEV: A Plea for Consistency." *The Bible Translator* 39 (1988) 126–29.

———. *Under the Southern Cross: The New Testament in Australian English*. Bloomington: WestBow, 2014.

[The] New American Bible. Nashville: Thomas Nelson, 1970. New Testament revised 1986. Revised Edition (NABRE), 2011.

The New American Standard Bible. Text ed. Chicago: Moody, 1971/1973.

The New English Bible. Cambridge: Cambridge University Press, 1970.

The New English Bible: New Testament. Cambridge: Cambridge University Press, 1961.

The New Testament of Our Lord and Saviour Jesus Christ. Translated out of the Greek: being the version set forth A.D. 1611 compared with the most ancient authorities and revised A.D. 1881. Revised Version. Cambridge: Cambridge University Press, 1881.

New World Translation of the Holy Scriptures. Rendered from the original languages by the New World Bible Translation Committee. New York: Watchtower Bible & Tract Society, 1961.

Select Bibliography

Newman, Barclay M. *Greek-English Dictionary of the New Testament*. London: United Bible Societies, 1971.
Newman, John Henry. *Lectures on Justification*. London: Rivingtons, 1838, ²1840. [Later editions bore the title *Lectures on the Doctrine of Justification* (³1874)].
Nida, Eugene A., and Johannes P. Louw. *Lexical Semantics of the Greek New Testament: A Supplement to the Greek-English Lexicon of the New Testament Based on Semantic Domains*. Atlanta: Scholars, 1992.
Nida, Eugene A., and Charles R. Taber. *The Theory and Practice of Translation*. Leiden: E. J. Brill, 1969.
Oden, Thomas C. *The Justification Reader*. Grand Rapids: Eerdmans, 2002.
Olin, John C., ed. *A Reformation Debate: Sadoleto's Letter to the Genevans and Calvin's Reply*. Grand Rapids: Baker, 1966.
Owen, John. "The Doctrine of Justification by Faith through the Imputation of the Righteousness of Christ; Explained, Confirmed, and Vindicated [1677]." In *The Works of John Owen, D.D.*, edited by William H. Goold, 5:1–400. Edinburgh: T. & T. Clark, 1855.
Paues, Anna Carolina, ed. *A fourteenth-century English biblical version, consisting of a prologue and parts of the New Testament edited from the MSS together with some introductory chapters on Middle English biblical versions (prose-translations)*. Cambridge: Cambridge University Press, 1902. [R.i. 1904 and 1909 without the introduction].
Perkins, William. *A Commentary on Galatians*. Edited by Gerald T. Sheppard. Introductory essays by Brevard S. Childs, Gerald T. Sheppard, John H. Augustine [Facsimile of *A Commentarie, or, Exposition vpon the fiue first Chapters of the Epistle to the Galatians* by William Perkins. London: Iohn Legatt, 1617.] R.i. Pilgrim Classic Commentaries. New York: Pilgrim, 1989.
———. *The Work of William Perkins*. Edited by Ian Breward. Courtenay Library of Reformation Classics. Abingdon: Sutton Courtenay, 1970.
Phillips, J. B. *Letters to Young Churches: A Translation of the New Testament Epistles*. With an introduction by C. S. Lewis. London: Collins/Fontana, 1955.
———. *The New Testament in Modern English: For Schools*. London: William Collins, 1960.
———. *The New Testament in Modern English*. Rev. ed. New York: Macmillan, 1972.
Piper, John. *Counted Righteous in Christ: Should We Abandon the Imputation of Christ's Righteousness?* Wheaton, IL: Crossway, 2002.
———. *The Future of Justification: A Response to N. T. Wright*. Wheaton, IL: Crossway, 2007.
Powell, Margaret Joyce, ed. *The Pauline Epistles Contained in MS. Parker 32, Corpus Christi College, Cambridge*. Extra Series no. 116. London: EETS, 1916.
Reid, Gavin, ed. *The Great Acquittal: Justification by Faith and Current Christian Thought*. London: Collins/Fount, 1980.
Reumann, John Henry Paul. *"Righteousness" in the New Testament: "Justification" in the United States Lutheran—Roman Catholic Dialogue*. With responses by Joseph A. Fitzmyer and Jerome D. Quinn. Philadelphia: Fortress, 1982.
The Revised English Bible. Oxford: Oxford University Press, 1989.
Ritschl, Albrecht Benjamin. *A Critical History of the Christian Doctrine of Justification and Reconciliation*. Edinburgh: Edmonston & Douglas, 1872. [E.T. by John S. Black of *Die christliche Lehre von der Rechtfertigung und Versöhnung*. 3 vols, 1870–74, vol. 1].

Select Bibliography

———. *The Christian Doctrine of Justification and Reconciliation.* Edinburgh: T. & T. Clark, ^{1}1874 ^{2}1883 ^{3}1888/1900. [ET by H. R. Mackintosh and A. B. Macaulay of *Die christliche Lehre von der Rechtfertigung und Versöhnung.* 3 vols, 1870-74, vol. 3].

Robertson, A. T. *A Grammar of the Greek New Testament in the Light of Historical Research.* Nashville: Broadman, 1934.

Rusch, William G. "How the Eastern Fathers Understood What the Western Church Meant by Justification." In *Justification by Faith: Lutherans and Catholics in Dialogue VII*, edited by Hugh George Anderson et al., 131–42. Minneapolis: Augsburg, 1985.

Salvation and the Church: An Agreed Statement by the Second Anglican-Roman Catholic International Commission ARCIC II. London: Church House, 1987.

Sanday, William, and Arthur C. Headlam. *A Critical and Exegetical Commentary on the Epistle to the Romans.* ICC. Edinburgh: T. & T. Clark, 1902.

Sanders, Ed Parish. *Paul and Palestinian Judaism: A Comparison of Patterns of Religion.* London: SCM, 1977.

———. *Paul, the Law, and the Jewish people.* Minneapolis: Fortress, 1983.

Schreiner, Thomas R. *Romans.* Baker Exegetical Commentary on the New Testament. Grand Rapids: Baker, 1998.

Schroeder, H. J., trans. *Canons and Decrees of the Council of Trent.* St. Louis: Herder, 1941.

Seifrid, Mark A. *Christ, Our Righteousness: Paul's Theology of Justification.* Downers Grove, IL: InterVarsity, 2000.

Snyder, Graydon F. "Major Motifs in the Interpretation of Paul's Letter to the Romans." In *Celebrating Romans: Template for Pauline Theology*, edited by Sheila E. McGinn, 42–63. Grand Rapids: Eerdmans, 2004.

Southern, Richard William. *Western Society and the Church in the Middle Ages.* Pelican History of the Church 2. Middlesex: Penguin, 1970.

Spurgeon, Charles Haddon. *The New Park Street Pulpit/Metropolitan Tabernacle Pulpit: Sermons Preached by C. H. Spurgeon.* Rev. ed. 62 vols. Pasadena, TX: Pilgrim, 1981.

Stendahl, Krister. "The Apostle Paul and the Introspective Conscience of the West." In *Paul among Jews and Gentiles*, 78–96. London: SCM, 1977.

Strong, James. *The Exhaustive Concordance of the Bible.* London: Hodder & Stoughton, 1894.

Stuhlmacher, Peter. *Gerechtigkeit Gottes bei Paulus.* Göttingen: Vandenhoeck & Ruprecht, 1966.

———. *Revisiting Paul's Doctrine of Justification: A Challenge to the New Perspective.* Downers Grove, IL: InterVarsity, 2001.

Stumme, Wayne C., ed. *The Gospel of Justification in Christ: Where Does the Church Stand Today?* Grand Rapids: Eerdmans, 2006.

Taylor, Kenneth Nathaniel. *The Living New Testament.* Wheaton, IL: Tyndale, 1967.

Torrance, Thomas F. *The Doctrine of Grace in the Apostolic Fathers.* Edinburgh: Oliver & Boyd, 1948.

Tyndale, William. *An Answer to Sir Thomas More's Dialogue, The Supper of the Lord, After the True Meaning of John VI and 1 Cor. XI, and Wm. Tracy's Testament Expounded* [1531]. Edited by Henry Walter. Parker Society vol. 3. New York: Johnson Reprint Corporation, 1968.

———. *The Beginning of the New Testament Translated by William Tyndale 1525.* Facsimile of the unique fragment of the uncompleted Cologne edition. With an introduction by Alfred W. Pollard. Oxford: Clarendon, 1926.

Select Bibliography

———. *A compendious introduccion/prologe or preface vn to the pistle off Paul to the Romayns*. Worms, 1526; r.i. Norwood, NJ: Walter W. Johnson, 1975.

———. *Doctrinal Treatises and Introductions to Different Portions of the Holy Scriptures*. Edited by Henry Walter. Parker Society vol. 1. New York: Johnson Reprint Corporation, 1968.

———. *Expositions and Notes on Sundry Portions of the Holy Scriptures, Together with the Practice of Prelates*. Edited by Henry Walter. Parker Society vol. 2. New York: Johnson Reprint Corporation, 1968.

———. *The New Testament, 1526*. R.i. [in facsimile] London: David Paradine, 1976.

———. *The New Testament. Translated by William Tyndale, 1534*. A reprint of the edition of 1534 with the translator's prefaces and notes and the variants of the edition of 1525. Edited by N. Hardy Wallis. Cambridge: Cambridge University Press, 1938.

———. *Tyndale's New Testament. Translated from the Greek by William Tyndale in 1534*. In a modern-spelling edition and with an introduction by David Daniell. New Haven, CT: Yale University Press, 1989.

———, et al. *Writings of Tindal, Frith, and Barnes*. London: The Religious Tract Society, n.d.

Vickers, Brian. *Justification by Grace through Faith: Finding Freedom from Legalism, Lawlessness, Pride, and Despair*. Explorations in Biblical Theology. Phillipsburg, NJ: P. & R., 2013.

Wallace, Daniel B. *Greek Grammar Beyond the Basics: An Exegetical Syntax of the New Testament with Scripture, Subject, and Greek Word Indexes*. Grand Rapids: Zondervan, 1996.

Waters, Guy Prentiss. *Justification and the New Perspectives on Paul: A Review and Response*. Phillipsburg, NJ: P. & R., 2004.

Westcott, Brooke Foss. *A General View of the History of the English Bible*. Edited by William Aldis Wright. 3rd rev. ed. New York: Lemma, 1972.

Westcott, Frederick Brooke. *St. Paul and Justification, Being an Exposition of the Teaching in the Epistles to Rome and Galatia*. London: Macmillan, 1913.

[Westminster Confession of Faith.] *The Confession of Faith; The Larger and Shorter Catechisms with the Scripture Proofs at large together with the Sum of Saving Knowledge . . .* [1647]. Foreword by Alexander Murray. Glasgow: Free Presbyterian, 1966.

Weymouth, Richard Francis. *The New Testament in Modern Speech*. An idiomatic translation into everyday English from the text of "The Resultant Greek Testament." Edited by Ernest Hampden-Cook. London: James Clarke, 1905.

Williams, Charles Bray. *The New Testament in the Language of the People*. New York: Bruce Humphries, 1937.

Wright, Nicholas Thomas. *Justification: God's Plan and Paul's Vision*. London: SPCK, 2009.

———. *The New Testament for Everyone*. London: SPCK, 2011.

———. "Translating δικαιοσύνη: A Response." *Expository Times* 125 (2014) 487–90.

Wycliffe, John, and John Purvey, eds., and trans. *The New Testament in English*. Translated by John Wycliffe 1382. Revised by John Purvey 1388. Sexcentenary edition. First exact facsimile of the First English Bible with an Introduction by Donald L. Brake. From Rawlinson 259 MSS. in the Bodleian Library Oxford, England. Portland, OR: International Bible Publications, 1986.

Scripture Index

Genesis	12	Mark	
12:3	18, 109	16:9–20	80
15:6	12, 16, 34, 104, 185, 188		
22:18	109	John	
		7:53–8:11	80
Exodus			
23:7	100	Romans	2, 12, 42, 53, 61–62, 66, 73, 95, 107, 163, 165, 174–5, 185–8
Psalms	103		
14:1–3	11	1:4	163
32:1–2	177, 179	1:5	16, 23, 163
50:6	10	1:7	22
53:2–4	11	1:9	23
143:2	104, 189–90	1:16–17	12, 23–24, 88, 92, 95, 107, 183
		1:17	18, 51, 61, 63, 65, 70, 79–80, 83–84, 86, 96, 101, 103–4, 164, 176, 178, 180
Isaiah	12, 103		
		1:18–3:20	108
Jeremiah		1:18	11, 28
31:34	188	2–3	21
		2:1–16	106
Ezekiel		2:3	185
18	106	2:5	14, 102
		2:13	17, 97, 176, 179
		2:17	101
Habakkuk		2:26	84, 185
2:4	51, 83–84, 95, 101, 104, 176, 178	3:4	10, 68
		3:5	103, 180
		3:10	4, 11

Scripture Index

Romans (continued)

Reference	Pages
3:19	4, 12
3:20–26	176–7, 179
3:20	11, 97, 101, 189–190, 192
3:21–31	24
3:21–26	72, 80–81, 107–8, 197–8
3:21–25	14
3:21–22	61, 79, 96, 103
3:21	19, 104, 181
3:22–25	101, 193
3:22	15, 49, 65, 181
3:23–24	13
3:23	4, 11
3:24–28	5
3:25–26	10, 79, 103
3:25	4, 11, 15, 22, 82
3:26	15, 49, 68, 77, 82, 84, 105
3:27–31	108
3:27–28	101, 193
3:28	185
3:30–31	101
3:30	84
3:31	12
4	15–16, 108, 187
4:2–6	177, 179
4:2–5	101, 193–4
4:2	101
4:3	12, 16, 34, 104, 183, 186
4:4	186
4:5	5, 16, 18, 20, 23, 68, 83, 99–100, 100n4, 161, 163, 167–8, 186
4:6–8	19
4:6	106, 186
4:7–8	177, 179
4:8	186
4:9	186
4:10–12	15
4:10	186
4:11	106, 183, 186
4:13	184
4:22	187
4:23	187
4:24	80, 187
4:25	4, 16, 102, 163, 168n6
5	11, 108
5:1–11	98
5:1–2	5
5:1	19
5:6–11	4
5:6	20, 23, 160
5:7	79
5:9–11	17, 19
5:9	14, 19
5:12	11, 28
5:15	128n2
5:16	61, 102, 128n2, 168n6
5:17	18, 79, 97, 99, 164–5
5:18	70, 79, 102, 168n6
5:19	23
5:20	128n2
6–8	5, 108
6	20, 88, 100, 108, 165
6:1–11	22
6:4	22
6:7	77, 79
6:11	22, 187
6:13	95, 164
6:16	95, 100, 164
6:18	95, 100, 164
6:19	14–15, 95, 100, 164
6:20	95
6:22	95
6:23	20
6:24	4
7	21
7:12	68
7:13	11
8:1–13	21
8:1–8	21
8:1	5, 19
8:3–4	20
8:9	14, 20
8:12–14	21
8:16	20
8:18	187
8:31–39	20
8:33	17
8:36	187
9–11	107–8

Scripture Index

9	23	Galatians	2, 12, 42, 48, 53, 62, 73, 95, 101n5, 107, 163, 165, 173, 185
9:4	83		
9:8	187		
9:30–33	101, 194	1:6–9	107
9:30	77–78, 108, 184	1:7	23
10:3–8	101, 194–5	1:11–17	107
10:3	80, 83, 181–2	1:13–2:14	107
10:5	182	1:15	18
10:6	184	2:7–9	18
10:9–10	12	2:15–21	24
10:9	15	2:16–3:29	107
10:10	77, 108	2:16	15, 49, 101, 189, 191
10:14–17	23	2:20	15, 49
10:14–15	16	2:21	77
10:14	15	3:2–3	19, 101, 192
10:15	23	3:3	48
10:17	16, 163	3:5	19, 23, 101, 192,
11:5–6	13	3:6	16, 34, 104, 185
11:13	18	3:8	17, 61
11:27	83	3:10–14	19
11:32	11	3:10	14, 19, 48, 101
14	17	3:11	51, 83–84, 97, 101, 104, 176, 178
14:3	17, 19–20, 98		
14:14	187		
14:23	15	3:13	14, 19
15	17	3:15	83
15:7	17, 19–20, 98	3:17	83
15:8–12	18	3:21–22	12
15:8–9	18	3:21	11, 83
15:14–15	18	3:22	11, 49
16:26	16, 23, 163	3:24	83
		3:26	15
		3:27	21
1 Corinthians		3:28	18
6:11	2, 95	4:4–5	13
14:8	88	4:4	22
		4:5	165
		4:21–31	12
2 Corinthians		4:24	83
3:9	2	5:3	12
5:17–21	19, 98	5:4	48
5:18–21	17	5:7	48
5:21	2, 95–96, 180	5:13–18	21
		5:22–25	21

Scripture Index

Philippians
3:4–9   95
3:6–9   101, 196
3:9   49, 181

1 Thessalonians   2

2 Timothy
2:2   76
3:17   76

Titus
3:3–8   2n2

Philemon   2

Hebrews
8:12   188

James
2   51

2 Peter
3:15–16   2n3
3:16   24n1

Greek Index

ἀγάπη, 13, 94
ἀδικία, 11
ἀκοή, 16
ἁμαρτία, 11
ἄνθρωπος, 76–77
ἀνοχή, 13, 94
ἀσέβεια, 11
ἀσεβής, 16
ἀφιέναι, 13, 94
δ-family, 1–2, 6–7, 9, 12, 53–54, 57,
    60–75, 77, 79–80, 82, 84–85, 89,
    93–110, 110n1, 161, 163, 165,
    165n4, 166, 168–9, 171, 173–5,
    197–8
δ-GR group, 18, 85, 87–89, 93–102, 104–
    5, 163, 165, 165n4, 171, 176–9
δ-R group, 69, 93–94, 102, 171
δικαι-stem, 93
δικαιοκρισία, 93, 102, 174
δίκαιος, 1, 14, 17–18, 54, 69, 75, 85, 93,
    96, 98, 100, 163–4, 173–5
δικαιοσύνη, 1, 8, 10, 14, 16, 18, 43, 54, 66,
    68–69, 72, 75, 77, 80, 82, 84–85,
    88, 93, 95–96, 98–100, 108, 161,
    163–5, 167, 169, 173–5
δικαιοσύνη αὐτοῦ, 103
δικαιοσύνη / θεοῦ, 94–95, 164–5, 180–81
δικαιοσύνη θεοῦ, 27, 63, 88, 92, 96, 99,
    103–4, 164, 168
δικαιοσύνη / πίστις, 99, 165, 183–4
δικαιοῦν, 1, 3–5, 16–18, 23, 27, 42–43, 54,
    61–62, 69, 72, 75, 77–78, 84–85,
    93, 96, 98–99, 101, 163–4, 166,
    168–9, 173–5
δικαίωμα, 84–85, 93, 102, 168n6, 174–5
δικαίωσις, 8, 15, 75n12, 89, 93, 102, 168,
    168n6, 169, 174–5
δωρεά, 13, 94
δωρεάν, 13
δώρημα, 13
ἔθνη, 94–95
ἐλεεῖν, 13, 94
Ἕλληνες, 94–95
ἐνώπιον αὐτοῦ, 97
ἔργα, 94
ζῆν, 94
ζωή, 94
κατάκριμα, 19
καταλλαγή, 98
καταλλάσσειν, 98
λογίζεσθαι, 36, 94, 185–8
μακροθυμία, 13, 94
νόμος, 94, 99
οἰκτίρειν, 13, 94
οἰκτιρμός, 13
ὀργή, 11, 14, 14n3, 28
παρὰ τῷ θεῷ, 17–18, 97
πιστ-stem, 104
πιστεύειν, 15, 94
πίστις, 15, 94, 99
πίστις Χριστοῦ, 15n4, 49
πλουτεῖν, 13
πλοῦτος, 13, 94
προσλαμβάνεσθαι, 17, 19, 98
ὑπομονή, 13
χάρις, 13, 94
χάρισμα, 13
χρηστός, 13
χρηστότης, 13, 94
χωρὶς νόμου, 19

Latin Index

gratia, 3
imputatem, 35
iustificare, 3, 4, 27, 29, 54, 57, 167
iustitia, 54, 57, 104, 167
iustitia Dei, 27.
iustus, 54, 57, 167
lectio divina, 26, 30
processus iustificationis, 31–33

reputatem, 35
simul iustus et peccator, 39
sola fide, 39
sola scriptura, 4
via media, 40
via moderna, 33
viator, 27, 27n4

Persons Index

Abraham, 12, 18, 109
Adam, 11, 38
Aland, Kurt & Barbara, 71, 75–76, 84
Albertus Magnus (Albert the Great) 31–32
Anderson, H. George, 44n22–25
Andrew of St-Victor, 31
Anselm of Canterbury, 30
Anselm of Laon, 31
Aristotle, 26–27, 31, 33
Augustine of Hippo, 3, 25–29, 29n5, 168

Barclay, William, 71, 85
Barnes, Robert, 36
Barth, Karl, 39, 39n17–18, 43
Beck, William F., 68
Beilby, James K., 49, 49n32–33
Bonaventure, 32
Bonner, Gerald, 29n5
Bratcher, Robert G., 43, 63, 66
Bray, Gerald, 108n9
Bruce, Frederick Fyvie, 85

Calvin, John, 35–37, 50, 56, 161
Carson, D. A., 2
Cassirer, Heinrich (Heinz) W., 72
Challonor, Richard, 57, 64
Chamberlin, William J., 67n11
Clifford, Alan C., 5n4
Coverdale, Miles, 55, 65
Cranmer, Thomas, 37
Cremer, Hermann, 41
Cyprian, 25

Daniell, David, 54n3–4
Dunn, James D. G., 103n7
Duns Scotus, Johannes, 33

Eddy, Paul Rhodes, 49n32–33
Erasmus, Desiderius, 34–35, 55

Farstad, Arthur L., 74–75
Fenton, Ferrar, 60–61
Finney, Charles Grandison, 41
Fitzmyer, Joseph A., 35n9
Frith, John, 36
Fulbert of Chartres, 30

Gardner, Paul, 108n9
Goodspeed, Edgar J., 61, 63
Gregory VII (Hildebrand), 26, 31
Gundry, Robert H., 24n2, 48, 48n30–31

Hart, Trevor A., 29n5
Hays, Richard B., 49
Headlam, Arthur Cayley, 42, 42n20
Henry VIII of England, 55
Hilary of Poitiers, 25
Hildebrand: *see* Gregory VII
Hodges, Zane C., 75
Hugh of St-Victor, 31

Irenaeus, 47

James I of England, 58
James VI of Scotland: *see* James I of England
Jeremias, Joachim, 107
Jerome, 28, 57
Jesus Christ, 26

Kingston, Simon, 82
Knox, Ronald A., 69
Küng, Hans, 39, 39n17, 43

215

Persons Index

Lanfranc, 30
Liddell, Henry George, 17n5
Longman III, Tremper, 74
Louw, Johannes P., 17n5, 43, 64, 97n2
Luther, Martin, 5, 29, 33, 33n7, 35–36, 50, 103–4, 107–8, 161

Mary I of England, 37
Matthew, Thomas, 56
McGrath, Alister E., 25n3, 50
Melanchthon, Philipp, 33–34, 34n8, 35, 35n10, 36, 161
Meyer, Heinrich August Wilhelm, 41
Moffatt, James, 60–61
Moore, Richard K., 5n5, 8n6, 13n2, 15n4, 40n19, 58n6-8, 65, 87n16, 94n1, 97n3, 100n4, 102n6, 103n8, 110n1, 128n2, 164n2, 165n3, 166n5
Moriaty, Joanna, 82
Moses, 101, 109
Moule, Charles F. D., 49

Nestle, Eberhard & Erwin, 71, 75–76, 84
Newman, Barclay M., 43, 64
Newman, John Henry, 40–41
Nida, Eugene A., 17n5, 43, 64, 86, 86n14-15, 87–88, 88n17, 97n2

Oden, Thomas C., 25n3
Olin, John C., 37n12

Paues, Anna Carolina, 54n1
Paul the Apostle, ix, 2, 5–8, 10–25, 28–30, 33, 39–40, 42, 46–50, 52, 54, 58, 62–63, 66–67, 70, 72–74, 82–83, 87–89, 91–92, 95, 105–160, 163–165, 168n6, 169, 191–8
Pelagius, 3, 25, 27, 29, 29n5
Peter Comester, 31–32
Peter Lombard, 31–32
Peter Manducator. *See* Peter Comester
Peter of Poitiers, 32
Peterson, Eugene H., 72
Phillips, J. B., 70
Piper, John, 51, 51n34
Plato, 31, 98
Powell, Margaret Joyce, 54n2

Reynolds (Rainolds), John, 58
Richard of St-Victor, 31
Ritschl, Albrecht Benjamin, 41
Robertson, A. T., 97n2
Rogers, John, 56

Sanday, William, 41, 42n20
Sanders, E. P., 46, 47n28, 48, 48n29, 49
Schroeder, H. J., 38n13–16
Schweitzer, Albert, 107
Scipio Africanus Major, 35, 35n11
Scott, Robert, 17n5
Simon, David Worthington, 42
Snyder, Graydon F., 25n3
Southern, Richard William, 29n6
Spurgeon, Charles Haddon, 40
Stendahl, Krister, 25n3, 107
Stevens, George Barker, 42
Strauss, Mark L., 74
Strong, James, 60n9
Stuhlmacher, Peter, 25n3, 103n7

Taber, Charles R., 86, 86n14–15, 87–88, 88n17
Taylor, Daniel, 74.
Taylor, Kenneth Nathaniel, 70–71
Tertullian, 25
Thomas Aquinas, 27, 31–32
Tischendorf, Constantinus, 59
Torrance, T. F., 25n3, 49
Tyndale, William, 36–37, 54–55, 55n3, 56–57, 104, 167

Wallace, Daniel B., 97n2
Weitzman, Ronald, 72
Westcott, Brooke Foss, 42, 58n5, 62
Westcott, Frederick Brooke, 42, 42n21, 62, 62n10, 63, 85
Weymouth, Richard Francis, 60–61
William of Ockham, 33
Williams, Charles Bray, 43, 63, 85, 89
Wright, Nicholas Thomas (Tom), 50–51, 51n35, 73, 82–83, 85
Wycliffe, John, 53

Youngblood, Ronald F., 79

216

Subject Index

America, North, 37
American Bible Society, ix, 43, 62–63, 66–67, 88, 162
American Standard Version, 59–60, 65, 69
Amplified Bible, The, 69
Anglicanism. *See also* Episcopalianism, 40, 56
Apocrypha, 58, 71
Apologists, 24
Apostolic Fathers, 24
assurance of salvation, 20, 38, 164
atonement. *See also* Jesus Christ: death, 47
Augsburg, 45–46
Augsburg Confession: *Apology*, 35
Authorized Version. *See* King James Version

baptism, 21–22, 27–28, 38, 40
baptism, infant, 26
Baptists, 63, 74
Barbarian invasions, 26
Bible, 73
Bible: authority, 4
Bible: English translation, 6, 55, 58, 65, 91, 161, 168–9, 197–8
Bible: English translations. *Listed under specific name of each version*
Bible: exposition, 27
Bible: fourfold sense, 31
Bible: glosses, 26, 30
Bible: inerrancy, 75
Bible: promotion, 90
Bible: publication, 90
Bible: reading, 28

Bible: scholarship, 90
Bible: study of, 27–28, 30–33
Bible for Today's Family, The, 67
Biblia Hebraica Stuttgartensia, 76
Biblica, 67
Bishop's Bible, 56–58
Black Death, 33
boasting, 101
booksellers, 90
British and Foreign Bible Society, ix, 62–63, 67, 71, 162

Calvinism, 37, 40, 161
cathedral schools, 26, 30
Catholic Church. *See* Roman Catholic Church
childhood, 26
Church: Eastern, 25
Church: Western, 1, 3–4, 6, 17, 25–26, 34
Church Dogmatics (Barth), 39, 39n18
circumcision, 12
clergy, secular, 30
Codex Sinaiticus, 59
Codex Vaticanus, 59
Committee on Bible Translation, 78–79, 81
Common English Bible (2011), 73, 83–84
Common Statement. See Justification by Faith. Common Statement
Constitutions of Oxford, 54
Contemporary English Version (1995), 67, 88, 168
context, 94
contractions, 84
contrition, 32
Council of Trent, 37–39

217

Subject Index

covenant. *See* God: covenant
covenantal nomism, 46–47, 101, 101n5
Coverdale Bible, 56, 58
curse, 14, 19

Dead Sea Scrolls, 47–48
deification, 25
Disciples of Christ, 83
doctrinal condemnations, 45
Douay Bible, 57, 64, 70, 87
Douay Old Testament, 57

ecumenical dialogues and conversations, 6, 43–46
England, 33, 36–37, 55, 57
English language, 6, 59–60, 90–91
English language: Middle English, 6, 53, 104, 167
English Standard Version, 73, 76–77, 85
Episcopalianism, 83
eternal life. *See* life, eternal
eucharist, 27–28, 40
Europe, 31, 33, 38
Evangelical/s, 49, 51, 71, 77
expiation, 51
Expanded Bible, The, 73–74

F-contexts, 95–96, 165, 171
faith, 5, 12, 14, 15–17, 23, 27, 29, 38, 48, 68, 94–96, 102, 104, 106, 109, 163–5, 188, 191–6
faith: a gift, 26
faith-righteousness, 183–4, 191–6
forgiveness. *See* God: forgiving
Form of Concord, 35
friars, 33
freedom, 39
freewill, 25, 32
functional equivalence, 169
Fundamentalism, 87, 90

Gaul, 25
Geneva, 37
Geneva Bible, 37, 56–58
Geneva New Testament, 37, 56
genitive case, 15n4, 49, 79, 96–97, 164
German/Germany, 33–34, 37, 104, 168

Glossa Ordinaria, 31
God: acceptance by, 17, 19–20, 27, 67, 70, 88, 98
God: adoption, 38
God: approval, 68, 88
God: compassionate, 13
God: covenant, 47, 50, 82–83
God: creator, 23, 26
God: elects, 22–23, 47
God: forbearing, 13
God: foreknowledge, 23
God: forgiving, 4, 13, 19, 23, 32, 109
God: generous, 13
God: gift, 13
God: gift of right relationship, 13, 109, 165
God: good, 13
God: grace, 3, 5, 13–14, 22, 25–28, 32, 38–39, 41, 46, 48, 102
God: initiator, 22–23, 47, 102
God: judge, 51
God: just, 4, 41
God: longsuffering, 13
God: loving, 13, 20, 22, 41, 164
God: merciful, 4, 13, 18, 41, 44, 47, 102, 164
God: patient, 13
God: promises, 44
God: redeemer, 23, 26
God: righteous, 10, 12
God: saving righteousness, 108
God: sending of Son, 108–9
God's Word, 68, 88, 168
God's Word to the Nations Bible Society, 68
good news (gospel), 5, 10–23, 39, 44, 88, 92, 94–95, 107, 109, 163, 166
Good News Bible, 43, 58, 66–68, 78, 85–87, 89, 99–100, 162
Good News for Modern Man. *See Good News Bible*
Good News New Testament, 43, 63, 89
Good News Publishers, 76
gospel. *See* good news
grace. *See* God: grace
Great Bible, 56

218

Subject Index

Greek language, 3, 4, 34, 55, 57, 66, 69, 84, 104
Greek New Testament: witnesses, 59
Greek New Testament, The, 71, 75–76
Greek New Testament according to the Majority Text, The, 75

HarperOne, 82
Hastings Dictionary of the Bible, 42
Hebrew/Aramaic languages, 55, 57, 66, 69
Historical New Testament, The (1901), 61
Hodder & Stoughton, 78
Holman Bible Publishers, 75
Holman Christian Standard Bible, 73–76, 85
Holy Spirit, 14, 19, 20–21, 23, 29, 109
humanism, 34

Iberian Peninsula, 26
inclusive language, 76, 78–79, 82
incorporation in Christ, 50
indulgences, 3–4, 29
infancy, 26
Institutes of the Christian Religion (Calvin), 36
International Bible Society, 67, 79
International Standard Version, 73
Islam, 27, 31
Israel, 50
Israel, New, 50

J-family, 6, 43, 54, 57, 60–61, 64, 66, 67–72, 74, 76–77, 80, 83, 85, 88, 104, 161, 167–8, 171
Jehovah's Witnesses, 64, 69
Jerusalem Bible, 65, 167
Jesus Christ: death, 4, 11, 14–15, 23, 25, 39, 41, 51, 94, 102, 108–9, 163–4
Jesus Christ: God's agent, 5, 44, 165
Jesus Christ: incarnation, 42
Jesus Christ: law, 24, 41
Jesus Christ; lordship, 109
Jesus Christ: merits, 36
Jesus Christ: resurrection, 15–16, 94, 109, 163–4

Jesus Christ: righteousness imputed, 5, 34–35, 40, 50, 161, 163, 188
Jesus Christ: Son of God, 109, 163
Jewish Christians, 101n5
Joint Declaration on the Doctrine of Justification (1997), 45
Judaism, 11, 47–49, 95, 101, 107
Judaizers, 48
justification, 1, 4–7, 27, 31–33, 38, 40, 44, 58, 75, 77, 87, 105, 162–6, 168, 168n6
justification: English translations, ix, 6–8, 53–92, 104–5, 161, 167–9, 197–8
justification: final, 51
justification: first, 161n1
justification: forensic view, 4–5, 34–35, 39–41, 161–2
justification: historical development, ix, 1, 3–8
justification: Paul's doctrine, 109
justification: process, 27
justification: realist view, 3, 5, 17, 35, 39–40, 100, 161–2, 167
justification: relational view, ix, 5–6, 41, 87–88, 96–98, 162–3
justification: role, 5, 9, 33, 106–8
justification: second, 161n1
Justification by Faith: Common Statement (1983), 44, 44n23n25, 46

King James Version, 15, 56–60, 67, 69–70, 75, 77–78, 87, 90, 168n6

L-contexts, 95–96, 165, 171
Latin language, 3–4, 25–26, 28, 31, 34, 54–55, 57, 66, 168
Law, 11–12, 14, 18–21, 23, 41, 47–48, 94–95, 101–2, 104, 109, 165, 191–6
law courts, 59, 102
Law-righteousness, 182, 191–6
lectionaries, 30
legal fiction, 5, 100
Letter to Diognetus, 24
Letters to Young Churches, 70
life, 94–95
life, eternal, 20

Subject Index

LifeWay Christian Resources, 74–75
Living Bible, The, 70–71
Living Bibles International, 70
Living New Testament, The, 70
Loci communes (Melanchthon), 34–36
Lockman Foundation, 69
Lollard Bible, 53–54, 167
Luther Bible Society, 68
Lutheranism, 1, 6, 43–46

manuscript tradition, 53–54
Mass. *See* Eucharist
Matthew Bible, 56
merit, 25, 27, 36, 39
Message, The, 72
Methodism, 83
Metropolitan Tabernacle Pulpit
    (Spurgeon), 40
Middle Ages, 3, 25–34
Mishnah, 47
Moffatt Bible, 61
monasticism. *See also* friars, 30
monasticism: Benedictines, 26, 30
monasticism: Celtic, 26, 30
monasticism: Cluniac, 30
monasticism: Dominicans, 27, 31, 65
monasticism: Franciscans, 27, 31, 33
monasticism: Victorines, 31
Moody Press, 70
MS Parker 32, 54

natural sciences, 31
nature, 27
Neo-Platonism, 31
NET Bible, 73, 77–78, 85
New American Bible (1970), 66
New American Bible (1987), 66, 87
New American Bible Revised Edition
    (2011), 6, 66, 73–74, 85, 87, 168
New American Standard Bible, 69, 105
New Century Version, 69, 74
New English Bible, 60, 65, 71
New English Translation. *See* NET Bible
New International Reader's Version, 73, 79–81
New International Version (1978), 58, 67, 79–81, 87

New International Version (1984), 67, 78–81, 87
New International Version (2011), 6, 67, 73, 81–82, 85, 87, 100, 168, 197–8
New Jerusalem Bible, 6, 64, 66, 87, 167–8, 197–8
New King James Version, 69, 87
New Living Translation, 71
New Revised Standard Version, 6, 65, 87, 168
New Testament, 47, 58, 66, 73
New Testament: A New Translation, The, 71
New Testament: canon, 5
New Testament: English translations, 6–7, 53–92
New Testament: Greek, 6, 55, 91
New Testament for Everyone, The, 73, 82–83
New Testament in the Language of the People, The, 43, 63
New World Translation, 69
New York Bible Society International, 67
non-Jews, 18, 95, 107
Novum Testamentum Graece, 71, 75–76, 84

obedience, 23, 26, 47, 163–4
Old Testament, 12, 17–18, 51, 55, 58, 66, 75, 102–4, 188
Orthodox Church, 65

pardon. *See* God: forgiving
Paris, 26, 32
participation in Christ, 50
patristic period, 24–26, 50
Paul: "New Perspective" on, 46–49, 51
penalty, 5
penance, 3, 27–28, 30, 32, 39
personal relationships, 96–98
Presbyterianism, 36, 83
processus iustificationis, 31–33
Prophetic Writings, 14, 104
Protestantism, 1, 4–5, 17, 35, 37–38, 40, 57, 64–65, 100, 108, 161n1, 162, 166–7
propitiation, 51
Puritanism, 37, 40, 164

Subject Index

R-contexts, 88–89, 94–101, 104, 165, 169, 171, 176–9
R-family, 6, 9, 43, 54, 60–61, 63–64, 66–72, 74, 76, 77, 80, 83–85, 88–89, 104, 161, 167–8, 172
reconciliation, 13, 17, 19, 42, 98
rectification, 61, 87, 100, 109, 166, 168
Rectification ('Justification') in Paul, in Historical Perspective, and in the English Bible, ix, 5n5, 8, 8n6, 13n2, 15n4, 40n19, 56n6–8, 73, 94n1, 97n3, 102n6, 103n8, 110n1, 128n2, 164n2, 165n3, 166n5
Reformation/Reformers, 1, 3–5, 26, 33–37, 40, 46, 50–51, 55, 164
Reformed tradition, 36, 43, 161
Renaissance, 4
repentance, 32, 38, 41
Revised Authorized Version, 69
Revised English Bible, 6, 11, 65, 87, 168
Revised Standard Version, 60, 65, 76
Revised Version, 59–60
Rheims New Testament, 56–57, 64, 88, 167
Rheims-Douai Bible. *See* Douay Bible
righteousness, 51, 105–6, 182–4
righteousness [moral], 4–5, 20, 23, 105–6, 109, 163–5
rightness [amoral], 96
Roman Catholic Church, 1, 6, 17, 34–35, 37, 40–41, 43–46, 56, 64–66, 71–72, 88, 100, 108, 161n1, 162, 167
Roman Empire, 3, 26, 30
Roman Empire: Eastern, 3
Roman Empire: Western, 3
Roman North Africa, 25

sacraments, 27–28, 32
salvation. *See also* assurance of salvation, 12, 18, 27–29, 38, 44, 47, 50, 94–95, 109
salvation: universal offer, 18, 94, 109.
salvation-history, 18
sanctification, 4, 17, 38, 40–41, 108–9, 161n1, 164
satisfaction, 25, 36
scholasticism, 26, 29–30, 36

scholasticism, Protestant, 36
Scotland, 36–37
Scriptures. *See* Bible
Sentences, 32
Septuagint (Lxx), 10, 62, 100
sin, 12, 15, 22, 25, 32, 98, 109
sin: original, 26, 28
sin: remission of, 32, 38
sin: universal, 11, 14
sins, venial, 39
Society of Biblical Literature, 77
Southern Epistles, 54
Spain, 31
SPCK, 82
substitution, 4–5
supernature, 28
Switzerland, 33, 37
synergism, 108

Talmud/s, 47
textual criticism, 59, 75
Today's English Version (TEV). *See Good News Bible*
theology, 27, 31–32
Today's New International Version, 67, 73, 78–82, 85
Torah. *See* Law
translation theory, 85
Translator's Translation, 63, 67, 71
Twentieth Century New Testament, The, 60–61

Under the Southern Cross, 9, 64, 95, 97, 99, 105, 110–60, 168, 197–8
United Bible Societies, 64
United Churches of Christ, 83
universities, 26, 32

Vatican Council II, 44
Voice, The, 73–74, 85
Vulgate, 26, 28, 34–35, 54–55, 57, 66, 69, 104, 167

works, good, 27, 38, 47–48
works of the Law. *See* Law

Zondervan Publishing House, 79

www.ingramcontent.com/pod-product-compliance
Lightning Source LLC
Chambersburg PA
CBHW070250230426
43664CB00014B/2482